Irish adventures in nation-buil

Manchester University Press

Irish adventures in nation-building

Bryan Fanning

Manchester University Press

Published by Manchester University Press
Altrincham Street, Manchester M1 7JA

www.manchesteruniversitypress.co.uk

British Library Cataloguing-in-Publication Data
A catalogue record for this book is available from the British Library

Library of Congress Cataloging-in-Publication Data applied for

ISBN 978 1 7849 9322 1 hardback

ISBN 978 1 7849 9323 8 paperback

First published 2016

The publisher has no responsibility for the persistence or accuracy of URLs for any external or third-party internet websites referred to in this book, and does not guarantee that any content on such websites is, or will remain, accurate or appropriate.

.

Typeset in Sabon and Gill Sans by
Servis Filmsetting Ltd, Stockport, Cheshire
Printed in Great Britain by
CPI Group (UK) Ltd, Croydon CR0 4YY

Contents

Foreword

The lyrics of a comic song by Wayne Kemp, 'One Piece at a Time', made famous by Johnny Cash, tells the story of a man who spends his life assembling Cadillacs in Detroit. He smuggles out components from different models one by one and assembles these into an odd-looking car of his own. The transmission is from 1953, the engine from 1973, and so on. This book brings together essays written during a far shorter period during which I also worked a number of other books including *The Quest for Modern Ireland: The Battle of Ideas 1912–1986* (2008), an analysis of influential Irish journals during this period, the second edition of *Racism and Social Change in the Republic of Ireland* (2012), which included examinations of groups sidelined by twentieth-century nation-building processes, and *Histories of the Irish Future* (2015), an intellectual history of Ireland and a history of understandings of Irish crises and predicaments from 1650 to our present time.

The essays that constitute *Irish Adventures in Nation-Building* are designed to fit together as a multi-disciplinary analysis of the making of modern Ireland. These focus on the intellectual, social, political, religious and economic ideas and processes that variously shaped Irish society, Irish nationalism and the Irish nation-state. Individual essays address key moments or influential debates and shifts in these. The structure of *Irish Adventures in Nation-Building* is mostly chronological, although some essays cover the entire century or so upon which the book is mostly focused. I am particularly indebted to the editors of the publications in which a number of these essays first appeared – *The Dublin Review of Books*, *The Irish Journal of Sociology*, *Studies*, *The Irish Studies Review* and *Taiwan in Comparative Perspective* – as well as to friends, colleagues and research collaborators for their support. In particular I wish to thank Bruce Bradley SJ, Denis Dillon, Maurice

Earl, Tom Garvin, Andreas Hess, Tom Inglis, Seán L'Estrange, Joan Maher, Ronaldo Munck, Rev. John McNeil Scott, Neil O'Boyle, Philip O'Connell, Fergus O'Donoghue SJ and Pilar Argáiz Vilar.

1

Adventures in nation-building

At the time of writing the Republic of Ireland is in the midst of a decade of centenary celebrations of key milestones in the foundation of an independent Irish nation-state. It is also struggling with the legacy of a prolonged economic crisis that has challenged some of the Republic's cherished narratives. Nations, Benedict Anderson has influentially argued, are imagined communities. And what is being imagined of course changes over time. My vantage point is that of a social scientist who is an avid reader of works on Irish literature and history by writers who are usually not avid readers of the social sciences. Disciplinary silos can be comfortable and comforting, but no one academic vantage point can claim to cover all the angles. Different disciplines present different maps and the trick is to learn how to these alongside one another. History as an academic discipline and studies of Irish literature offer the most frequently consulted maps of the Irish story. Economists have a lot of influence in an era where the national interest tends to be calculated in financial terms, but this was not always so. The various social sciences study society, its institutions and social problems but often pay insufficient attention to historical contexts. No single attempt at synthesis can wrap everything up neatly but when the object of study is literally common ground, in this case the territory that calls itself the Republic of Ireland, efforts to join some of the dots such as this are worthwhile. The essays that follow focus on literature as well as on social and economic policy, on historical scholarship as well as what the social sciences tell us about Irish society and the Irish nation-state.

The approach in *Irish Adventures in Nation-Building* is firstly to offer a map that locates the main nation-building projects that have shaped Ireland across two centuries and then to focus mostly on the last century in the chapters that follow. Collectively these essays chart the main shifts in dominant ideas and shifting cultural, economic and political circumstances during the last hundred years. Topics considered range from why Patrick Pearse's ideas about education were ignored to why Ireland has been recently so open to large-scale immigration, from the case for isolationism in support of de-colonisation to how and why Ireland came to be defined as an open economy. What is being examined are shifting representations of nation-building goals set out in seminal periodicals, books and government reports. For the most part the focus is on mainstream vantage points and critiques of these.

Some of the early chapters examine the influence of Catholicism and the common cause it found with cultural nationalism in post-independence Ireland. Subsequent chapters address contestations of post-colonial isolationism by liberals who were also nationalists. Later chapters examine the emergence of a new economic nation-building project from the late 1950s. The vantage points examined include those of prominent revolutionaries, cultural nationalists, clerics, economists, sociologists, political scientists, public intellectuals, journalists, influential civil servants, political leaders and activists who weighed into debates about the condition of Ireland and where it was going. Most of these were men and, for the most part, their perspectives were privileged ones. Some chapters focus on where women, Travellers, vulnerable members of society and, most recently, immigrants figure in the mainstream narratives that profess to tell Ireland's story.

Anderson's approach to the study of nationalism and nation-building is predicated on the argument that similar sociological processes can be found in different contexts. Nationalism and nation-building projects have also come to preoccupy academics in different countries in similar ways. They, no less than the politicians and officials of nation-states, are protagonists in processes of nation-building. As put by Anderson:

> For a fair part of the past two hundred years, narrating the nation seemed, in principle, a straightforward matter. Armies of historians, good and bad, helped by folklorists, sociologists, statisticians, literary critics, archaeologists, and of course, the State, produced a vast arsenal of work to help existing or future citizens imagine the biography, and the future, of their political communities. There could be every conceivable difference in method, approach, data base, and political viewpoint, but these 'historians' typically understood their texts as 'documents of civilisation', or stories of progress, however meandering, because the nation was always, and without much question, regarded as historically factual and morally good. There are all kinds of political and other reasons that allow us to be confident that the flow of such work will continue indefinitely, since

nation-states require it, and in the broad public arena, the legitimacy of the nation-state is still generally accepted, even insisted upon.[1]

Scholars have produced and will continue to produce a flow of academic output preoccupied with nationalism and national identity as contributions to ongoing thinking and re-thinking of national problems and national dilemmas.

Anderson argues that nationalisms cannot be understood in isolation from the older political forms such as kingdoms and empires from which these emerged. The earliest form of nationalism, which Anderson refers to as creole nationalism, grew out the expansion of some of these empires. In a 1994 essay he discussed the 1682 memoir of an American-born non-English 'Englishwoman' Mary Rowlandson, who, though she had never been within three thousand miles of England, described the English cattle and English fields of her home in Massachusetts.[2] Anderson saw the seventeenth-century non-Spanish Spaniards of southern America as another example of what he calls creole nationalism. Such creole nationalism denotes nationalism pioneered by settler populations from the Old Country, who shared its religion, language and customs but increasingly felt alienated from it. Examples include the United States and various Latin American countries that became independent in the late eighteenth and early nineteenth century but also there are more recent examples such as French Canadian separatism and, of course, the Irish case. A key characteristic of creole nationalisms has been their blending of settler and indigenous peoples and traditions.[3] Although the focus of this book is mostly on the last century or so it is important to bear in mind that Ireland's twentieth-century nation-building projects stood on the foundations of earlier ones.

Anderson also highlights what he terms official nationalism. This kind of nationalism came about as a reactionary response to popular nationalisms from below that were directed against rulers, aristocrats and imperial centres. An example here was Imperial Russia, where the Tzars ruled over many ethnic groups and religiously different communities and where the ruling elite spoke French. It was only from the 1880s that this elite professed a Russian nationalism and promoted this amongst its diverse subjects. In similar ways, French, English and German elites pushed official nationalisms and sought for example to impose the French language on Italian-speaking Corsica, to anglicise Ireland and to Germanise parts of Poland. These top-down official nationalisms promoted imperial cultures within which subject peoples were to become, for example, French or British, albeit second-class members of such nations.[4] The post-colonial Irish nation-state was built on such pre-independence legislative, institutional and linguistic foundations.

Various sociologists besides Anderson have focused on the spread around the world of nationalism as ideology, of the nation-state as an institution and of a limited repertoire of nation-building processes. Amongst these, Ernest Gellner depicted the nation as a product of the Great Transformation which dissolved all ancient, isolated communities into modern industrial societies, which required a solidarity based on an abstract, literacy-based culture. As put by Gellner:

> A major and distinctive change has taken place in the social conditions of mankind. A world in which *nationalism*, the linking of the state and of 'nationally' defined culture, is pervasive and normative is quite different from one in which this is relatively rare, half-hearted, unsystematised and untypical. There is an enormous difference between a world of complex, intertwined, but not neatly-overlapping patterns of power and culture, and a world consisting of neat political units, systematically and proudly differentiated from each other by 'culture', and all of them striving, with great measure of success, to impose cultural homogeneity internally. These units, linking sovereignty to culture, are known as nation-states. During the two centuries following the French revolution, the nation-state became a political norm.[5]

He was wrong, Anderson argued, to emphasise so strongly the role of industrialisation as a historic source of nationalism. For example, many of the places where nationalism flourished during the nineteenth century, including Ireland, Hungary and Poland, had experienced very little industrial development.[6] Clearly, industrialisation has been part and parcel of processes of nation-building. The military-industrial complex of the United States after the Second World War (the term was coined by President Dwight Eisenhower in 1961) had its predecessors amongst Europe's great powers in the run-up to the First World War: the mass production of armaments went together with industrial expansion, mass education and social hygiene aimed at ordering populations. But Anderson in turn has overstated the case against Gellner whilst agreeing with the essence of much of what he has to say about the relationships between nationalism and modernity. Industrial capacity has not proven to be a precondition for linguistic nationalism aimed at creating monoglot communities or even the propagation of a sense of shared mass identities through the expansion of education and print technologies or for the copying of this repertoire of nation-building techniques around the world.[7]

For Gellner, the core characteristics of industrial society included the emergence of high culture as the pervasive operational culture for

society as a whole. Modern societies had to adopt a standardised culture
in order to function. Access to the standardised culture – a high culture
insofar as it was defined by print technologies and a complex repertoire
of shared meanings – became a precondition for employment and social
participation.[8] Gellner defined nation-building as the process of achieving such cultural standardisation. Even where national cultures were
apparently modelled on folk cultures these were also expressions of
modernity. The valorisation of folk traditions by nationalist intellectuals
and the use of these as the basis of nationalist ideology resulted in something new. Even where mass cultures evoked the ideals of traditional
society these did so in distinctly modern ways.[9] Leaders were forever
evoking ideals of community and tradition whilst engaged in decidedly
modern forms of identity formation. They used, as Gellner put it in a
review of a book about Irish nationalism by Conor Cruise O'Brien, the
language of *Gemeinschaft* in the pursuit of *Gesellschaft*. Nationalist
movements championed folk culture but what they in fact created was a
codified version of this expressed through literacy and mediated through
mass education.[10] In effect, both cultural and economic forms of nation-
building are expressions of modernity and are often intertwined.

In the Irish case, pre-Reformation and post-Reformation English
colonialisms preceded any conception that Ireland was a distinct nation.
Waves of colonial settlement during the seventeenth century led to the
dominance of what came to be termed during the eighteenth century
the Irish Ascendancy, the Protestant descendants of colonial settlers.
Their dominance was exemplified by ownership of most of the lands of
Ireland and by Penal Laws that excluded Catholics from landownership,
the professions and politics. A definite rupture with the pre-seventeenth-
century social and political order has since been emphasised by most
Irish nationalist historians.

In his account of the emergence of creole nationalism Anderson iden-
tifies parallels between the early colonisation of America and the post-
seventeenth-century colonisation in the Irish case.[11] Efforts to promote
a viable Protestant patriotism in Ireland can be traced to the end of the
seventeenth century. This began with arguments that an Irish parliament should be established under the control of the Irish Protestant elite.
Most notably, Jonathan Swift argued, in a series of 1720s pamphlets and
satires that became seminal nationalist texts, that Ireland was badly run
from London. Many of his complaints concerned colonial taxes imposed
on the Protestant Irish (an issue that similarly inflamed the Thirteen
Colonies half a century later) rather than the removal of political and
property rights from the Catholic majority. In 1782 the Irish Parliament
was restored under the control of the Protestant Ascendancy. Edmund

Burke in his late-eighteenth-century writings on Ireland argued that the Ascendancy parliament could have no legitimacy whilst it excluded Catholics. In the 1760s he described anti-Catholic laws as unjust to a large majority of the population and, as such, as undermining the perceived legitimacy of the Constitution. A society could weather injustice towards some of its members and remain stable. Injustice towards a large majority of the population served to undermine social cohesion because legitimacy was a necessary bedrock of any viable constitution.[12]

Three decades later the Penal Laws had to some extent been relaxed but Ascendancy intransigence worked to marginalise the Catholic majority to the greatest extent possible.[13] An unsuccessful rebellion in 1798, inspired by the French Revolution, precipitated the end of the Ascendancy parliament and an Act of Union in 1801, which introduced direct rule from London with Irish political representation in the Westminster Parliament. Subsequent waves of Irish nationalism built on the Protestant patriot tradition but these came to be predominantly focused on concerns of the Catholic majority. In a sense creole or settler political identities persisted in the north of Ireland, which remained part of the United Kingdom when a twenty-six-county Irish Free State (which later became the Republic of Ireland) was established.

During the early nineteenth century a Catholic nationalist political party led by Daniel O'Connell successfully contested the Penal Laws, and once these were repealed in 1828, Catholics, who constituted the majority of the Irish population, became more influential. The Great Famine during the 1840s led to the death of about one million and precipitated large-scale emigration and land reforms. The Famine combined with the influence of European romantic nationalism (a Young Ireland movement influenced, for example, by Young Italy) rejected the parliamentary/constitutional nationalism of O'Connell. By the 1860s revolutionary nationalists, seeking Irish independence (as distinct from home rule or rights for Catholics), were strongly influenced by emigrant Irish living in the United States (the Fenians). During the 1880s, political agitation focused successfully on land reform (the Land League). The second half of the nineteenth century also saw a huge rise in the influence of the Catholic Church, which emerged as the main provider of education and social services. By the end of the nineteenth century the Catholic peasantry had become a mostly conservative land-owning class. The dominant Catholic political movement, the Irish Parliamentary Party, focused on achieving home rule through alliances with the Liberal Party in the Westminster Parliament.

The late nineteenth century saw the emergence of new cultural nationalist movements, such as the Gaelic League, dedicated to restoring the

Irish language and the Gaelic Athletic Association, dedicated to replacing 'foreign' sports with Irish games. In effect these movements sought to promote new shared mass identities that were distinctly Irish and that could be mobilised in support of nationalist claims for political autonomy. To a considerable extent the Catholic education system embraced this cultural nationalism. Catholicism and cultural nationalism both became key elements of the modernisation of Irish society and identity.

The war of independence was followed by a civil war (1922–23) and partition. The focus of this collection of essays is upon bounded debates and conflicts within the jurisdiction of the Republic, but the ongoing influence of the north and of post-partition aspirations for a united Ireland also needs to be acknowledged. Partition resulted from the terms of the truce that ended the war of independence but also triggered a civil war. The 1937 Constitution of the Irish Free State included commitments to the unification of Ireland. Specifically, Article 2 stated: 'The national territory consists of the whole island of Ireland, its islands and the territorial seas.' The real audience for political anti-partition rhetoric was the population of the Free State.[14] Fianna Fáil (trans., 'The soldiers of destiny'), the dominant political party between 1932 and 2007 (with some short periods in opposition), had emerged from the anti-Treaty side during the civil war. The party's founder, Éamon de Valera, had been the nationalist political leader during the war of independence. He was also the sole surviving leader of the 1916 Rising. For de Valera or Fianna Fáil, appearances of compromise on the question of partition would not have been possible. Yet, crucially, the Irish Free State/ Republic of Ireland never sought to exercise this claimed sovereignty. Anything that might decisively undermine partition was ruled out. For example, Irish political parties, including Fianna Fáil, did not organise north of the border. Nor before the post-1969 northern conflict did the Republic seek to interfere in the north on behalf of oppressed Catholics. Leading members of Fianna Fáil who were implicated in efforts to provide weapons to the IRA at the beginning of the Northern Ireland conflict were sacked from the Republic of Ireland government although one of these, Charles Haughey, later became Taoiseach (trans., 'Prime Minister').

Following the 'Good Friday' Northern Ireland Agreement in 1998 and a referendum, Articles 2 and 3 of the Republic of Ireland Constitution were revised so as to remove the claim to sovereignty over the whole island of Ireland. Revised Article 3 retained the ideal of a united Ireland but emphasised the principle of consent: 'It is the firm will of the Irish Nation, in harmony and friendship, to unite all the people who share the territory of the island of Ireland, in all the diversity of their identities and traditions, recognising that a united Ireland shall be brought about only by peaceful means with the consent of a majority of the people, democratically expressed, in both jurisdictions in the island.'

The Irish Free State (from 1948 the Republic of Ireland) was for several decades ideologically dominated by Catholicism and 'Irish-Ireland' cultural nationalism. For a period this advocated cultural and economic isolationism and, in effect, it sought to de-colonise Ireland. Irish-Ireland nationalism came symbolically to dominate the new state from the 1920s to at least the 1960s. However, the Irish-Ireland nation-building project proved unsuccessful at arresting economic stagnation and ongoing emigration. From the 1950s it was contested by a developmental modernising one, which came to emphasise economic and human capital reproduction as utilitarian nation-building goals. The institutional narrative of Irish developmental modernisation has tended to focus on influential state-of-the-nation reports seen to exemplify emerging new political and economic orthodoxies. Protectionism unravelled during the 1950s, when import substitution policies proved unable to sustain employment.[15]

The emergence of a supposed new developmental paradigm was signalled by the high-profile publication in 1958 of a report entitled *Economic Development*. Its significance was that it institutionalised the perception that protectionism did not work. An OECD/Irish Government 1965 report *Investment in Education* has been credited with jolting the focus of Irish education from character development and religious formation to one on economic development and the human capital needed for industrial development. *Investment in Education* (1965) amounted to a paradigm shift which broke earlier approaches to education aimed at reproducing Catholicism and Gaelic culture. In sociological terms a modernisation of belonging occurred that prioritised human capital over forms of cultural capital.[16] By this I mean the attributes, habits, attitudes and dispositions required of people in order that they might fit into Irish society had changed. In terms of the politics of nation-building the Republic of Ireland had entered a new phase that was also, in a sense, a return to dominance of liberal political economy goals of the kind rejected by cultural nationalists in the post-Famine period.

Outline of the book

In an age of apparently unprecedented globalisation, transnational interconnections and cosmopolitan aspirations, this book examines the case for research focused on nation-states. When it comes to the Republic of

Ireland such a focus is complicated by the existence of Northern Ireland and by the Irish diaspora. Generations of southerners who perhaps never visited the north believed in a united Ireland. Millions of people who consider themselves Irish do not live in the Republic of Ireland. Yet, as argued in Chapter 2 ('In defence of methodological nationalism') there are compelling justifications for methodological nationalism: research and analysis focused on the jurisdiction of a nation-state. The nation-state remains a necessary unit of analysis not least because it is a unit of taxation and representation, a legal and political jurisdiction, a site of bounded loyalties and of identity politics. We still study the world by comparing census data and other kinds of information focused on nation-states. We still live in a world where, as Sinisa Malesevic puts it, 'everybody is expected to possess a distinct national identity'. He argues that nationalism in twenty-first-century Ireland is even more powerful and socially embedded than it was in de Valera's Ireland.[17] Nationalisms and national identities and the nation-building processes that create and re-create these remain important fields of research.

Chapter 3 ('Patrick Pearse predicts the future') considers what kind of Ireland Pearse wanted to bring about. He was executed after the 1916 Rising and has been a totemic figure since. In 1906 Pearse wrote an essay about what Ireland might be like in 2006. This is examined along with his subsequent writings on social issues. Pearse has been celebrated as an educationalist but had no influence on Irish education. The reasons why are addressed in Chapter 4 ('Paul Cullen's devotional revolution'), which describes how from the mid-nineteenth century the Catholic Church came to dominate education. Pearse proposed a model that was very different from the already dominant Catholic model that did much to incubate modern Ireland.

Beyond this, Catholicism offered a distinct response to modernity aimed at competing with the two main secular ideologies: liberalism and socialism. Catholic social thought was taught as political science; it promoted vocationalism as an alternative to both individualism and statism, though with little success in the Irish case compared, say, to that of Portugal under António de Oliveira Salazar, from 1932 to 1968. Vocationalism was mostly ignored as a blueprint for Irish political institutions, other than having some influence on composition of the Irish Seanad (Senate). But Catholic social thought came to dominate Irish sociology during the same period.[18] It offered a software of ideas that variously influenced de Valera's 1937 Constitution and the corporatist model known as social partnership that agreed economic and social policies during the Celtic Tiger era.

Catholic social thought offered ideological justifications for keeping the state out of education and healthcare and from interfering in families and communities. Ireland was for the first half-century after independence dominated by the Church, but Ireland, at one stage the only Catholic democratic country in the world, was never a theocracy. Chapter 5 ('A Catholic vision of Ireland') examines the nature of its influence and how this declined. In parallel, Chapter 6 ('Catholic intellectuals'), through an analysis of articles in the Jesuit journal *Studies* published between 1912 and 2012, examines how Catholic perspectives intersected with other strands of intellectual life in Ireland. *Studies* hosted the mainstream social, economic, constitutional and political debates that shaped the new state. Within such debates there were often many shades of opinion. Manichean accounts of conflicts between Catholic conservatives and champions of modernisation make little sense in a society where the liberals and the modernisers were also mostly Catholics.

The focus in Chapter 7 ('The limits of cultural nationalism') is on an argument that played out between Michael Tierney and Daniel Binchy about *King of the Beggars* (1938), a biography of Daniel O'Connell by Sean O'Faoláin.[19] The intellectual argument rehearsed in Chapter 7 illustrates conflicts within post-independence Ireland about the extent to which cultural de-colonisation was feasible or even desirable. A modern Irish culture, Tierney argued, could be built on the old Gaelic culture but a viable political system could not. O'Connell's contribution to the modern Irish nation was, Tierney argued, a philosophically utilitarian one that readily discarded this legacy. That O'Connell's constitutional nationalist movement occurred alongside Gaelic cultural decline was to be regretted. Tierney's thesis was that the Irish revolution had politically internalised that which it supposedly stood against. Utilitarianism included acceptance of the English language as well colonial legal and political institutions that had no alternative Gaelic antecedent. Tierney, according to Tom Garvin, anticipated Anderson and Gellner by a generation in his analysis of how modern nationalities were invented.[20] For their part, Binchy and O'Faoláin were critical of how romantic nationalism had influenced the politics of and intellectual life in the new state.

Chapter 8 ('Hidden Irelands, silent Irelands') examines related disputes between Daniel Corkery, the pre-eminent cultural nationalist intellectual in the decades after independence, and two of his former protégés, O'Faoláin and Frank O'Connor, who both opposed the isolationism of the new state. Some of their work was banned but, as is the way with these things, their reputations in Ireland were bolstered by international success. For O'Faoláin censorship was not the problem *per se* but was a symptom of a wider cultural and intellectual malaise that made it difficult to discuss Irish society realistically. Irish social problems were, he argued, obscured by the ideological mist of romantic nationalism. This, he maintained, was epitomised by Corkery's *The Hidden Ireland*, a hugely influential text he saw as legitimising cultural isolationism and censorship.[21]

Chapter 9 ('Liberalism and *The Bell*') examines the periodical that O'Faoláin hoped would gaze unflinchingly on the realities of contemporary Irish life. For all *The Bell* has been celebrated in accounts of twentieth-century Irish modernisation it was at times progressive with a small 'p', conservative with a small 'c' and liberal with a small 'l'. In this it was true to its time and place, a mostly rural insular Ireland, a young country still preoccupied with cultural nation-building and still uneasy about defining itself in terms of progress and economic growth. Ireland had its conservative revolutionaries and its Catholic conservatives. It also had fairly conservative liberals.

Three chapters address the emergence of the economic nation-building project that more than half a century later remains the dominant one. Chapter 10 ('Behind the Erin curtain') examines the standard mythic account, one that venerates de Valera's successor Sean Lemass and a generation of patriotic technocrats led by T.K. Whitaker, for sweeping aside the blockers of progress who, as the title of Tom Garvin's 2004 book implies, were preventing the future.[22] It was of course not as simple as that. Yes, the 1950s witnessed the emergence of a new nation-building narrative that emphasised economic development. However, its core elements included ideas of progress that had played out in Ireland for more than a century. Amongst these was the liberal utilitarianism of O'Connell's time and the opinions of liberal political economists on how the Irish might be improved – that is, change their character and habits – in order to be fit for purpose in a modern economy. The new post-1950s nation-building project drew on ideas that had been, to some extent, sidelined by cultural nationalism. An ideological conflict between culture and economy, one that had played out for more than a century amongst Irish nationalists of various kinds, ended with the apparent supremacy of economic nationalism.

Chapter 11 ('The new young Irelanders') examines the emergence of a new liberal elite preoccupied with political, social, economic and educational reform. They were members of Tuairim (trans., 'Opinion') an organisation that published pamphlets, described by its founder Donal Barrington as a cross between the Fabian Society and the Young Ireland movement. Many of its members were or went on to become leading members of the judiciary, influential economists and politicians.

Women have been marginalised in most of the debates that shaped Ireland even where they were directly affected by them. One of the most picked-over episodes in twentieth-century Irish history has been the conflict surrounding the Mother and Child Scheme. It played out as a conflict between male clergy and a male politician, Noël Browne. The most prominent polemics that attacked the scheme were written by men, yet it was obviously a conflict about the place of women in Irish society. Chapter 12 ('Women and social policy') examines this conflict as a starting point of an analysis of the place of women in post-independence Ireland.

The focus of Chapter 13 ('New rules of belonging') is on the emergence of social policy efforts to regulate and control a category of Irish people who were being displaced by economic modernisation. The chapter argues that the *Report of the Commission on Itineracy* (1963) is no less seminal a text than those setting out plans for economic development which are usually emphasised by historians. The characteristics associated with the itinerants (or Travellers) in prevailing stereotypes were pretty much the same as those used to describe most Irish people during the nineteenth century by those seeking to justify colonialism or anxious to improve the condition of the Irish by changing their habits and behaviour. A line can be traced from the prescriptions of the Commission on Itineracy back to the writings of nineteenth-century economists preoccupied with the improvement of the Irish.

Chapter 14 ('Partisan reviews') examines a number of the main Irish periodicals that have provided outlets for Irish public intellectuals and journalists since the beginning of the twentieth century. Whilst some of these periodicals championed reportage and were committed to investigative journalism many were explicitly partisan in the doctrines and ideologies they championed. The list of periodicals covered includes nationalist ones such as *The United Irishman* edited by Arthur Griffith and *The Leader* edited by D.P. Moran, *The Irish Citizen*, which was published by the Irish Woman's Franchise League, and *The Irish Statesman*, which was aimed at the Free State's Protestant minority, along with more recent seminal magazines including *Hibernia*, which focused on the northern conflict, and *Magill*, which did so also but also critiqued the political culture of the Republic. Taken together, these periodicals covered the main fringes of political and intellectual life in the Republic of Ireland.

Three chapters address the rise and fall of the Celtic Tiger, the name given to a period of rapid economic growth that was likened to the performance of East Asian 'tiger' economies that also saw huge social change, including large-scale immigration. There are, as Anderson put it, a limited repertoire of nation-building techniques, but different permutations of these of course are found in different countries. Chapter 15 ('Tales of two tigers') compares the emergence of Ireland's economic nation-building project with the case of Taiwan. Ireland abandoned post-colonial isolationism to become one of the world's most open economies, dominated by foreign capital. Taiwan, by contrast developed its economy along the lines advocated by de Valera during the economic war with England, where the emphasis was on protectionism and domestic ownership of capital. Unlike the Irish case, Taiwanese cultural nation-building coincided with a strong emphasis on economic nation-building. The focus is on upon comparing and contextualising the respective nation-building choices and predicaments of both countries in order to understand the Irish case better.

Chapter 16 ('The sociology of boom and bust') examines structural explanations for Ireland's economic success as distinct from ideological narratives. It examines the institutional contexts of economic nation-building. These include corporatist modes of organisation that enabled consensus about national goals. Chapter 16 also examines the role this 'social partnership' played in bringing about Ireland's most recent economic crisis.

Chapter 17 ('Immigration, the Celtic Tiger and the economic crisis') examines the most striking manifestation of social change during the same period. It considers how Irish responses to large-scale immigration might be explained in terms of the politics of nation-building. Following the Northern Ireland Agreement the Constitution was amended to state (Revised Article 2) that was the entitlement and birthright of every person born on the island of Ireland to be part of the Irish nation. This was changed following the 2004 Referendum on Citizenship. In the Referendum almost 80 per cent of voters in the Republic voted to remove this automatic birthright from the Irish-born children of immigrants. Seemingly, most Irish citizens did not consider such Irish-born children part of the Irish nation. This outcome points to a strong sense of nationalism in twenty-first-century Ireland. Malesevic, in his analysis of Irish nationalism, argues that nationalist ideology and practice have actually intensified over the last several decades and that today's nationalism is more powerful and socially embedded than that present during de Valera's time.[23] Chapter 18 ('The future of Irish identity') examines how and to what extent this might indeed be the case. This conclusion chapter examines what has changed in what were, or what were once meant to be, the main planks of a distinctive Irish identity.

Notes

1 Benedict Anderson, *The Spectre of Comparisons: Nationalism, Southeast Asia and the World* (London: Verso, 1998), p. 333.

2 Benedict Anderson, 'Exodus', *Critical Inquiry*, 20.2 (1994), 314–327, p. 315.

3 Benedict Anderson, 'Western Nationalism and Eastern Nationalism', *New Left Review*, 9.2 (1998), p. 2.

4 Anderson, 'Western Nationalism and Eastern Nationalism', p. 3.

5 Ernest Gellner, 'The Coming of Nationalism and Its Interpretation: The Myths of Nation and Class', in Gopal Balakrishnan (ed.), *Mapping the Nation* (London: Verso, 1996), p. 105.

6 Anderson, 'Exodus', p. 317.

7 Benedict Anderson, 'Introduction', in Gopal Balakrishnan (ed.), *Mapping the Nation* (London: Verso, 1996), pp. 3–10.

8 Gellner, 'Coming of Nationalism', p. 107.

9 Gellner, 'Coming of Nationalism', p. 128.

10 Ernest Gellner, *Nations and Nationalism* (Oxford: Blackwell, 1983), p. 57.

11 Benedict Anderson, 'To What Can Late Eighteenth-Century French, British, and American Anxieties Be Compared?', *The American Historical Review*, 106.1 (2001), 1281–1289, p. 1283.

12 See Burke's, 'Tracts on the Popery Laws' (unpublished 1760–65), in Edmund Burke, *Letters, Speeches and Tracts on Irish Affairs*, ed. Matthew Arnold (London: Macmillan, 1881).

13 Edmund Burke, *A Letter to Sir Hercules Langrishe, Bart, M.P., on the subject of the Roman Catholics of Ireland, and the Propriety of Admitting them to the Elective Franchise, Consistently With The Principles Of The Constitution As Established in 1792*, 3 January 1792.

14 Thomas Bartlett, *Ireland: A History* (Cambridge: Cambridge University Press, 2010), pp. 425–426.

15 Cormac O'Grada and Kevin O'Rourke, 'Economic Growth in Ireland Since 1945', in N. Crafts and G. Toniolo (eds), *Economic Growth in Europe since 1945* (Cambridge: Cambridge University Press, 1996), p. 141.

16 Bryan Fanning, 'From Developmental Ireland to Migration Nation: Immigration and Shifting Rules of Belonging in the Republic of Ireland', *Economic and Social Review*, 41.3 (2010), 395–412.

17 Sinisa Malesevic, 'Irishness and Nationalism', in Tom Inglis (ed.), *Are the Irish Different?* (Manchester: Manchester University Press, 2014), p. 11.

18 Bryan Fanning and Andreas Hess, *Sociology in Ireland: A Short History* (London: Palgrave Pivot, 2015), pp. 28–34.

19 Sean O'Faoláin, *King of the Beggars: A Life of Daniel O'Connell, the Irish Liberator* (Dublin: Poolbeg, 1980).

20 Tom Garvin, 'Foreword', in Martin Tierney (ed.), *Michael Tierney: A Classicist's Outlook: Michael Tierney: 1894–1975* (Dublin: privately published, 2002).

21 Daniel Corkery, *The Hidden Ireland: A Study of Gaelic Munster in the Eighteenth Century* (Dublin: Gill and Macmillan, 1970 [1924]).

22 Tom Garvin, *Preventing the Future: Why Was Ireland So Poor For So Long?* (Dublin: Gill and Macmillan, 2004).

23 Malesevic, 'Irishness and Nationalism', p. 11.

2

In defence of methodological nationalism

In 1992 Francis Fukuyama declared the end of history, suggesting that with the fall of the Berlin Wall liberalism had triumphed as the political and economic paradigm across a globalised world.[1] In 1994 Yasemin Soysal amongst others and with less fanfare argued that an era of post-national citizenship had arrived.[2] The development of discourses of universal human rights had extended into the nation-state from beyond. Rights no longer strictly depended on nation-states. Cosmopolitan ideals expressed through human rights conventions had reached into nation-states. States bought into these on behalf of their citizens but also acknowledged the rights of denizens. In liberal democratic states both civil rights and some social rights to welfare goods and services like education and health care came to be largely disconnected from formal citizenship. Borders were being dismantled within the European Union. Money and information moved instantaneously around the world. Airfares became cheaper. People started to migrate in new waves to countries to which they had no historic connection, colonial or otherwise.

The new globalisation paradigm implied that, by comparison, the cultures of the past were homogeneous, certain, bounded and fixed. The new watchwords were 'hybridity', 'fluidity' and 'complexity', as if human societies had never before experienced such characteristics.[3] Influential intellectuals including Jurgen Habermas, John Rawls and Ulrick Beck emphasised how cosmopolitan humanism had come to influence norms of international reciprocity.[4] The new cosmopolitan theorists argued that the nation-state was being challenged by the formation of transnational political and legal structures and the onset of global risks that no state could address on its own.[5] Yet human rights continued to depend on what nation-states did about them under their laws. Cosmopolitanism was not a new notion. It was an Enlightenment idea – advanced notably by Immanuel Kant in *Perpetual Peace* (1795) – that had been sidelined by rise of nationalism as the dominant solidarity ideology of the nineteenth and twentieth centuries and by the rise of the nation-state as the main vehicle of political, civil and social rights. Universal principles continued to sit uncomfortably with nation-state politics.

For example, the asylum-seeker issue became politicised in a number of EU member states as a challenge to nation-state sovereignty.[6] The Irish response was to transfer all responsibility for the welfare of asylum seekers to the government department responsible for security and borders. In Ireland as elsewhere the right to seek asylum set out in the UN Convention on the Rights of Refugees (1951) was trumped by the carrier liability legislation and other border controls aimed at frustrating the exercise of this right. Irish citizens, even cosmopolitan ones, expected the Irish state to be capable of defending national sovereignty by being able to control borders. This expectation might be understood as a social fact, to use Émile Durkheim's terminology, about nation-states.[7] When Ireland ratified the Convention in 1956 its obligations to refugees were theoretical. When tested by real refugees Irish responses fell short of cosmopolitan or human rights ideals. The new waves of migration that are the focus of studies of transnationalism elicited responses that can only be understood through some focus on host nation-states. The politics of immigration in Ireland as elsewhere suggest cognitive distinctions between 'nationals' and 'non-nationals', dominant senses of community rooted in earlier phases of nation-building, the persistence of ethnic chauvinism alongside open labour markets, the invisibility of large immigrant communities going about their transnational lives within a national imaginary that barely notices their existence.[8]

The intellectual rejection of nationalist beliefs does not necessarily prompt reflexive scrutiny of one's own everyday nationalist practices or even – assuming for a moment that sociologists can stand outside of society – scrutiny of the bounded empathies and shared 'us and them' presumptions of their fellow citizens. These are summarised by Andreas Wimmer and Nina Glick Schiller in the following terms:

> Modern nationalism fuses four different notions of peoplehood that had developed separately in early modern Europe. These are: the people as a sovereign entity, which exercises political power by means of some sort of democratic procedure; the people as citizens of a state holding equal rights before the law; the people as a group of obligatory solidarity, an extended family unit knit together by obligations of mutual support; and the people as an ethnic community undifferentiated by distinctions of honour and

prestige, but united though common destiny and shared culture. These four notions of peoplehood are fused into one single people writ large. Democracy, citizenship, social security and national self-determination are the vertexes of a world order of nation-states as it matured after the Second World War.[9]

Similar social processes clearly affect different nation-states. Sociological theory is clearly useful in trying to understand these. But explanations lie in the detail. Alongside generic processes of social change there is a need to address specific contexts. The great European sociologists Karl Marx, Max Weber and Émile Durkheim knew this and acknowledged such contexts in their work even if their theories have often since been applied without reference to specific national contexts. To quote the opening sentence of their contemporary Leo Tolstoy's novel *Anna Karenina*: 'Happy families are all alike; every unhappy family is unhappy in its own way.'

Cages, containers and bounded communities

Much of my own work considers the Republic of Ireland as an object of understanding and a unit of analysis. One strand is exemplified by books with titles like *Racism and Social Change in the Republic of Ireland* (2012), *New Guests of the Irish Nation* (2009) and *Immigration and Social Cohesion in the Republic of Ireland* (2011). Another, focused on Irish intellectual history, is exemplified by books like *The Quest for Modern Ireland: The Battle of Ideas 1912–1986* (2008) and *An Irish Century: Studies 1912–2012* (2012). But I am also co-editor of *Globalization, Migration and Social Transformation*, a collection that emphasised the global and diasporic contexts of twenty-first-century Irish diversity.[10] And I was a founding editor of *Translocations*, an online journal with a similar emphasis on locating the Irish case in trans-national contexts or as put by my co-editor Ronaldo Munck: 'Ireland in the World, the World in Ireland'.[11] *Translocations* had the following manifesto:

> While it is a 'trans' journal, *Translocations* is not another global studies journal disembodied and non-grounded. We are a trans-locational journal in the belief that global processes can only take shape in particular locations.[12]

The turn towards transnationalism has given rise to more fluid and pluralist understandings of migration compared to the old 'push-pull' theories that dominated economic and sociological interpretations.[13] Yet, transnationalism as a phenomena 'does not swirl blithely free of the political spaces of nation-states'.[14] According to Anthony Smith, a sociologist of nationalism, 'the world nation-state system has become an enduring and stable component of our whole cognitive outlook'.[15] As put by Ulrick Beck, the nation-state came 'to constitute the container of society and the boundary of sociology'.[16] Methodological nationalism is a term used by sociologists to refer to social inquiry which is bounded by political borders. The term was coined by Hermino Martins in 1974 to refer to how statistics and social science research based on these came to focus on 'national communities' as the natural unit of social analysis.[17] Social science came to equate society with the nation-state, and conflate national interests with the purposes of social science.[18] It has taken for granted that the boundaries of the nation-state delimit and define the unit of analysis. Such presumptions have reflected and reinforced the identification that many scholars maintain with their own nation-states. Such methodological nationalism equated societies with nation-states and these as setting the parameters of social science analysis.[19]

Nationalism as an ideology assumed that humanity is naturally divided into a limited number of nations, which on the inside organise themselves as nation-states and, on the outside, set boundaries to distinguish themselves from other nation-states. The influence of such thinking in the Irish case can be seen in the emergence of the 1840s Young Irelander movement which like its European equivalents promoted national literatures, histories and music. Their efforts to promote cultural distinctiveness sought to assert that the Irish were a distinct nation deserving of their own nation-state.

During the nineteenth century states sought to cage nations, and ethnic groups sought states that demarcated those who shared the same culture and language from other cultural and linguistic groups. Nation-building goals of fostering cultural homogeneity and the creation of new mass identities co-existed alongside other forms of social modernisation. Sociologists who have focused on nationalism have emphasised shifts from *Gemeinschaft* to *Gesellschaft* within national containers. Such modernisation theory saw nation-building as a crucial component of developing an effective modern society, one capable of political stability and economic development.[20] The educationally transmitted, literate shared cultures of modern industrial states emerged along national lines.

In Ireland as elsewhere the nation-state came to be portrayed as the most fundamental category of social and political organisation. Yet the Irish nation-state is less than a century old. The ideological conceptions of nation that were poured into its creation resulted in a political entity that some Irish nationalists opposed because as a container it left out six northern counties. From such a perspective the Irish nation and the Irish nation-state are not coterminous. A civil war after the war of independence did not settle the question even if what became the Republic of Ireland became a distinct political container and a specific unit warranting sociological analysis. The sociological imagination which developed during the nineteenth century came to be implicitly shaped by nation-state perspectives on society, politics, law, justice and history.[21] Michael Mann argues that our primary twenty-first-century social cage remains the nation-state.[22] In the Irish case this is a cage or container (Ulrick Beck's term) that, for better or worse, excludes Northern Ireland and the millions of the Irish diaspora.

In recent decades social theorists like Smith, Mann, Ernest Gellner and Benedict Anderson have explicitly focused on nations and nationalism as sociological phenomena. Classical sociological theory postulated accounts of social relations and social change from one social structural type to another. The industrial revolution had been the seismic event of the early nineteenth century. It precipitated social change with no obvious link to political borders or inter-ethnic conflict. Smith has argued that the leading sociologist students of such change – Marx, Durkheim and Weber – spectacularly failed to develop conceptualisations of nationalism comparable to their classic analyses of capitalism, industrialisation, rationalisation and bureaucratisation. Gellner also has argued that such sociology, in its efforts to understand such change, placed little emphasis on nationalism.[23] It would be more accurate to suggest that nationalism was never the main focus of such sociology, that within the social sciences more generally nationalism hid in plain sight. Nationalism both influenced how social science developed in specific contexts yet was often ignored as phenomenon. As put by Seán L'Estrange:

> The human and social sciences do not have a great track record when it comes to nationalism. Not only have most disciplines allowed themselves to be shaped according to the 'national idea' of the particular society from which its practitioners have been drawn, thus creating distinct 'national traditions' in what are putatively universal scientific disciplines, but neither have they been particularly good at subjecting nationalism to systematic scrutiny with the full range of resources at their disposal.[24]

Max Weber's sociology emphasised shifts from traditional to bureaucratic, legal and professional forms of organisation and authority in what he saw as an ongoing process of rationalisation in economy and society. But he also classified racial identities, ethnicity and nationality in ways that highlighted common presumptions shared between these. Racial identities were predicated on presumptions of common inherited and inheritable traits understood to derive from common descent. Ethnicity referred to human groups that entertain a belief in their common descent because of similarities of physical type or of customs or of both, or because of memories of colonisation or migration. Weber emphasised that ethnic identities depended upon such belief; it did not matter whether or not an objective blood relationship existed. Whether racial, ethnic or national differences were real or not was irrelevant to Weber. What mattered was the consequences of such beliefs for how societies were organised and segregated. He noted that beliefs in ethnic identities often came to set limits upon how a community was politically defined.[25] Yet, ethnicity, as Weber understood it, only came to be a widely used concept from the 1980s.

Durkheim emphasised how patterns of social solidarity shifted with the division of labour in society. In peasant societies the basis of social interaction was the resemblance of one person's life to their neighbour's. The division of labour required by the industrial revolution altered this. Ferdinand Tonnies similarly postulated a shift from *Gemeinschaft* to *Gesellschaft*, terms that respectively denote communal identities based on similarity of ways of life and the complex social orders and interdependencies of the industrial era. The specific empirical focus of Tonnies's work was on Germany.[26] Durkheim, for his part, hoped that his sociology would help France to deal with the social crises thrown up by modernisation, the *anomie* that he saw as accompanying the unravelling of traditional communal social order.[27]

Marxism viewed capitalism as a global system, one that had been preceded by feudalism and would be succeeded by socialism. History for Marxists unfolded as the story of class conflict. They expected (or hoped) that national loyalties would be rejected by the exploited working class in favour of class consciousness; national loyalties, it was argued, made no more rational sense than for prisoners to develop feelings of loyalty towards jailers. But this was to underestimate, Gellner wrote in 1964 in sympathy with such Marxist analyses, the power and hold of the dark atavistic forces in human nature.[28] Marxists envisaged that nationalism and patriotism would be swept aside by proletarian internationalism. But nationalism no less than religion became the opium of proletariats. Nationalism in the Irish case, more so than in most places, won out over class consciousness.[29]

Marx and Friedrich Engels gave some thought to how Irish nationalism might help to bring about socialism. In an 1882 letter to Karl Kautsky, reflecting on the revolutions of 1848, Engels wrote that it was 'historically impossible for a great people' to seriously address their internal circumstances 'so long as national independence is lacking'.

Engels had come to believe that socialism could only be realised through nation-states. He argued the Irish 'were not only entitled but duty-bound to be national before they are international'.[30] In Ireland nationalism won out over socialism not least because Catholic social thought was designed explicitly to compete with the appeal of socialist ideals. Socialists around the world may have sung 'The Internationale' but in 1924 Joseph Stalin proclaimed the necessity of socialism in one country. In the Soviet Union the Second World War came to be called the Great Patriotic War. Obituaries for state socialism after 1989 proclaimed the end of history, meaning the dominance of liberalism as a social, economic and political engine of progress. But the spread of free markets was accompanied by new manifestations of nationalism. Yugoslavia split into warring nations. Serbians engaged in a programme of ethnic cleansing aimed at creating a mono-ethnic nation-state uncontaminated by non-nationals. In some other parts of Europe – Germany in the aftermath of the Second World War and Ireland chastened by the northern conflict – cosmopolitan political and intellectual elites have sought to keep a lid on atavistic expressions of nationalist sentiment.

The nation-states and host cultures that find themselves disrupted by immigration cannot be understood as static entities. For example, in the Irish case an 'Irish-Ireland' cultural nation-building project dating from the nineteenth century came to be displaced gradually from the mid-twentieth century by an economic developmental nation-building project, a victory of liberal utilitarianism over cultural nationalism that found expression as economic nationalism. This impacted not just on the goals of the Irish state (sometimes now referred to by media commentators as 'Ireland PLC') but arguably also upon the habitus of Irish citizens. But the kinds of social change that preoccupied sociologists during the second half of the twentieth-century – for example relating to urbanisation, individualism, secularisation and attitudes to sexuality – also reflected transnational patterns of social change. There is much about everyday life in twenty-first-century Ireland that is generically modern and pretty indistinguishable from day-to-day existence in many other Western countries be it shopping at Lidl or Aldi, the organisation of work, the use of social media or watching box sets on DVD or Netflix.

Nevertheless, perceptions that significant cultural differences persist between nation-states find ongoing expression in political responses to immigration. For example, ethnic nepotism, a term that refers to feelings of primary solidarity with co-ethnics or fellow citizens, can be identified in justifications for nation-states giving some immigrants lesser rights and entitlements to welfare goods and services.[31] Ethnic nepotism was exploited politically during the 2004 Citizenship Referendum to accentuate cognitive distinctions between 'nationals' and 'non-nationals' in a context where citizens were overwhelmingly drawn from the majority host ethnic group. Almost 80 per cent of Irish nationals who voted in the 2004 Referendum seemingly endorsed ethnic nepotism. Furthermore, an *Irish Times* opinion poll in January 2006 suggested that almost 80 per cent of voters wanted a system of work permits to be reintroduced for citizens from the ten new European Union member states coming to Ireland.[32] The findings of the Irish National Election Study (INES) 2002–07 were that some 62.4 per cent of respondents in 2002 (falling to 58.8 per cent in 2007) agreed or strongly agreed that there should be 'strict limits' on immigration.[33] Gradations of rights between citizens and non-citizens, immigrant 'guest' workers, 'illegal' workers, refugees and asylum seekers have emerged in a number of Western countries that as recently as a century ago operated few restrictions on immigration. In such a context citizenship becomes not just a set of rights, but also a mechanism of exclusion.[34]

Whereas sociological metaphors depict nation-states as cages and containers, those of nationalists refer to motherlands, fatherlands and homeland security. Where cosmopolitan critics of nationalism have depicted it as a pathogen, Benedict Anderson has emphasised how nationalism from the inside has been framed by the language of love:

> In an age where it is so common for progressive, cosmopolitan intellectuals (particularly in Europe) to insist on the near-pathological character of nationalism, its roots in fear and hatred of the Other, and its affinities with racism, it is useful to remind ourselves that nations inspire live, and often profoundly self-sacrificing love. The cultural products of nationalism – poetry, prose fiction, music, plastic arts – show this love very clearly in thousands of different forms and styles.[35]

'Nationalism is not a moral mistake', Craig Calhoun adds, for all that it has been implicated in atrocities and makes people think of arbitrary boundaries and contemporary global divisions as ancient and inevitable.[36] Cosmopolitan theorists, Calhoun suggests, underestimate the work done by nationalism and national identities in organising human life as well as the politics of the contemporary world. They treat nationalism as 'a sort of error smart people will readily move beyond – or an evil good people will reject'. Their theories 'grasp less well than they should the reality of the contemporary world'.[37] But, 'in failing to attend well enough to nationalism, ethnicity and related claims to solidarity, the otherwise attractive cosmopolitan visions have also underestimated how central nationalist categories have been to political and social theory, to practical reasoning about democracy, to political legitimacy and the nature of society itself'.[38] Take nationalism seriously, he argues, especially if you don't approve of it.

Notes

This chapter is an edited version of Bryan Fanning, 'In Defence of Methodological Nationalism: Immigration and the Irish Nation-State', *Irish Journal of Sociology*, 21.1 (2013), 1–16.

 1 Francis Fukuyama, *The End of History and the Last Man* (London: Penguin, 2002).
 2 Yasemin N. Soysal, *Limits of Citizenship: Migrants and Postnational Membership in Europe* (Chicago: Chicago University Press, 1994).
 3 Andreas Wimmer and Nina Glick Schiller, 'Methodological Nationalism, the Social Sciences and the Study of Migration: An Essay in Historical Epistemology', *International Migration Review*, 37.3 (2003), 576–610, p. 596.
 4 Robert Fine and Will Smith, 'Jurgen Habermas's Theory of Cosmopolitanism', *Constellations*, 10.4 (2003), 469–487; Ulrick Beck, 'The Cosmopolitan Perspective: Sociology of the Second Age of Modernity', *British Journal of Sociology*, 51.1 (2000), 79–105.
 5 Robert Fine and Vivienne Boon, 'Cosmopolitanism: Between Past and Future', *European Journal of Social Theory*, 10.1 (2007), 5–16.
 6 Eleonore Kofman, 'Citizenship, Migration and the Reassertion of National Identity', *Citizenship Studies*, 9.1 (2005), 453–467, p. 459.
 7 Bryan Fanning, *Immigration and Social Cohesion in the Republic of Ireland* (Manchester: Manchester University Press, 2011), p. 39.
 8 A.M. Suskucki (ed.), *Welfare Citizenship and Welfare Nationalism* (Helsinki: Nordwel, 2011).
 9 Andreas Wimmer and Nina Glick Schiller, 'Methodological Nationalism and Beyond: Nation-State Building, Migration and the Social Sciences', *Global Networks*, 2.4 (2002), 301–334, p. 309.
10 Bryan Fanning and Ronaldo Munck (eds), *Globalisation, Migration and Social Transformation: Ireland in Europe and the World* (London: Ashgate, 2011).
11 Ronaldo Munck, 'Ireland in the World, the World in Ireland', in Fanning and Munck (eds), *Globalisation, Migration and Social Transformation*, p. 3.
12 *Translocation: Migration and Social Change: An Irish Inter-university Open Access E-journal*, www.imstr.ie.
13 Munck, 'Ireland in the World', p. 9.
14 Gavan Titley, 'Media Transnationalism in Ireland', *Translocations*, 3.1 (2008), 29–49.
15 Anthony D. Smith, *Nationalism in the Twentieth Century* (Oxford: Martin Robinson, 1979), p. 21.
16 Ulrick Beck, 'How Not to Become a Museum Piece', *British Journal of Sociology*, 56.3 (2005), 335–343, p. 338.
17 Hermino Martins, 'Time and Theory in Sociology', in John Rex (ed.), *Approaches*

to Sociology: An Introduction to Major Trends in British Sociology (London: Routledge and Kegan Paul, 1974), p. 274.

18 Anthony D. Smith, 'Nationalism and Social Theory', British Journal of Sociology, 34.1 (1983), 19–38.

19 Daniel Chernilo, 'Social Theory's Methodological Nationalism: Myth and Reality', European Journal of Social Theory, 9.5 (2006), 5–22, p. 6.

20 Craig Calhoun, Nations Matter: Culture, History and the Cosmopolitan Dream (London: Routledge, 2007), p. 37.

21 Michael Mann, 'The Emergence of Modern European Nationalism', in John A. Hall and I.C. Jarvie (eds), Transition to Modernity: Essays on Power, Wealth and Belief (Cambridge: Cambridge University Press, 1992).

22 Michael Mann, The Dark Side of Democracy: Explaining Ethnic Cleansing (Cambridge: Cambridge University Press, 2005).

23 Ernest Gellner, Encounters with Nationalism (Oxford: Blackwell, 1994), p. 9.

24 Seán L'Estrange, 'Commentary: Excavating Nationalism in Archaeology', Archaeological Review from Cambridge, 27.2 (2012), p. 189.

25 Max Weber, Wirtshaft und Gesellschaft, first published posthumously in 1922, trans. E. Matthews in W.G. Runciman (ed.), Max Weber: Selections in Translation (Cambridge: Cambridge University Press, 1978).

26 Ferdinand Tonnies, Community and Civil Society, ed. Jose Harris (Cambridge: Cambridge University Press, 2001).

27 Steven Lukes, Emile Durkheim (New York: Harper Row, 1972), p. 80.

28 Ernest Gellner, Thought and Change (London: Weidenfeld and Nicolson, 1964), p. 148.

29 Mann, 'Emergence of Modern European Nationalism'.

30 Friedrich Engels, Letter to Karl Kautsky, 7 February 1882.

31 Kenan Malik, Strange Fruit: Why Both Sides are Wrong on the Race Debate (London: One World, 2008).

32 Irish Times, 22 January 2006.

33 Michael Marsh and Richard Sinnott, Irish National Election Survey [INES] 2002–2007: Data Description and Documentation (Dublin: Trinity College Dublin and University College Dublin, 2009), www.tcd.ie/ines/files/code-book_27_05_2009.pdf (accessed on 27 October 2015).

34 Christian Joppke, 'How Immigration is Changing Citizenship: A Comparative View', Ethnic and Racial Studies, 22.4 (1999), 629–632.

35 Benedict Anderson, Imagined Communities: Reflections on the Origins and Spread of Nationalism (London: Verso, 2006), p. 141.

36 Calhoun, Nations Matter, p. 1.

37 Calhoun, Nations Matter, p. 7.

38 Calhoun, Nations Matter, p. 80.

3

Patrick Pearse predicts the future

On 4 August 1906, in *An Claidheamh Soluis,* which translates as the sword of light (or light sabre), Patrick Pearse wrote a piece in English imagining the Ireland of 2006. He was dozing one evening in his garden when the postman arrived, laid a bundle of letter and papers on the table and saluted him. 'You have Irish?' Pearse replied. He had not known that any of the local post-office staff spoke Irish. 'To be sure I have, Sir' the postman replied with a note of surprise in his voice. 'If I hadn't it's a small chance I'd have of my present job.' This was the first sign that there was something amiss, or all too right. He took the postman's remark as a piece of sarcasm but then he noticed the man's uniform. It was a very neat dark green. On the collar in small letters of white metal, was the cryptic inscription 'P na hE'. It stood for Post na hÉireann, the postman explained with a note of surprise as he departed.[1]

The narrator turned to his bundle of post. Every item was addressed in Irish. The familiar pencilled translation into English of Irish addresses was absent. The postmarks too were in Irish. Puzzled, he picked up a copy of *An Claidheamh Soluis* from the bundle. It was larger than usual. Every word was in Irish. Advertisements and all! *An Claidheamh* was now a daily broadsheet. The issue in his hand was dated 4 August 2006. Fearing this was a dream he wasted no time in gleaning as much about twenty-first-century Ireland as possible.

One article announced the opening of the Oireachtas (trans., 'Parliament') by the Ard Rí (trans., 'High King') at a ceremony to be attended by the Emperor of the French and the President of the Russian Republic. There would be a royal procession from the Palace of the Nation – dignitaries followed by detachments of the National Guard (*Fianna Éireann* in Irish) and the Boy-Corps of the Palace down Sráid Dhomhnaill Uí Chonail (Daniel O'Connell Street) and across O'Connell

Bridge. The ministries and other public buildings along the route would be decorated. There was no mention of the General Post Office. Dignitaries in the procession would include the President and officers of the Gaelic League, the adjudicator and officials of the Oireachtas, members of the Irish Academy and the Bards in their robes. When the procession reached the Hyde monument in Plas an Chraoibhín the Herald of Ireland would proclaim the Peace of the Gaels. The Bard of Ireland would invoke the spirit of Gaelic Thought and Imagination and the Ard Rí would declare Oireachtas in session. The National Hymn would be intoned. Another article described dramatic changes in climate and to the environment:

> It must be remembered that – as a result of the draining of the bogs and the re-forestation of the country – the temperature of Ireland has risen several degrees within the last century; which explains why it is now possible for us to hold nearly all our gatherings, whether for business or for pleasure, in the open air. We who are used to a Baile Átha Cliath of shady boulevards and open-air cafes can hardly realise that our city had neither boulevards nor cafes in 1906. People then paraded sun-baked streets in summer and ploughed their way through sludge in winter; whilst they resorted for 'refreshment' to evil-smelling dens known as 'public-houses', which no decent woman would enter.

Pearse then turned to the parliamentary column, which reported a debate about a bill for the compulsory teaching of Japanese as a second language in seaport towns and cities. This reflected the growing importance of Japanese as a commercial world language. The Minister of Education opposed the bill, recalling that it was once maintained that English would become the dominant world language when it was now only spoken by a few peasants in Somersetshire. How had this come about? The conquest of England by the Russian republic and the splitting up of the British Empire into independent kingdoms and republics soon destroyed the commercial value of English. It had never been a valuable language in intellectual terms. *An Claidheamh Soluis* described the language policy of the Irish state as based on two longstanding principles. Every child had a right to be taught its own mother-tongue. Every child ought to learn in addition at least one other language:

> Almost the first act of the Revolutionary Government of 19– (the figure was unfortunately blotted) had been to establish a national education system embodying the two principles he had referred to. Under that system Irish was regarded as the vernacular or 'first language' over one-third of the total area of the country, English being regarded as the vernacular over the remaining two-thirds. In the first-named area English, French, or German

was taught as a 'second language'; in the other, Irish was the 'second language' almost universally adopted, though a few schools, chiefly in the North East, adhere to French or German for a few years. Ireland, as they were aware, rapidly extended its vernacular area, with the result that, in a generation and a half, it completely ousted English as 'first language'. The conquest of England by the Russian republic and the splitting up of the British Empire into independent kingdoms and republics soon destroyed the commercial value of English.

This collapse of Britain had provided the impetus for the abandonment of English as a second language in Ireland in all but three schools, two in Beál Feirste (Belfast) and one in Rath Ó Maine (Rathmines). The parliamentary report recorded that there had been laughter as this was noted by the Minister of Education. Policy in 2006 was for the teaching of no compulsory second languages. The same imagined 2006 article also noted a review of a history of the National University: 'founded by public subscription in 1911, – *before* the War of Revolution, in which, by the way, its students played a prominent part.'

Pearse imagined this twenty-first-century Ireland several years before he became a self-appointed prophet of revolutionary blood-sacrifice nationalism. My aim here is to consider the kind of material future Pearse imagined Ireland might have in isolation, insofar as this is feasible, from what his former pupil, secretary, 1916 Rising comrade and biographer Desmond Ryan described as the frequent harking on bloodshed that became monotonous in his speeches, 'with an almost sinister frequency towards the end'.[2] Pearse was born in 1879. He joined the Gaelic League when he was sixteen years old and moved quickly up its ranks. In 1903 he became the editor of *An Claidheamh Soluis*, its newspaper. In 1909 he founded St Edna's school for boys. He came to political nationalism only in the last few years of his life.

In various *Claidheamh Soluis* editorials Pearse insisted on the primary importance of the Gaelic revival over all other kinds of 'national work':

When the position of Ireland's language as her greatest heritage is once fixed, all other matters will insensibly adjust themselves. As it develops and *because* it develops, it will carry all kindred movements with it, Irish art, Irish dancing, Irish games and customs, Irish industries, Irish politics – all these are worthy objects. Not one of them, however can be said to be fundamental.

When Ireland's language is established, her own distinctive culture is assured ... All phases of a nation's life will most assuredly adjust themselves on national lines as best suited to the national character is safeguarded by its strongest bulwark.[3]

In his later writings Pearse played John the Baptist to what he envisaged as his own Christ-like martyrdom for the cause of Irish Freedom. But freedom to do what? Nationalists of Pearse's generation pursued a Gaelic linguistic revival to make the case for Irish political autonomy and imagined that home rule would provide a means of securing the Gaelic revival: 'To some it held out the delightful prospect of Orange boys and Orange girls being forced to learn Irish', he wrote in his 1912 essay *The Murder Machine*: 'To others it meant the dawn of an era of commonsense, the ushering in of the reign of a "sound modern education" suitable to the needs of a progressive modern people.' If the former was delightful, the latter appalled him.[4]

The Murder Machine set out Pearse's pedagogical vision, honed as the headmaster of St Edna's, the experimental school he founded in 1909 after he stepped down as editor of *An Claidhmeamh Soluis*. He attacked Ireland's 'filthy' utilitarian education system, 'a lifeless thing without a soul', which aimed to turn men and women into 'mere Things' for sale.[5] Education had come to be conceived of as some sort of manufacturing process for turning out citizens according to certain approved patterns. The example he gave focused on the moulding of middle-class Catholic children, for only a very small percentage of children attended secondary schools at the time:

> Our children are the 'raw material'; we desire for their education; 'modern methods' which must be 'efficient' but 'cheap'; we send them to Clongowes to be 'finished'; when 'finished' they are 'turned out'; specialists 'grind' them for the English Civil Service and the so-called liberal professions; in each of our great colleges there is a department known as the 'scrap heap' though officially called the Fourth Preparatory – that limbo into with the *débris* ejected by the machine is relegated.

Pearse had never been sent to Clongowes, the elite Catholic school founded by the Jesuits to which Irish Party leaders sent their sons, though he was an external examiner in Irish history for the school. He attended the middle-class Westland Row Christian Brothers school in Dublin. The 'murder machine' Pearse railed against took its raw material, remoulded it and ejected it 'with all the likeness of its former self crushed from it'. The actual school he attended prepared him for formal examinations by sticking to the curriculum and pushing pupils to learn every subject by rote. But the machine, as his biographer Ruth Dudley Edwards put it, 'did not eject Pearse. He was an intelligent, exceptionally industrious boy, who adapted successfully to the system, whatever his later reservations.'[6] After he completed his Intermediate examinations at the age of sixteen the school employed him as an Irish teacher.

What was being 'murdered' Pearse claimed in 1913 was the spiritual-ity, as he saw it, of the Irish nation.[7] The 'murder machine' was at once an instrument of British policy and, even more pernicious, an instrument of progress. A section of the essay was headed 'Against Modernism'. Never averse to hyperbole Pearse claimed that the old Irish, 'two thou-sand years ago', had the best and noblest education system ever known amongst men. Here he meant the schools described in the legends of Cúchulainn. In lectures and his essays he was, as one of his friends Joseph Holloway put it, 'indiscriminately eulogistic to absurdity' about the literary merits of the Gaelic sagas that he came to treat as history.[8] As put by his biographer Ruth Dudley Edwards:

> No modern historian would assert that these stories were other than fables, but pioneering Irish historians in the previous three centuries, including Keating, O'Donovan and O'Curry, believed them to be authentic. By 1900, the attentions of continental scholars had been turned on Irish literature and severe blows had been struck at the acceptance of stories of figures like Finn as historical fact. Pearse had read these modern scholars, but could not bring himself into line with their findings. He arraigned himself uncom-promisingly alongside the 'euhemeristic' historians – those who treated supernatural beings as real historical characters.[9]

The purpose of Pearse's mash-up of myth and history, of mythic ancient Ireland – of the uncertain history of early Christian Ireland, of a senti-mentalised pre-seventeenth-century Gaelic aristocratic Ireland and of chauvinistic accounts of post-1798 patriot movements – was to marshal a pantheon of Irish heroes to inspire the youth of twentieth-century Ireland to patriotic sacrifice:

> If our schools would set themselves that task, the task of fostering once again knightly courage and strength and truth – we should have the begin-nings of an educational system. And what an appeal an Irish school system might have! When we were starting St. Edna's I said to my boys: We must re-create and perpetuate in Ireland the knightly tradition of Cúchulainn, 'better is a short life with honour than a long life with dishonour'; 'I care not if I were to live my life but one day and one night, if only my fame and my deeds live after me'; the noble tradition of the Fianna, 'we the Fianna, never told a lie, falsehood was never imputed to us'; 'strength in our hands, truth on our lips, and cleanness in our hearts'; the Christ-like tradition of Colmcille 'if I die it shall be from the excess of love I bear the Gael.' And to that antique evangel should be added the evangels of later days: the stories Red Hugh and Wolfe Tone and Robert Emmet and John Mitchel and O'Donovan Rossa and Eoghan O'Growney. I have seen Irish boys and girls moved inexpressibly by the story of Emmet or the story of Anne Devlin, and I have always felt it to be legitimate to make use for educational pur-poses of an exaltation so produced.[10]

Colmcille's excessive love for the Gael, *The Murder Machine* had approvingly declared a few pages earlier, had been 'so excessive as to annihilate all thought of self, a recognition that one much give all, much be willing to make the ultimate sacrifice'.[11] Teachers had to be capable of so inspiring their pupils. For 'so priest-like an office' nothing less than 'the highest souls and noblest intellects of the race' would do. In *The Murder Machine* he likened his ideal schoolmasters to Christ, their pupils to Christ's disciples.[12]

Pearse described his ideal school as a 'child republic' but the kind of freedom he proposed for teachers suggested an authoritarian system where they determined what their pupils needed to learn. St Edna's, the school he established, had boy officials elected by the pupils themselves but these seem to have been invested with less responsibility than was usual in the prefect system operated by British public schools.[13] James Larkin sent his three sons there. Pearse took them in following the Dublin Lockout in 1913. Larkin's son Jim, in his memoir, recalled the regime in the school as strict, living conditions as Spartan, the food as scarce and the heating as deliberately minimal during winter. The belief was that the boys should keep themselves warm through exercise.[14] None of this suggests that St Edna's operated an especially harsh regime by the standards of the time.

As an essay *The Murder Machine* operated on two registers. Beneath the thicket of Pearse's overstated, exaggerated, extravagant and hyperbolic prose (this barrage of synonyms is warranted) there was some consideration about what might be feasible. The case he made for educational reform, he declared, was no more than 'a plea for freedom within the law'.[15] Teachers ought to be free to decide what their pupils needed to learn and not be required to submit to the stultifying uniformity of a state examination system. In a future independent Ireland, under an Irish Minister for Education, the education system would be drawn into 'a homogeneous whole' that included Ulster. Pearse advocated a bilingual school system. Ireland was six-sevenths English-speaking with an Irish-speaking seventh. Irish nationalists would restore Irish as a vernacular to the English-speaking six-sevenths and would establish Irish as the national language of a free Ireland. Irish would be language of instruction in the Irish-speaking one-seventh with English taught as a second language. But where English was the home language it must of necessity be the 'first language in schools'. In such cases Irish would be a compulsory 'second language' but it would be used as a medium of instruction from the outset.[16]

Pearse called for an Ireland, 'not merely free but Gaelic as well'. By those criteria, Conor Cruise O'Brien pithily observed in 'The Embers of Easter', a 1966 essay on the legacies of the 1916 Rising, it came to be 75

per cent free and 0.6 per cent Gaelic, well down from the one-seventh
Pearse estimated it to be in 1912.[17] The Irish state that fell short of the
Republic Pearse proclaimed in 1916 banished him to the margins of its
own national pageants even as Pearse's image came to be commemorated
on postage stamps and street names. The 1966 commemoration of the
1916 Rising centred more on James Connolly, who with Pearse had co-
authored the 1916 Proclamation of an Irish Republic. The Proclamation
declared the right of the people of Ireland to the ownership of Ireland
and poignantly declared that all children of the nation would be cherished equally. Pearse never presented convincing arguments as to how
the revolution he advocated might realise such social goals.

In his October 1913 *From a Hermitage* essay, the Hermitage being
the estate where St Edna's was situated, he pondered the prevalence
of poverty and hunger in Dublin. He described himself as not smart-
ing under any burning personal wrong (other than belonging to an
enslaved nation). He calculated that one-third of the people of Dublin
were underfed, that half the children attending Irish primary schools
were undernourished, that twenty thousand Dublin families lived in
one-room tenements, yet he could not quite bring himself to agree with
James Larkin's 'unwise' methods of addressing such hideous wrongs.
The root of the problem he insisted in October 1913 lay in foreign domination, not ruthless capitalism.

His response to such inequalities was to assert that Ireland was
capable of feeding twenty million, that a free Ireland would drain the
bogs, would harness the rivers, nationalise the railways and would
promote commerce.[18] This echoed his sketch of twenty-first-century
Ireland set out in 1906 in *An Claidheamh Soluis*, where all social problems had evidently disappeared by 2006, where everyone spoke Irish,
where the Irish had stopped drinking and where even the climate had
improved, all because Ireland had become free.

The widespread view was that Pearse was 'a spinner of phrases without
a practical spark in him', an accusation from which Desmond Ryan
tried with difficulty to defend him.[19] Ryan was the editor of Pearse's
works including his political writings and an account of his work at St
Edna's, *The Story of a Success*. This comprised a series of articles from
An Macnaomh (trans., 'The Youth'), the school magazine edited by
Pearse. Parts of *The Story of a Success* – various phrases, sentences and
arguments – were reworked into *The Murder Machine* although the tone
of both texts was, for the most part, quite different. Where *The Murder
Machine* mostly denounced what he was against, *The Story of a Success*
described what Pearse hoped to achieve at St Edna's. He took pride in
the pedigree of pupils that the school attracted.

I admit that our opportunities were unique. In no other school in Ireland can there be, in proportion to its size, so much of the stuff out of which men and nations are made. There is hardly a boy of all our seventy who does not come from a home which has traditions of literary, scholarly or political service.[20]

Denis Gwynn, son of the Irish Party MP Stephen Gwynn, was described by Pearse as gallant and noble in the Cúchulainn pageant put on by the school in 1909. Pearse hoped the boys would remain under Cúchulainn's spell, but Gwynn served in the British Army on the Western Front rather than in the GPO and became a notable academic critic of the physical-force nationalism professed by Pearse. Other past pupils went on to be part of independent Ireland's great and good, and a number – like Kenneth Reddin, who became a judge in 1922 – took the side of the Free State in the civil war against those uncompromising republicans who saw themselves as Pearse's successors. Joseph Sweeney, a Donegal pupil elected as a Sinn Féin TD there in 1920, was one of a number what Pearse styled the Boy-Corps of St Edna's who joined the 1916 Rising as runners. He later became a Major-General in the Irish Army. Pearse sought to produce a new elite filled, as put it in the Christmas 1910 issue of *An Macnaomh*, with the spirit that sent Robert Emmet with a smiling face to the gibbet. In this he was only partly successful.

His target in *The Murder Machine* was the state, with its emphasis on exams and standardised curriculum. He argued that monopoly control of public examinations in secondary schools, exercised since the Intermediate Education Act of 1898, gave the state virtual control of the secondary curriculum. But the schools themselves were overwhelmingly owned and run by the Church. Pearse for the most part ignored the elephant in the room that was the denominational school system though he referred twice to the complicity of the Church 'in running the murder machine'. There was the aforementioned reference to the Jesuit-run Clongowes and a passing one to the role of the Catholic Church in main-taining 'a portion of the machinery'.[21] An intense battle for the control of education for Catholics had been decisively won by the Church during the second half of the nineteenth century. The mass expansion of the primary school system had been levered by dedicated teaching orders such as the Christian Brothers. There were few private schools – what in England were called public schools – where pedagogical innovation might take place at the discretion of a head teacher.[22] Pearse's educational vision floundered to some extent for the want of a more English school system and to a greater extent in the face of Catholic educational ideals, which were no less intensely pursued in Church-run schools than those of Pearse at St Edna's.

During his years as editor of *An Claidheamh Soluis* Pearse clashed with the Catholic Church over what he saw was inadequate support for the Irish language from the hierarchy who did not support making Gaelic mandatory in seminaries. Pearse being Pearse, his criticism was intemperate.[23] Pearse was a cultural nationalist first and a Catholic only in far second place. His personal mythic structure incorporated Christ alongside Cúchulainn into an idea of sacrifice for nation. His 1906 vision of Ireland's future in *An Claidheamh Soluis* cut the Church out of the picture. The culmination of Pearse's imaginary 2006 procession of poets in priestly robes was the invocation of the 'spirit of Gaelic Thought and Imagination' – a *Geist* not Christ – of a nation in worship of itself.

Such thinking was anathema to many Irish Catholic intellectuals of his time and the Catholic clergy who dominated education after his death.[24] A number of 1915 articles in the Jesuit periodical *Studies* attacked the German equivalent of what Pearse advocated in *The Murder Machine*: a *Kultur* of state, nation and *Volk* idolisation manufactured in school and camp.[25] The Church was clear that the duty of schools was 'to train children to love and fear God'. Seminaries and Catholic secondary schools of the time described themselves as in the business of recruiting soldiers for Christ. Pearse had no monopoly in martial language. But other Irish schools did not put Cúchulainn on a par with Christ.

After independence the government sought to gaelicise education, along the lines advocated by Pearse in the few passages of *The Murder Machine* that made specific policy proposals, but there was no impetus to follow Pearse's pedagogical programme. Pearse had made a serious study of educational innovations in other European countries – especially Belgium, which had developed a bilingual school system. He disapproved of corporal punishment and of learning by rote. The Christian Brothers might have venerated Pearse but the main pedagogical tool of many poorly educated Brothers was the leather strap. Their schools were variously aimed at building the Catholic professional middle class, recruiting more Christian Brothers, ordering the lives of the poorer classes and warehousing unwanted and vulnerable children on behalf of the state.

Pearse idealised the surviving remnants of the Irish-speaking peasantry of Connaught, where he went to learn and practise his Irish, but had little of understanding of the poverty that forced many to learn English in order to be able to find employment in Ireland or emigrate. The folk tales they recounted to visiting writers and Gaelic students made them conduits to Ireland's mythic past. As put by Ruth Dudley Edwards, after giving a number of examples of his incomprehension of the difficulties of their everyday lives: 'To him they were the repository

of the noble tradition of the Gael, and it bewildered him that they did
not find complete satisfaction in the fulfilment of this sacred duty.'[26] The
economic pressures upon Irish-speaking communities continued in the
generations following Pearse's death despite government assistance for
Gaelteacht areas.

For most of the hundreds of thousands of Irish children obligated
to study Irish all though their primary and secondary education, the
language did not take. It had no utilitarian purpose except to secure
state jobs and positions in teacher-training colleges. The majority of
pupils did not use Irish in their homes. The teaching of Irish was often
bad and was hampered intellectually by the small range and volume
of available literature compared to thriving European languages such
as English, French or German. Simply put, there was just not enough
great stuff to read. Eighteen-year-old James Joyce briefly attended Irish
classes given by the twenty-year-old Pearse at University College, but
seems to have been put off by the experience. Joyce gave up his Irish
lessons, according to his biographer Richard Ellman, because Pearse
found it necessary to exalt Irish by denigrating the English language.[27]
The Irish literature upon which Pearse heaped hyperbole was mostly
mediaeval and whilst there was nothing wrong with that it was hardly
made for twentieth-century audiences. In a 1913 essay Pearse asserted
(a key word in his lexicon) that the *Táin* was greater than the *Iliad*, that
the story of Diarmuid and Gráinne was more psychologically acute than
Ibsen's *Hedda Gabler*, but found few if any takers for such claims.[28]
Pearse and other revivalists wrote stories, plays and poems for modern
audiences. Irish-language literature found its niche, but a recurring
feature of debates about the future of the Irish language after independence was that these, by necessity, took place in English. The free Irish
people mostly chose to read novels and newspapers in English. Writers
as different as Canon Sheehan, Frank O'Connor, James Joyce, John
McGahern and Maeve Binchy all wrote about what it was to be Irish
in English. People went to the cinema where English became, once the
talkies arrived, the language of romance and adventure. Their great-
grandchildren most probably know more about *Lord of the Rings* or
Game of Thrones than the *Táin*.

Notes

This chapter was previously published in the *Dublin Review of Books*, 20 May
2013.

1 Patrick Pearse, *An Claidheamh Soluis*, 4 August 1906.
2 Desmond Ryan, *Remembering Sion* (London: Arthur Barker, 1934).

3　*An Claidheamh Soluis*, 27 August 1904.

4　Patrick Pearse, *The Murder Machine*, in *Collected Works of Pádraic H. Pearse: Political Writings and Speeches* (Dublin and Belfast: Phoenix, 1917), p. 23.

5　Pearse, *Murder Machine*, pp. 7–10.

6　See Ruth Dudley Edwards, *Patrick Pearse: The Triumph of Failure* (Dublin: Irish Academic Press, 2006), p. 13.

7　Pearse, *Murder Machine*, p. 16.

8　Edwards, *Triumph of Failure*, p. 29.

9　Edwards, *Triumph of Failure*, p. 38.

10　Pearse, *Murder Machine*, p. 39.

11　Pearse, *Murder Machine*, p. 25.

12　Pearse, *Murder Machine*, p. 23.

13　Norman Atkinson, 'The Educational Ideas of Patrick Pearse, 1879–1916', *Comparative Education Review*, 11.1 (February 1967), p. 71.

14　James Larkin, *In the Footsteps of Big Jim: A Family Biography* (Dublin: Blackwater Press, 1995).

15　Pearse, *Murder Machine*, p. 36.

16　Pearse, *Murder Machine*, pp. 45–47.

17　Conor Cruise O'Brien, 'The Embers of Easter', *Irish Times*, 7 April 1966.

18　Pearse, *From a Hermitage, October 1913* in *Political Writings*, pp. 178–181.

19　Patrick Pearse, *The Collected Works of Padraic H. Pearse: Vol 4*, ed. Desmond Ryan (Dublin: Phoenix, 1924), p. 132.

20　Pearse, *Collected Works*, p. 6.

21　Pearse, *Murder Machine*, p. 10.

22　Atkinson, 'Educational Ideas of Patrick Pearse', p. 79.

23　Edwards, *Triumph of Failure*, p. 76.

24　Alfred O'Rahilly, 'The Influence of German Philosophy', *Studies*, 4.16 (1915), 563–577.

25　Alfred O'Rahilly, 'Ideals at Stake', *Studies*, 4.13 (1915) 16–33, and M.F. Fagan, S.J, 'Kultur and Our Need of It', *Studies*, 4.14 (1915), 169–184.

26　Edwards, *Triumph of Failure*, p. 53.

27　Richard Ellman, *James Joyce* (Oxford: Oxford University Press, 1959), p. 62.

28　Patrick Pearse, 'Some Aspects of Irish Literature', *Studies*, 2.5 (1913), 810–822.

4

Paul Cullen's devotional revolution

Paul Cullen (1803–73) was perhaps as important a maker of modern Ireland as Daniel O'Connell and in the decades after O'Connell's death, when parliamentary nationalism languished in the doldrums, he was Ireland's most important Catholic leader. O'Connell built a polity out of a peasantry mobilised parish by parish and achieved Catholic emancipation. Cullen arrived on the Irish scene almost two decades later, loosened the link between the Church and nationalist politics and left as his legacy a near-century of Catholic power. This era of Catholic dominance in its final phase was exemplified by Archbishop John Charles McQuaid, a successor to Cullen as Catholic Archbishop of Dublin. McQuaid was, in many respects, cut from a mould forged by Cullen.

Cullen was born in Prospect, County Kildare. He studied in Carlow but at seventeen years of age enrolled in the College of Propaganda in Rome. Between 1832 and 1850 he was rector of the Irish College in Rome, where he counted John Henry Newman as one of his protégés. In 1850 he was appointed Archbishop of Armagh and from 1852 until his death was Archbishop of Dublin. His voluminous papers, previously and partially published in five idiosyncratic volumes by Peadar Mac Suibhne, are only now getting the systematic attention they deserve. They offer a crucial primary source for understanding the formation (in every meaning of this word) of modern Ireland. Cullen has been the focus of ongoing scholarship for several decades now. This is surveyed by Colin Barr's chapter in *Cardinal Paul Cullen and His World*, a 2011 volume edited by Dáire Keogh and Albert McDonnell, in which a number of historians address Cullen's life and times and legacies. Barr cites Joe Lee's cartoon of Cullen as a sort of Tammany Hall machine boss, 'the pope's chief whip in Ireland', with a 'feline sensitivity for the levers of power in the Vatican'.[1]

Cullen has not always been dealt with well by Irish historians. A key reason, according to Barr, was that in crucial respects Cullen was not an Irishman. He was moulded and shaped in Rome. His project was the promotion of ultramontane Catholicism rather than of any particular Irish national destiny. He was neither a Castle Catholic nor a nationalist one. If asked where he stood on the national question Cullen might answer that this was to ask the wrong question. His conflicts with Protestantism were transnational and transcendental, even if these took place on Irish soil. In an important sense he differed from his successor McQuaid, who clearly saw himself a force in Irish political life. In his afterword to the book, Gearóid Ó Tuathaigh, drawing on points made by several contributors, argues that Cullen was neither the prime mover nor the sole creator of Ireland's devotional revolution.[2] But one of the problems of a book of essays that place the same man at the centre of each of these is that the result will almost inevitably place him at the centre of his time. In Cullen's case this is justifiable.

Cullen's London *Times* obituary described him as undistinguished as a theologian, a writer or a preacher, but an agent of great change who typified better than any other prelate the vast change that had come over the spirit of the Catholic Church in Ireland. He was, according to Emmet Larkin (in a chapter entitled 'Paul Cullen: The Great Ultramontane'), an ecclesiastical imperialist who governed as if in a perpetual stage of siege. Such a man could not, Larkin argues, have had the play of mind or broad sympathies of a great intellectual. Cullen was defined, and in turn defined the Catholic Church in Ireland, through his fixed and narrow focus, his militant temper. He was, according to his *Times* obituary 'fervently sincere, single-minded, devout, unflinching, distrustful of culture'.

If Cullen was a father of modern Irish Catholicism he was in turn moulded by Pius IX, who could claim to be the father of the modern papacy and, with it, modern Roman Catholicism more generally. As explained by Eamon Duffy (in 'The Age of Pio Nono: The Age of Paul Cullen') the centralising response of the Church to the nineteenth century – to liberalism, socialism, secularism and modernity more generally – could be traced back in theory to the Council of Trent. But Pius IX, during his thirty-year papacy, presided over a global standardisation of how Catholic doctrine was taught in schools and how Catholic morality was enforced everywhere. The Church's politics and those of many Catholics were conservative for reasons Edmund Burke would have understood. In France, the First Republic had been politically anti-clerical and had disestablished the Church. Pius VI had been imprisoned by French troops in 1798. In 1848 Pius IX had to be smuggled out of Rome in disguise. By 1870 the last of the Papal States had been subsumed into the Kingdom of Italy. That same year Pius IX introduced the doctrine of ultramontanism or papal infallibility. He was voted infallible in 1870 by just 535 of the 1,084 ecclesiastics eligible to cast a ballot. Cullen considered anti-infalliblists to be heretics and was an important advocate of the doctrine of papal infallibility.

Cullen's great accomplishment, Oliver Rafferty emphasises (in 'The Ultramontaine Spirituality of Paul Cullen'), was a devotional revolution in Ireland. Cullen as an institutional builder presided over the building of many churches, schools and religious communities. But he also redefined, as Rafferty and a number of other contributors emphasise, Irish public spirituality.[3] Cullen's Catholicism was defined by a sense of the Church *conta mundi*: contempt for the world beyond the Church, a belief that it was engaged in a life or death struggle against this world. He personally witnessed and was shaken by the exile of Pius IX from Rome in 1848. His spirituality was defined by devotion to the Blessed Virgin and, in almost equal measure, veneration of the person of the pontiff. Ciarán O'Carroll (in 'The Pastoral Vision of Paul Cullen') describes how Cullen inaugurated devotional patterns that impressed him profoundly during his sojourn in Rome.[4] Altars and shrines to the Blessed Virgin were introduced in every church and chapel in the country; May devotions were promoted. Clergy were encouraged to decorate their churches in the Italian style. Cullen promoted the stations of the cross and many churches were adorned with images of these. He focused on religious renewal through retreats and an extensive programme of parish missions, led by religious orders that he promoted such as the Redemptorists.

Old folkways were driven out by new orthodoxies. Whereas Saint Patrick supposedly drove the snakes from Ireland and converted pagan festivals into Christian ones, Cullen modernised a church that the suppression of Catholicism had turned into an untended garden. Priests of the previous generation had been active in politically mobilising Catholics and active in supervising their education, but expressions of religious worship – celebrations of the sacraments and funerals – were not housed in churches to the extent these came to be under Cullen's influence.

A number of chapters emphasise Cullen's influence upon Catholicism in countries with emigrant Irish communities. Rory Sweetman (in 'Paul Cullen and the Remaking of Catholicism in the Antipodes') describes how Cullen had lobbied the Pope for an Irish mission there with at least one Irish bishop, in competition with a French mission which he argued had failed.[5] Cullen's closeness to Rome helped in various turf wars and also in achieving dominance over other bishops in Ireland.

Gerard Moran (in 'Paul Cullen and the Irish emigrant world') cites correspondence in which Cullen emphasised the benefits of mass emigration
for expanding the influence of the Church in the United States. Cullen
used his influence to keep this Irish Catholic diaspora loyal to Rome.[6]
The ideological enemy in particular was militant Fenian nationalism.
Matthew Kelly (in 'Providence, Revolution and the Conditional Defence
of the Union: Paul Cullen and the Fenians') quotes an 1861 pastoral
letter which attacked secret societies. Their machinations, under the
pretence of promoting human liberty, were held responsible for promoting drunkenness, the violation of the rights of property and the worst
excesses of the French Revolution. Kelly emphasises how peripheral
Fenianism was compared to Catholicism.[7] Nationalist politics after
O'Connell lacked the institutional strength he gave it. The Church under
Cullen filled both an institutional vacuum and an ideological one. Cullen
for his part believed that Catholic emancipation had created the political
structures that would enable not just the redress of Catholic grievances
but the creation of a theocratic state. Andrew Shields (in 'Paul Cullen
and the Irish Conservative Imagination') suggests that Cullen's hostility
to nationalism, his own deep-rooted respect for established authority,
put him effectively on the same side as many political opponents of
Catholicism and insofar as he was demonised by these enemies of the
Church it was because he was the most effective champion of Catholic
interests that they had to face since O'Connell.[8]

Mary E. Daly's chapter on Dublin in the age of Cullen describes how
what had once been a Protestant capital was now very much a Catholic
city, though much of this change had occurred during the episcopate of
Daniel Murray, who was Archbishop when Catholic emancipation was
realised, and who worked co-operatively with his Established Church
counterpart Archbishop Richard Whately. If anything distinguished the
age of Cullen from that of his predecessor it was the abandonment of
Murray's pragmatic ecumenicalism in areas such as the governance of
education.[9]

Cullen had close collaborators rather than close friends. One of these
meetings of minds, as Anne-Marie Close puts it, was with Margaret
Alyward, foundress of the Holy Faith Sisters. Alyward was a close
ally in his campaigns against Protestant proselytisers. She founded an
orphanage, St Bridget's, that went on in Cullen's words to save several
hundred children from 'the fangs of the proselytizer'. Both agreed on
the need for Catholic institutions to prevent children from falling into
the wrong hands. Alyward shared Cullen's contempt for the national
system of education. Both believed that the education of all Catholic
children, including the children of the poor, ought to be the preserve of

the Church.[10] The dangers of proselytisation as continually emphasised by Cullen were almost certainly exaggerated. Mac Suibhne describes how in 1839 Archbishop Murray commissioned an evaluation by Rome on the national school system as a means of supporting his case against the demands of some Catholic leaders, notably Archbishop McHale of Tuam, for a system of Catholic denominational schools. Murray was on the Education Board and with his counterpart Richard Whately defended the compromise system both had helped broker.[11] The evaluation was conducted the following year by Cullen, who concluded at the time that the schools 'could not have been more Catholic than they are'.

Many of the chapters have ponderous titles of the kind academics are wont to give to their conference papers – this book began as a conference – each superfluously naming Cullen. These include 'Catholic Dublin: The Public Expression in the Age of Paul Cullen' and 'Paul Cullen, J.J. McCarthy and Holy Cross Church, Clonliffe: The Politics and Iconography of Architectural Style'. Some of these long titles are intriguing – 'Amiens, Brisbane and Crimea: Paul Cullen and the Mercy Mission that Led to the Establishment of the Mater Hospital in Dublin' – or manage to nail the essence of their thesis ('Not... an equal, but... one of his subjects': John Henry Newman's Perception of the Archbishop of Dublin'). There are some great photographs of the iconography of the Cullen era and the book is beautifully produced. Whilst there is a clear logic to its structure the flow is hardly seamless. Too many of the twenty-seven authors paint similar portraits of Cullen for it to constitute an Irish Rashmon. The lack of conspicuous disagreement between contributors is striking. Rather, they attest individually and collectively to his single-mindedness.

Cullen was the human face of the Catholic civilisational juggernaut that hit post-Famine Ireland. The achievement of this book is to provide a dense (as distinct from insubstantial) mosaic of this world. Cullen unsurprisingly dominates every chapter of *Cardinal Paul Cullen and His World* but the reader is told again and again that Cullen was a type, the product of a specific social milieu who found common cause with those of similar beliefs and institutional affiliations. The absence of reference to the sociological literature on the role of Catholicism on the modernisation of Ireland is to be regretted. But champions of sociology should no more fault historians for not being sociologists than fault Cullen for not being a nationalist. Cullen was the determined champion of the devotional revolution he believed Ireland needed to save itself from the world, Protestantism and the wrong kinds of Catholicism roughly in that order. According to the sociologist Tom Inglis there were three methods by which the priest acted as a civilising agent in Irish society:

The first was his mere physical presence as a civilised, disciplined and well-mannered Catholic being. He was a model of morality and civility, a shining example of what could be produced from a tenant farmer background. He interacted with the poorest of the people, bringing civility and morality to into their humble abodes. The second method had to do with the transformation of the priest from a social functionary who officiated at the major rites of passage. E.g. birth, marriage and death, into a rigorous disciplinarian who through pastoral visitation and confession began to supervise and control all aspects of social life. The third method was the dissemination of a detailed body of Catholic doctrine and practice, first through confraternities and book societies, and later through schools, hospitals and homes.[12]

Various accounts suggest that Irish rural society in the early nineteenth century placed little emphasis on physical modesty. Openly sexual ribaldry was apparently commonplace and was part and parcel of communal events such as May Day festivals and wake-games at funerals. The changes that the Church sought to impose on marriages and sexual practices were aimed at instilling shame and guilt about the body. The Catholic Church sought to impose the new civility, and morality amongst the people was by fostering rigid adherence to its rules and regulations. Obedience towards priests was fostered by the imposition of legalistic rules of religious and moral conduct on rules that applied to religious observance and sacraments and on public morality focused on repressing sexuality.[13] So it wasn't just a matter of Cullen laying the law or regimenting the priesthood. Church-building and the construction of schools provided spaces in which moral discipline could be exercised.

It was in churches, according to Inglis, that most Irish people learned to control their bodies and exercise moral disciple through civil behaviour: 'Etiquette and good manners became associated with going to church and fulfilling rules and regulations.' There were rules about dress and cleanliness, silence and posture.[14] New forms of religious practice mostly of Roman origin were emphasised during the post-1850 devotional revolution, including the rosary, novenas, benedictions, devotion to the Sacred Heart and the Immaculate Conception, processions and retreats. These worked to regularise religious practice, as did the use of catechism.[15]

On Cullen's watch the Catholic Church gained what Inglis calls a moral monopoly and in exercising this it addressed the functional needs of post-Famine Irish society. Irish Catholics began to adhere to the rules and regulations of the Church in order to improve their standard of living. If tenant farmers were to prevent subdivision of their smallholdings from generation to generation, they had to ensure that their sons and daughters variously deferred marriage, remained celibate or emigrated. The fourth option, followed by more and more young Irish people during the second half of the nineteenth century, was to join a religious order. And it was these religious orders, according to Inglis: 'the priests and nuns and brothers, and the teachers under their supervision, who instilled into the uncouth, boorish Irish children of the nineteenth century all the manners and habits which we today regard as standard social practices. It was they who took over the task of making the Irish into a clean-living, orderly, well-managed, self-controlled, literate people. They were the forces which girded the bent and unruly bodies of the Irish and fashioned them into fine, upstanding, moral citizens.'[16]

Notes

This is a slightly expanded version of a review of Dáire Keogh and Albert McDonnell (eds), *Cardinal Paul Cullen and His World* (Dublin: Four Courts Press, 2011), previously published in *Studies*, 101.401 (2012), 78–85. The additional text cites the work of Tom Inglis on the sociology of post-Famine Catholicism.

1 Colin P. Barr, '"An Ambiguous Awe": Paul Cullen and the Historians', in Keogh and McDonnell (eds), *Cardinal Paul Cullen and His World*, p. 425.
2 Gearóid Ó Tuathaigh, 'Reassessing Paul Cullen: An Afterword', in Keogh and McDonnell (eds), *Cardinal Paul Cullen and His World*, pp. 435–444.
3 Oliver P. Rafferty SJ, 'The Ultramontane Spirituality of Paul Cullen', in Keogh and McDonnell (eds), *Cardinal Paul Cullen and His World*, pp. 61–77.
4 Ciarán O'Carroll, 'The Pastoral Vision of Paul Cullen', in Keogh and McDonnell (eds), *Cardinal Paul Cullen and His World*, pp. 115–129.
5 Rory Sweetman, 'Paul Cullen and the Remaking of Catholicism in the Antipodes', in Keogh and McDonnell (eds), *Cardinal Paul Cullen and His World*, pp. 377–400.
6 Gerard Moran, 'Paul Cullen and the Irish Emigrant World', in Keogh and McDonnell (eds), *Cardinal Paul Cullen and His World*, pp. 166–178.
7 Matthew Kelly, 'Providence, Revolution and the Conditional Defence of the Union: Paul Cullen and the Fenians', in Keogh and McDonnell (eds), *Cardinal Paul Cullen and His World*, pp. 308–328.
8 Andrew Shields, 'Paul Cullen and the Irish Conservative Imagination', in Keogh and McDonnell (eds), *Cardinal Paul Cullen and His World*, pp. 205–214.
9 Mary E. Daly, 'Catholic Dublin: The Public Expression in the Age of Paul Cullen', in Keogh and McDonnell (eds), *Cardinal Paul Cullen and His World*, pp. 130–145.
10 Anne-Marie Close, 'A Meeting of Minds? Margaret Aylward and Paul Cullen', in Keogh and McDonnell (eds), *Cardinal Paul Cullen and His World*, pp. 216–230.

11 Peadar Mac Suibhne, *Paul Cullen and His Contemporaries*, vol. 4 (Kildare: Leinster Leader, 1974).

12 Tom Inglis, *Moral Monopoly: The Rise and Fall of the Catholic Church in Ireland* (Dublin: University College Dublin Press, 1998), p. 142.

13 Inglis, *Moral Monopoly*, p. 145.

14 Inglis, *Moral Monopoly*, p. 146.

15 On the use and influence of catechisms see Bryan Fanning and Tom Garvin, *The Books that Define Ireland* (Dublin: Merrion, 2014), pp. 36–43.

16 Inglis, *Moral Monopoly*, p. 157.

5

A Catholic vision of Ireland

In his 1911 novel *The Dawn of All*, Robert Hugh Benson, an English priest who converted to Catholicism (his father had been the Archbishop of Canterbury), imagined a future where most of the world had done the same. *The Dawn of All* recounts the story of a former priest living in a future atheistic 1973, who regains consciousness in a London hospital, in an England where the Reformation and secularism have been reversed. In this vision, religion had no influence in society and priests had no relevance. In the remainder of the book Benson's imaginary future changes dramatically. It becomes one in which Catholic social and political thought has been implemented worldwide, where the great political economists of the day consult cardinals and where Ireland has been turned into the contemplative monastery of Europe.

At the beginning of the twentieth century Catholic thinkers were preoccupied with the threats that secular, liberal and social ideals presented to religiosity. In his 1907 novel *Lord of the World*, Benson had imagined a future world dominated since 1917 by socialism, freemasonry and secular science. In this future, England had assented to Catholic home rule in Ireland and encouraged its Catholic population to emigrate there. Catholicism had declined everywhere except in Rome and in Ireland, where appearances of a woman in blue were reported at Marian shrines.[1] The ideas behind Benson's respective utopia and dystopia were in keeping with wider Catholic intellectual responses to the threat of modernity.

English Catholics like Benson and Hillaire Belloc viewed the survival of Catholicism in post-Reformation Ireland as a historical miracle. Ireland's distinctive religious history – Penal Laws followed by Catholic emancipation and a devotional revolution – looked much like post-Reformation Europe in reverse. Catholic churches were mostly newer than Protestant ones and Catholic schools had been integral to the nation-building project that would lead to Irish independence. The Protestant Church of Ireland was disestablished in 1871 and had lost much of its political influence. By the time of independence the Catholic Church was on the cusp of a level of influence that could only be imagined as science fiction elsewhere in much of the English-speaking world.

But the Church was unwilling to depend on miracles for its future survival. In 1870 Pope Pius IX invented the doctrine of papal infallibility as a bulwark against modernism. Intellectually, the Church drew on Thomism – Aristotelian natural law philosophy as Christianised by Thomas Aquinas – for its rebuttals of liberalism and socialism. The turn of the century witnessed the rise to dominance of neo-Thomist orthodoxy in seminaries and the repression of dissident thinkers associated with modernism. The mobilisation of Thomism in the 1891 papal encyclical *Rerum Novarum* 'on the condition of the working classes' provided the basis for specific political and social prescriptions that were at once an expression of interest group politics and an ontological conflict with secular modernity.

Rerum Novarum acknowledged a spirit of revolutionary change in politics and economics and, whilst recognising the 'misery and wretchedness pressing so unjustly on the working classes', sought to divert an impoverished Catholic working class away from socialism.[2] But it harked back to a time before the Enlightenment when liberalism and individualism did not exist. It idealised the pre-capitalist Middle Ages as the form of society that most epitomised the Christian ideal of social solidarity.

That the Catholic ideal was a pre-Reformation one was unsurprising. It was similar to that of Protestant conservatives opposed to the impact of industrialisation such as Thomas Carlyle, who in his 1843 book *Past and Present* argued that European peasants fared better under the stable hierarchies of feudalism than their descendants were doing under industrial capitalism.[3] The Catholic critique of modernity intellectually mirrored Émile Durkheim's *The Division of Labour in Society*, which emerged in 1894, a few years after the publication of *Rerum Novarum*. Durkheim described the unravelling of traditional 'mechanistic' forms of social solidarity and their replacement by more complex 'organic' interdependencies. Mechanistic solidarity was grounded in resemblance. Individual members of society resembled each other because they cherished the same values and held the same things sacred.[4] Society was coherent because individuals led very similar lives. Durkheim's German contemporary Ferdinand Toinnes referred to this as *Gemeinschaft*. This archetype had much in common with the mediaeval one of social cohesion beloved by neo-Thomists – people lived and died in the village in which they were born, within visual range of the same Church steeple, sharing the same beliefs. Durkheim's preoccupation with the moral basis of social solidarity shared much with natural law understandings of the social order. Durkheim employed the concept of *anomie* to depict the ruptures in social solidarity and the sense of belonging that came with the decline of established religious moral authority.[5] The shift from traditional mechanistic interdependencies or *Gemeinschaft* to new, yet to be fully realised forms of social solidarity was for Durkheim a sociological puzzle. It was understood by many European Catholic thinkers as an existential crisis.

The Catholic sociology of Catholic power

The battle for the survival of Catholic Ireland – a society that had come into being following the repeal of the Penal Laws and the Famine, and one in which the Catholic Church came to exercise what Tom Inglis calls a moral monopoly[6] – was framed by Catholic thinkers in explicitly sociological terms for several decades after independence. For more than half a century Catholic sociology articulated influential visions of Ireland's future. These are represented here by the writings of two key figures. Father Edward Cahill (1868–1941) was Professor of Sociology at the Jesuit Milltown Institute: he was a close friend of his former pupil and later Taoiseach Éamon de Valera. The last significant sociological defender of Catholic Ireland was Rev. Jeremiah Newman (1926–95), who became Professor of Sociology at Maynooth in 1953 and a long-standing editor of the doctrinally Catholic journal of sociology *Christus Rex*. Sociology for both was the science of reproducing Catholic Ireland from one generation to the next. Both emphasised the role of law in enforcing Catholic public morality and thereby enforcing social norms that were in accordance with Catholic ideals.

Cahill made the case for the kind of society fictionalised by Benson at a time when Catholic public morality was being increasingly reflected by the laws and Constitution of the Irish state. Although most of the parliamentarians of the Free State were Catholics, there were limits to the extent to which the new state passed Church doctrine into law. In 1923, three private member bills aimed at prohibiting divorce put before the Dáil were blocked by William T. Cosgrave's government. Cosgrave was personally in favour of upholding the values of the Catholic majority, yet he was unwilling to prohibit divorce because this was seen to infringe upon the rights of the Protestant minority. But Catholic public morality became increasingly reflected in the laws of the state over time.

The importation of contraception was prohibited by a 1935 Act, and de Valera's 1937 Constitution prohibited divorce.[7]

Cahill was in regular correspondence with de Valera when the latter was drafting what would become the 1937 Constitution. Cahill's 701-page *Framework of a Christian State* (1932) was the most substantive post-independence elaboration of Catholic social and political thought. He distinguished Catholic sociology from the secular kind popularised by the French positivist philosopher Auguste Comte. Catholic sociology, whilst it might make use of statistics, rested on principles of natural law which were unchanging and knowable to reason. By definition, Catholic sociology excluded theories that studied religion as a social construct. To a considerable extent Catholic sociology was promoted in Irish universities to ensure that Catholic students would not be exposed to intellectual justifications of secularism.[8] *The Framework of the Christian State* was intended 'primarily for students of social science who accepted the Church's teaching'.[9] It explained and elaborated upon papal encyclicals that pontificated about the place of religion in public life, the family, education, the interrelations between capital and labour, the functions of the state and its relations with the Church.

The initial intellectual project of Catholic sociology was to combat the influence of socialism. Cahill's *Framework of a Christian State* discussed at length the history of socialist ideas, theories of surplus value and dialectical materialism. But the battle against socialism in the Irish case had long been won. On 29 January 1916, in *The Workers' Republic*, James Connolly praised a 'splendid speech' by the Capuchin priest Father Laurence in Dublin to an audience of Catholic working men and women. Connolly professed himself to be unable to identify any fundamental differences between Laurence's views and those of Irish socialists. In declaring this, he was undoubtedly trying to encourage the Catholic Irish working class to embrace socialism. Connolly echoed the language of Catholic natural law: 'We accept the family as the true type of human society. We say that as in the family the resources of the entire household are at the service of each, as in the family the strong does not prey upon the weak.'[10] Connolly, if not naive, was whistling in the dark. After his execution following the 1916 Rising, various efforts were made by Catholic intellectuals to either co-opt or dismiss his legacy. A 1919 article 'Socialism and Catholic Teaching' in the Irish Jesuit journal *Studies* by Peter Finlay SJ argued that the programme of Connolly's Irish Republican Socialist Party was one that Leo XIII had explicitly condemned. However, in *The Social Teachings of James Connolly* (1921), the first major study of his writings by another Jesuit, Lambert McKenna, a trenchant critic of Marxism, claimed some of Connolly's socialist principles were in accordance with Catholic social thought.[11] In the absence of a realistic socialist threat the main focus of Catholic sociology was to understand and combat social change that might foster secularism.

de Valera invited Cahill to draft a preamble to the 1937 Constitution. In their correspondence Cahill argued that 'a constitution for Ireland should be, if not confessedly Catholic (which may at present not be feasible) at least definitely and *confessedly Christian*'.[12] A number of provisions (Articles 40 to 44) covering social policy, the family, divorce, the role of women and the status of children, all reflected Catholic social thought. Cahill and de Valera's ideal Ireland had much in common. de Valera's famous St Patrick's Day speech of 1943 had evoked a Catholic, anti-materialist, rural social ideal that was very much in keeping with *Rerum Novarum* and Cahill's *Framework for a Christian State*.

> The ideal Ireland that we would have, the Ireland that we dreamed of, would be the home of a people who valued material wealth only as the basis for right living, of a people who, satisfied with frugal comfort, devoted their leisure to the things of the spirit – a land whose countryside would be bright with cosy homesteads, whose fields and villages would be joyous with the sounds of industry, with the romping of sturdy children, the contest of athletic youths and the laughter of happy maidens, whose firesides would be forums for the wisdom of serene old age. The home, in short, of a people living the life that God desires that men should live.[13]

Cahill had emphasised the fundamental importance of rural family life to the survival of the Church and the Irish nation, a perspective which dominated Catholic social thought in Ireland until the 1960s. He argued that the urban poor were especially threatened by immorality and vice and that extreme poverty and poor housing conditions – worse in Dublin than almost anywhere in Europe – undermined family life. In 1926 more than a quarter of Dublin's families lived in one-room tenements.[14] Cahill argued that the emphasis had to be on checking rural depopulation and stabilising rural communities. He made the case for programmes that would sustain viable small farms including rural co-operatives and restricting ownership of land to people willing to live on it.[15] The root causes of emigration and urbanisation were deemed to be the concentration of the most fertile land in the ownership of the great ranchers who did not cultivate it, and insufficient protection for native producers. This was also de Valera's diagnosis. Other causes identified by Cahill included the dreariness of rural life and the lack of Catholic rural organisations that might improve living conditions and promote social cohesion. He also blamed the education system, the unchristian press and the cinema for inculcating distaste for rural life.

Newman's sociological focus from the late 1950s was on the impending decline of Irish Catholicism. In a 1959 book review in *Christus Rex* Newman observed that students of what was 'commonly called "Sociology" in Ireland – that is as taught by him – would be very confused by how the subject was defined in other countries'.[16] As editor of *Christus Rex* he kept secular theoretical sociology at bay through censorship until the last 'glasnost' issue of the journal in 1970 before it was re-launched as *Social Studies*. In a remarkable article in the final issue he referred to a plethora of secular sociologists whose works *Christus Rex* had deliberately never discussed or reviewed.[17] Newman's own best-known sociological analyses focused on rural Limerick where he grew up, and the decline in vocations at Maynooth where he took holy orders and was later in charge of the spiritual formation of seminarians. He argued that in the face of ongoing rural decline, the only way to conserve rural population was, 'paradoxical though it may seem', to develop a number of towns in each county with adequate social and cultural facilities.[18] Newman formulated an index of social provision for towns and villages in County Limerick. This quantified the availability of public utilities, different kinds of commercial activities (the presence of various kinds of shops, banks etc.), public transport, 'places of assembly' (social facilities such as churches, libraries, public houses, cinemas) and social organisations. In short Newman's proposal was to concentrate on building up a number of sustainable communities in the county. Newman's sociology extolled the virtues of *Gemeinschaft*, the community life of the family and the locality, of the village, the smaller town, the owner-occupied shop, the rural church as the best incubator of priests and good Catholics.

Social change and Catholic public morality

By the time *Christus Rex* folded, Fianna Fáil, under de Valera's successor Sean Lemass, had embraced a new nation-building project focused on economic development. The period of influence of Catholic social thought had coincided with a period of Irish-Ireland, of a post-colonial cultural nation-building project which emphasised economic isolationism and efforts to promote the Irish language. However, in a 1961 article in *Christus Rex*, Lemass, the new Taoiseach, explicitly rejected the Catholic vision of a frugal, anti-materialistic rural-centred society championed by Cahill and de Valera. Lemass blamed emigration on 'the insufficiency of our efforts to develop a completely attractive way of life for all elements of the national community, and adequate opportunities of employing individual talents in Ireland to earn livelihoods equivalent to those which emigrants hope to find elsewhere'. Contrary to the prevailing view in *Christus Rex* he did not believe that emigration could be ended by urging people to willingly accept less than could be obtained elsewhere.[19]

Newman argued that spiritual life and individual faith were sustained by social habits that could be damaged by removal from a society within which religious norms prevailed. Urban life and the impersonal social structures of modernity made community intangible and made faith difficult. He argued that with the decline of Irish *Gemeinschaft*, a legally enforced public morality offered the only potential bulwark against the acceleration of secularisation. The state, he argued, had a duty to Ireland's Catholic majority to enforce Catholic public morality.

The Catholic ideal, he insisted in his book *Studies in Political Morality* (1962), was for an established Church. It should never surrender this ideal in theoretical discussions on Church–state relations. More generally it should never surrender the primacy of theology to political theory. He faulted progressive American theologians for having done so. The demands of the Church of Christ on the state, he argued, were fundamentally doctrinal; they stemmed from the uncompromising source of theological truth.[20] Catholics were required to accept Catholic doctrine. From a Catholic doctrinal perspective the focus had to be on the political implications of theological truth rather than the other way around:

> Special recognition of the church may be necessary to secure these interests to the full in a state in which the vast majority is Catholic. It is not a question of seeking what *can* be secured from the State but what *ought* to be granted if the people's spiritual interests are to be adequately looked after in so far as their government is competent to do so. On the side of the State this, in turn, re-echoes its duty of doing whatsoever is necessary in pursuit of the political common good. It is simply erroneous to suggest that the limitation of the State to catering to the exigencies of public order means that it cannot grant special recognition to the Church.[21]

In the Irish case, where the Church enjoyed a special position closer to the ideal than in many other polities, other issues came to the fore. There had, Newman insisted, to be limits to religious tolerance. The rulers in a state consisting almost entirely of Catholics had a duty to influence legislation of the state in accordance with Catholic teaching. This included a duty to defend the religious patrimony of the people against every assault that sought to deprive them of their faith.

By the 1970s it was clear that Catholic goals in Ireland could no longer be pursued by episcopal insistence on the primacy of Church authority in Church–state relations. The decline of vocations meant that the threats of modernity to Irish Catholicism were no longer external. There would soon be, Newman anticipated, pressure for legislation to permit divorce. He depicted this pressure as a 'minority right' issue and argued that the state in a predominantly Catholic society had a duty to protect Catholic values:

> What I am getting at is the need for a patterned sociological framework which will give support to the religious and moral beliefs of the average man and thus help him live his life in accordance with them. What he needs, if you will, is a prop to his weakness, but then this is the purpose of all society in all its domains. Political society or the State is no exception. Its legal system represents a fabric of social values that are intended to sustain the individual through social living. This is the function of a constitutional provision which prohibits divorce in a society composed predominantly of people who believe it wrong to practice it.[22]

Laws that enforced Catholic public morality protected the Catholic social fabric. In a 1969 *Christus Rex* article, he described the prohibition of divorce in Ireland as part of the framework provided by the Irish State that supported the conformism of the average man.[23] Newman argued that the emphasis of Vatican II on participation of the laity in the Church and other reforms would not ensure future high levels of religious observance in the way that had been made possible by laws underpinned by Catholic moral teaching. So defending the constitutional status quo was a priority. Social change, he believed, was inevitable. But the pace of change was fast enough without increasing it by changes to the Constitution which would, he believed, further undermine Catholicism in Ireland. As he put it, in a 1969 article in *Christus Rex*:

> That diehard traditionalism is bad for society, and that there is need for a liberal stimulus to counter it, is a sound general political principle. But it should be related to society as found in the concrete. Thus the contribution of the liberal stimulus is unquestionably valuable in the context of a backward looking, quite closed, conservative society. At the other extreme, in that of a wholly liberal permissive society, there is need rather for the fostering of a sound conservativism. Today in our mixed – partly conservative and party liberal Irish society – it seems to me that one should be unusually careful about introducing a liberal stimulus in the direction of secularisation. Where has this led Britain even in our own time – from a proud empire to a giggling society?[24]

Newman believed that the pressure for divorce legislation and for secularisation went hand in hand. In the Irish case, Catholic politicians who advocated legislation on divorce tended to do so on grounds of promoting religious pluralism. But they needed to understand that in countenancing divorce they were also endorsing the secularisation of Irish society by undermining public morality. He made similar arguments against legislation in favour of contraception and abortion. He argued that the law was a crucial bulwark against the erosion of Catholic public morality and that this in turn was one against the erosion of Catholic faith.

Catholic visions and the distinctive Irish case

Ireland was never a theocratic state but, according to Paul Blanchard in *The Irish and Catholic Power* (1954), it came closer to one than any other Western democracy during the twentieth century. Ireland was clearly a democracy but, as put by Blanchard, an unofficial Church–state alliance permitted ecclesiastical dictatorship and political democracy to live side by side 'without any sense of incongruity'.[25] Ireland was the only democracy where the Church enjoyed such status. By contrast, the political order Robert Hugh Benson envisaged was a highly schematic version of the vocational state: people were represented through guilds and different professions had different colour uniforms. Some elements of this found expression in Mussolini's Italy. But it was Salazar's Portugal that came closest to the ideal Catholic vocationalist state. Vocationalism was discussed from the 1870s by Catholic thinkers as a means of preventing the kinds of class conflict that fostered socialism. It was endorsed by an International Conference of Catholic Sociologists held in Germany in 1893.[26] As explained in a 1938 article in the *Irish Monthly* by Rev. Cornelius, who was Professor of Theology and Political Theory at Maynooth:

> The vocational guild, therefore serves a double purpose. First, it knits the employers and the workers of the same occupation together and so acts as a corrective to the class antagonism natural when only the conflicting interests of the two classes are emphasised as at present. Secondly it plans the economy of the occupation as a whole, with an eye both to the needs of the community and the good of the various bodies in the occupation. In this way it relieves the State of duties which it has ordinarily neither the competency nor the qualifications to carry out.[27]

But by then it was clear that vocationalism had only a limited influence in the Irish case. In the 1930s, it offered General O'Duffy's Blueshirt movement an off-the-shelf political programme. But the Blueshirts never gained power and the era came to be politically dominated by de

Valera and Fianna Fáil. By the time the corporatist state found political champions like O'Duffy, Ireland's most influential Catholic intellectuals had moved on. For example, Alfred O'Rahilly, a long-time
supporter of vocationalism, argued that it was unnecessary in a 1935
article in *Studies* on constitutional reform.[28] Ireland, in any case, did
not have a socialist problem that needed vocationalist solutions. Cahill's
Framework of a Christian State had placed little emphasis on vocationalism *per se*. He was a republican nationalist who had been criticised
by fellow clergy for holding IRA sympathies during the civil war.[29] But
so too were some other leading clerical proponents of Catholic social
thought like the Jesuit Timothy Corcoran, the Professor of Education at
University College Dublin.

Catholic social thought failed to translate into a coherent political
programme in the Irish case not just because it was backed by the losing
side of 1930s electoral politics. Tony Fahey has convincingly argued
that the central thrust of papal social teaching, which strove to find a
middle way between what the Vatican saw as the extremes of *laissez
faire* capitalism and state socialism, had only limited relevance to social
conditions in Ireland: 'Outside of the industrialised north-east of the
island, capitalism had failed to take off in Ireland and the socialist movement scarcely developed beyond the embryonic stage. The main targets
of attack for Catholic social teaching were thus either weak or largely
absent in Ireland – or were present primarily as external conditioning
circumstances.'[30] Cahill and Newman saw the defence of rural life and
Catholic public morality as more crucial to the survival of Catholicism
than such continental Catholic political experiments.

The Church political ideal, Newman argued in 1961, was for
something like the Republic of Ireland, a Catholic society in which
the Church had considerable influence upon the state and where the
state established through constitution and laws a public morality that
accorded with Catholic teaching. In the case of the United States, where
Catholics were in the minority, the Church nevertheless held on to the
ideal of a Church–state relationship that would enshrine Catholic doctrine in law. But this influence was clearly on the wane and the Church
was on the cusp of losing its moral monopoly over Irish life. The tyranny
of a Catholic majority at the heart of Newman's political philosophy
had come to be replaced by the tyranny of a secularising majority that
now needed to be resisted.

The Church also had to deal with pressures for reform from some
clergy and laity. Brian Moore's 1972 novel *Catholics* imagined a future
that would have horrified Newman. The book was set in what seems to
be the year 1999 where, following Vatican IV, the monks in a monastery

off the coast of Kerry were to be censured for practising traditional Catholicism. The Church no longer believed in miracles ('Lourdes is no longer in operation'), there had been ecumenical compromises with other faiths – a merger with Buddhism was on the cards – and the Mass was officially regarded as nothing more than a symbolic act.[31] For a time it must have looked like liberation theology and folk masses in the post-Vatican-II climate might lead to further Church reform and doctrinal compromise. However, the long papacy of Pope John Paul II and that of his successor Benedict XIV, formerly Joseph Ratzinger, have been characterised by a neo-conservative doctrinal emphasis on a universally binding natural law and the teaching of absolute moral norms. The political playbook of the Catholic Church in twenty-first-century Ireland resembles the one Newman described as fitting countries where Catholics were in a minority. In such cases, he insisted, they should hold on to the ideal of a Catholic public morality, never compromising on its contents, whilst pragmatically accepting the status quo and playing a long game.

Notes

This chapter was previously published as Bryan Fanning, 'A Catholic Vision of Ireland', in Tom Inglis (ed.), *Are the Irish Different?* (Manchester: Manchester University Press, 2014).

1 Robert Hugh Benson, *Lord of the World* (London: Sir Isaac Pitman and Sons, 1907); Robert Hugh Benson, *The Dawn of All* (St Louis: B. Herder, 1911).
2 *Rerum Novarum* (1891) cited in Edward Cahill, *The Framework of a Christian State* (Dublin: Gill and Son, 1932), p. 148.
3 Thomas Carlyle, *Past and Present* (London: Chapman and Hall, 1843).
4 Émile Durkheim, *The Division of Labour in Society* (London: Macmillan, 1984).
5 Émile Durkheim, *Suicide: A Study in Sociology* (New York: Free Press, 1951).
6 Tom Inglis, *Moral Monopoly: The Rise and Fall of the Catholic Church in Modern Ireland*, 2nd ed. (Dublin: University College Dublin Press, 1998).
7 John Whyte, *Church and State in Modern Ireland 1923–1979*, 2nd ed. (Dublin: Gill and Macmillan, 1980), p. 37.
8 Bryan Fanning, *The Quest for Modern Ireland: The Battle of Ideas 1912–1986* (Dublin: Irish Academic Press, 2008).
9 Cahill, *Framework of a Christian State*, p. xiii.
10 James Connolly, 'The Programme of Labour', *The Workers' Republic* (29 January 1916).
11 Lambert McKenna SJ, *The Social Teachings of James Connolly* (Dublin: Catholic Truth Society, 1920).
12 Dermot Keogh, 'The Jesuits and the 1937 Constitution', in Bryan Fanning (ed.),

An Irish Century: Studies 1912–2012 (Dublin: University College Dublin Press, 2012).

13 Quoted in Dermot Keogh, *Twentieth-Century Ireland: Nation and State* (Dublin: Gill and Macmillan, 1994), pp. 133–134.

14 Cahill, *Framework of a Christian State*, p. 663.

15 Cahill, *Framework of a Christian State*, pp. 321–325.

16 Jeremiah Newman, 'Review of Joseph H. Fischer, Sociology (University of Chicago Press, 1958)', *Christus Rex*, 13.3 (1959), 220–221.

17 Jeremiah Newman, 'Progress and Planning', *Christus Rex*, 23.3 (1977), 173–186; see Bryan Fanning, *Quest for Modern Ireland*, p. 133.

18 Jeremiah Newman, 'Report of the Limerick Rural Survey', *Christus Rex*, 15.1 (1961), 20–22.

19 Sean F. Lemass, 'Social Factors and Emigration', *Christus Rex*, 15.1 (1961), 16–19.

20 Jeremiah Newman, *Studies in Political Morality* (Dublin: Scepter, 1962), p. 240.

21 Newman, *Studies in Political Morality*, p. 265.

22 Newman, *Studies in Political Morality*, p. 178.

23 Jeremiah Newman, 'Socio-Political Aspects of Divorce', *Christus Rex*, 23.1 (1969), 5–15.

24 Jeremiah Newman, *Conscience Versus Law: Reflections on the Evolution of Natural Law* (Dublin: Talbot, 1971), p. 182.

25 Paul Blanchard, *The Irish and Catholic Power: An American Interpretation* (Boston: Beacon Press, 1954).

26 Cornelius Lucey, 'The Vocational Group Movement', *The Irish Monthly*, 66.778 (1938), 221–237, p. 235.

27 Lucey, 'Vocational Group Movement', p. 227.

28 Fanning, *Quest for Modern Ireland*, p. 104.

29 Patrick Murray, *Oracles of God: The Roman Catholic Church and Irish Politics 1922–37* (Dublin: University College Dublin Press, 2000), p. 174.

30 Tony Fahey, 'The Catholic Church and Social Policy', in Seán Healy and Brigid Reynolds (eds), *Social Policy in Ireland* (Dublin: Oak Tree Press, 1998), p. 418.

31 Brian Moore, *Catholics* (London: Cape, 1972).

6

Catholic intellectuals

The Jesuits launched their journal *Studies* in March 1912. In its first decade *Studies* reflected the Catholic constitutional nationalism that became displaced by Sinn Féin. After the war of independence and the civil war it hosted the mainstream social, economic, constitutional and political debates that shaped the new state. Both the conservative and liberal wings of the Catholic bourgeois who dominated politics and academia set out their thinking in *Studies*. A catholic intent was signalled by its initial subtitle: 'An Irish Quarterly Review of Letters, Philosophy and Science'. The stated object of *Studies*, set out in the first issue, was to 'give publicity to work of a scholarly type, extending over many important branches of study, and appealing to a wider circle of cultured readers than strictly specialist journals could be expected to reach'. Specifically, it sought to address general modern literature, comprising both critical and original work; Celtic, Classical and Oriental subjects; historical questions that had some bearing on religious and social issues; philosophy, sociology, education, and the experimental and observational sciences. In 1912 Catholic intentions hardly needed to be advertised. In time the subtitle became shortened to 'An Irish Quarterly Review' with the accompanying explanation of the remit of *Studies*: 'It examines Irish social, political, cultural and economic issues in the light of Christian values and explores the Irish dimension in literature, history, philosophy and religion.'

In the pages of *Studies* the polarised conflict between Catholicism and liberalism claimed by some accounts of Irish modernisation break down. The Irish century it exemplifies reveals symbiosis as well as conflict between both intellectual traditions. Catholicism had found political common ground with nineteenth-century liberalism; in the decades after independence both favoured a minimal state; Catholics were economic liberals and vice versa. In *Studies*, prompted by the northern conflict, clerics came to advocate constitutional pluralism on issues such as divorce. *Studies* had moved well to the left of the political mainstream by the 1980s; its critique of the economic crisis of that decade focused very much on the damage to social cohesion engendered by market forces.

Many leading academics published extensively in *Studies*. For example, Michael Tierney, Professor of Classics and later President of University College Dublin (UCD), contributed fifty-five articles between 1922 and 1953. These accounted for most of his academic output and included many public intellectual contributions to Irish debates. George O'Brien, the leading economist of his generation, published thirty-three articles in *Studies* between 1914 and 1947. Timothy Corcoran SJ, the dominant educationalist of his day, contributed thirty-eight essays between 1912 and 1941.

In recent decades *Studies* can legitimately claim outsider status; the decline of Catholic power and expansion of various media moved the centre of Establishment debates elsewhere. Tierney's successors in twenty-first-century university management actively dissuade Irish scholars from contributing to Irish periodicals like *Studies*. Instead they are expected to exclusively to target international specialist journals; by definition 'international' excludes Irish periodicals; inadvertently such an international focus sponsors provincialism. In recent decades Catholic ideas have found expression as dissidence where once these represented the Irish status quo. Scepticism about neo-liberalism and commitment to social justice set *Studies* apart from the rightward shift of the Irish political mainstream. In an Ireland stifled by damaging complacencies, its new place outside the mainstream has been both honourable and interesting.

Corcoran, the first editor, was close to Éamon de Valera and a mentor to the future Archbishop John Charles McQuaid.[1] In the post-1912 period he was unofficial leader of the Sinn Féin caucus at the university.[2] In this he was at odds with the main thrust of political opinion within *Studies* as exemplified by his fellow professors (and former students at Clongowes) Thomas Kettle and Arthur Cleary. However, in 1916 *Studies* became temporarily caught up in the wave of emotion that followed the post-Rising executions. It responded with a series entitled 'Poets of the Insurrection'. Thomas McDonagh's patriotism, as evident in his poems, was described as a 'furnace glow of passion'. Joseph Mary Plunkett drew admiration for proclaiming that he was dying for God and the honour of Ireland.[3] John F. MacEntee was described as 'a genuine if immature poet', who hated 'all that the word "England" means to an enlightened and patriotic Irishman', yet was passionately fond of English literature, architecture and art.[4] Each was described at the time as an exemplar of Catholic piety and true patriotism. MacEntee, who survived 1916, changed his first name to Seán and set aside poetry for a long career in politics. The summer 1916 verdict on Patrick Pearse was that he was a better short story and prose writer than he was a poet. Some of his poems were 'so simple that one may not say much about them'. However, he was portrayed as a brilliant educationalist (subsequent appraisals in *Studies* would say propagandist) in his use of school pageants to foster simultaneously a patriotic and religious spirit amongst his pupils. Subsequent scathing reappraisals – enough to comprise a hefty anthology – saw nothing Christ-like in Pearse's invocation of patriotic blood sacrifice, a theme Pearse was gearing up to in his sole contribution to Studies, 'Some Aspects of Irish Literature (1913)'.[5]

Tom Kettle perished on the Western Front within weeks of the Rising. As Professor of Political Economy and essayist he exemplified the distinctive fusion of Catholic and liberal ideas which influenced much that *Studies* published about economics for half a century. Arthur Cleary's obituary in *Studies* described him as 'the most brilliant mind of the generation that succeeded Parnell'. Kettle, Cleary emphasised, was 'at all relevant times a constitutionalist, a parliamentary nationalist, but with a highly developed dramatic sense', rooted in the orthodoxy of the Irish Party of Davitt and Parnell, but also part of a cosmopolitan movement, that existed as an undeveloped alternative to the 'Irish-Ireland' ideology of which D.P. Moran was the prophet. A casual observer, Cleary argued, would describe this incorrectly as 'socialistic'. What this amounted to was 'an effort to apply cosmopolitan ideas of regeneration (often without any clear idea of what they were)' to social conditions – 'in fact, an aspiration towards modern "progress" of the less brutal kind'.

One of Cleary's contributions to *Studies*, 'Votes for Irish Youth' (1915), exemplified such progressive liberalism; Cleary's concern was with finding a political mechanism to provide an impetus against the exploitation of children in the Irish labour market. The context was the campaign of the suffragettes whose demands he supported.[6] The alternative to romantic nationalism presented in *Studies* was one that emphasised no practical reform in the living conditions of Irish people. The solutions to Ireland's problems, a 1919 article on the housing conditions of dock workers implied, lay more in better urban planning than political ideology.[7] In the decades that followed, with the rise of communism and fascism abroad and threats to parliamentary democracy at home, *Studies* held fast to its focus on reform of a less brutal kind.

Cleary's eulogy for Kettle appeared in December 1916. Just weeks before his own death in France, he described meeting his friend in Dublin following the executions; 'his whole conversation was of MacDonagh and the others who had been put to death in Low Week, of the fortitude they had shown. He felt very bitterly ... He died in a different way for a different cause.'[8] Other appreciations for Kettle followed. One from 1966, by Denis Gwynn, places him as the social and intellectual milieu from which *Studies* also emerged.[9] Gwynn had been a pupil of Kettle's at UCD and also one of Pearse's at St Edna's; he came from similar bourgeois stock; his father had been an Irish Party MP.

Gwynn was wounded on the Western Front and invalided home in 1917. John Redmond's son died in France. In 1920 *Studies* had published an article by Henry Gill SJ, a much-decorated former member of the Irish Guards (DSO and MC), which described events during his time as Catholic chaplain to the 2nd Royal Irish Rifles. His account of his quest referred to the death of another Jesuit chaplain to the Irish Guards, a fellow aficionado of the history of Irish regiments. Such commemoration of Irishmen who died in the Great War, Catholic Redmonites as well as Protestants, was driven underground by the versions of nationalism that came to dominate ideologically post-1912 Irish politics. Hostility to the commemoration of Armistice Day and Remembrance Sunday became, to some extent, institutionalised within the new state.[10] In 1993, the seventy-fifth anniversary of the Armistice, an Irish head of state attended a Remembrance Sunday service for the first time.

The First World War, the Irish war of independence and the subsequent civil war received little contemporary attention in *Studies*. An article assessing the journal on its seventy-fifth anniversary in 1986 attributes this to an early decision that *Studies* should be characterised by reasoned and detached criticism. One exception was Daniel Corkery's eulogy 'Terence MacSwiney: Lord Mayor of Cork' (1920), following MacSwiney's death from hunger strike in Brixton prison. Corkery saw him as cut from the same cloth as Pearse when it came to patriotic fervour and self-sacrifice.[11] AE's sober 'Lessons of Revolution' (1923) was more characteristic of the *Studies* viewpoint. The champions of physical force, he argued in a 1923 essay, had poisoned the soul of Ireland: 'The very children in the streets play at assassination, ambush and robbery.'[12]

After independence *Studies* published many articles on the implications of Catholic social thought as set out in the papal encyclicals *Rerum Novarum* (1891) and *Quadragesimo Anno* (1931). A key contributor here was Alfred O'Rahilly, Professor of Mathematics and later President of University College Cork. Article after article struggled with

the practicalities of corporatist and vocationalist alternatives to socialism and capitalism. Whilst many articles disparaged socialist political
experiments, many were genuinely informative. Whilst Catholic social
thought proposed a conservative political project this should not be mis-
taken for a crude anti-modernist one. O'Rahilly's first article in *Studies*
had been a defence of Darwinism from a Catholic perspective;[13] his
second contribution was a very fine survey of works by Nietzsche that
had yet to become available in English.[14]

Virginia Crawford's 'The Rise of Fascism and What it Stands For'
(1923) noted the apparently successful corporatist restructuring of trade
unions and the establishment of vocationalist councils, all along lines
mooted by Catholic thinkers. However, this was leavened by a scathing account of fascist terrorism. Their methods 'were those of the Black
and Tans'. She described how lorries filled with armed *fascisti* would
concentrate at a given signal on a socialist municipality, setting fire to
labour halls and co-operative stores, destroying and looting property
unhindered. Mussolini, she reported, had restored religious teaching in
the schools ('not that he is a practicing Catholic but he accepts Italy as
a traditional Catholic country and believes that religion is beneficial for
the masses') but any Irish admirers she argued, would be wise to copy
the extreme caution of the Vatican in its dealings with the new Italian
state.[15]

By the time a corporatist state (the replacement of democracy with
vocational representation) was mooted by General O'Duffy it found
little support in *Studies*. Significantly, Michael Tierney, a key intellectual figure in *Cumann na nGaedheal* and a founder of Fine Gael, wrote
nothing in *Studies* in the course of some fifty-five articles that advocated
corporatism or vocationalism. In 1935 O'Rahilly argued that the corporate state was dead as a political idea, and rightly so.[16] There was no real
point to a vocational Senate with, say, one doctor, one professor, a few
industrialists, some farmers, shopkeepers and workers and so on. Dáil
Éireann was as things stood probably just as diverse. Instead the emphasis had to be on the adoption of a Christian constitution protecting, as
he put it, 'our natural and religious rights and embodying our social
aspirations'. The main institutional success of Catholic social thought
lay with the insertion of natural law principles into the sections of the
1937 Constitution on family (Articles 40–44) and into the Preamble of
the Constitution.

In March 1933 Daniel Binchy, who had been the Irish Minister to
Germany from 1929 to 1932, published a perceptive analysis of the rise
of Adolf Hitler. It was written before the March 1933 elections which
cemented Hitler's political domination over Germany. Binchy detailed

plans, outlined in *Mein Kampf*, for the withdrawal of citizenship from Jews and the confiscation of their property.[17] Subsequent articles in *Studies* also contested Nazi racial theories. 'The Nazi Movement in Germany' (1938) by Rev. Denis O'Keeffe, then Professor of Ethics and Politics at UCD, rubbished Nazi racial theories as 'pseudo-scientific nonsense'. He described their claims as characteristic of extreme forms of nationalism. There was, he observed, 'a natural tendency for nations to seek an escape from the inadequacies of the present in a mythical past. This is a common experience in all countries. But it requires a portentous absence of humour to accept the theory in the form given to it in Nazi literature – in this form it is altogether pathological.'[18]

Post-independence Irish Catholicism is now often depicted as monolithically repressive. Yet a strong distaste for any of the authoritarian political experiments of the twentieth century – extreme nationalism at home, fascism and communism abroad – characterised the early decades of *Studies*. A large number of articles examined the rise of state socialism. Most were inevitably critical; many were genuinely informative about Marxist ideas; some were clearly awed by the Soviet experiment. In 1926, 1929 and 1932 *Studies* published reports by visitors to Soviet Russia. The first example, 'Two Months in Soviet Russia' by Violet Connolly described a delightful 'pulse of life' behind the shabby character of day-to-day existence, noting only in passing that prospective émigrés recounted alarming stories about 'the latest communist enormities'.[19] In 'Reflections After Visiting Russia' (1929) Peter Somerville came away by no means certain that communism would be an economic failure.[20] In 1932 the economist John Busteed insisted that the Soviets had accomplished colossal tasks.[21]

A 1938 symposium in *Studies* (it is examined here in Chapter 7), in which a number of writers responded to an article by Michael Tierney, adroitly captured the then intellectual politics of cultural nationalism and isolationism. Tierney's piece was an attack on the intellectual legacy of Daniel O'Connell. Binchy to some extent sided with Sean O'Faoláin, whose book on O'Connell, *King of the Beggars*, was the object of discussion. O'Faoláin had in turn challenged the core arguments of Daniel Corkery's *The Hidden Ireland*, the most celebrated intellectual defence of cultural isolationism. Both books were proxies for post-independence ideological conflicts between liberals and cultural isolationists.

Like Corkery, Tierney championed a Catholic cultural 'restoration' that would turn back the clock on nineteenth-century utilitarianism and liberalism and other 'great heresies' of the previous three hundred years. Both imagined in their respective thought experiments turning back the clock on the Reformation and on the post-Reformation destruction of Gaelic Catholic culture. Tierney found little fault with O'Faoláin's account of the genesis of the modern Irish nation. Gaelic League platforms were built on 'faked tradition' but this did not, he argued, warrant a denunciation of the older Gaelic society that pre- ceded the political Irish nation. The foundations of modern Ireland laid down by O'Connell were ones built on an indigenous cultural vacuum. O'Connell's Benthamite ideas justified the abandonment of Gaelic for the 'superior utility of the English tongue'.

Tierney's solution, like Corkery's, was to promote a cultural restora- tion even though he accepted that whatever might be restored would not be authentic. Many successful civilisations were built, Tierney explained, on attempts to 'recover literary, linguistic and artistic tradi- tions that were not always genuinely ancestral to them'. The vanished Gaelic past then, however unreal, was a necessary ideological bulwark against the cultural void of individualism and utilitarianism. But Tierney also acknowledged that such cultural restoration did not fulfil the insti- tutional needs of a nation-state. The invocation of a mythic past some- times worked as symbolic politics but not as a basis of policy making.

After independence, Irish economic policy was anti-protectionist. A punctilious observance of British economic orthodoxies, including the doctrine of free trade, prevailed. For example, a 1924 article by C.H. Oldham, Professor of National Economics at UCD, lambasted the assumption that protectionist tariffs would foster industrial develop- ment. Oldham pointed to the incapacity of the Irish home-market to absorb the whole of industrial output. Exports were crucial for the survival of Irish manufacture. Protectionism would be inflationary because imported raw materials were needed. Economic development, he argued, could only be sustained by *laissez faire* policies and by resisting a sentimental chauvinism towards Irish goods.[22] In 1927 John Busteed advised that tariffs 'were part of a larger complex problem and in themselves produced endlessly complex reactions'. On their own they could not solve the problems of the Irish economy.[23]

From the outset *Studies* was very much preoccupied with economics; its second editor Thomas Finlay SJ went on to become UCD Professor of Political Economy. In 1932 Finlay's protégé and successor at UCD, George O'Brien, invited John Maynard Keynes to give the first memo- rial Finlay lecture, which was published the following year in *Studies*.[24] The lecture had been attended by de Valera and his cabinet as well as by W.T. Cosgrave and former members of his government. Keynes, when later recalling his visit to Dublin, described Cosgrave as very much the nineteenth-century liberal.[25] In a 1953 *Studies* gave a platform to Patrick Lynch to argue for Keynesian planning and offer reassurances about growing state activism. *Studies* published a number of seminal articles advocating an economic developmental role for the state. Lynch argued for realistic debate about the need for some state activism. Many critics of state interventionism sheltered behind 'the lingering shadows of economic liberalism to deny positive economic functions to a government'. Their views were, he argued, based on an incorrect reading of classical economics and on a convenient disregard of economic history. Economic arguments were one thing – these depended on time and place – and ideology was another. Lynch quoted Keynes: 'Practical men who believe themselves to be quite exempt from any intellectual influences, are usually the slaves of some defunct economist.' Indeed, much of what he had to say owed much to Keynes. Economic liberalism had been bankrupt since the Great Depression. Lynch emphasised the impracticality of *laissez faire* ideology ('the only untried utopia' because it had never naturally occurred in the world).[26] In a 1963 article, Lynch described his preferred approach as 'non doctrinal state activity'.[27] It was one distinctly derived from the ideological models of liberal Keynesian economics and Catholic social thought. His influential argument was that when it came to state planning and development there was no conflict of interest between Church and State.

A number of articles in *Studies* had railed against the spectre of a welfare state. The 1951 'Mother and Child Scheme' as proposed by Noël Browne was vilified in several (see Chapter 12). But nuanced analyses of the British post-war plans were also published. In 1944 George O'Brien contributed three such articles. The first, 'Capitalism in Transition', argued that the great age of capitalism had passed. Reform had won out over revolution; future societies would be more egalitarian than before with less poverty and no 'pauperism'. This new social security would, he suggested, come at a cost to society:

> People will be less forward-looking. Social security will provide against the risks and hazards of life ... The falling birth-rate and the gradual ageing of the population will reduce the importance of the family as a unit in the social structure. Saving, the typical Victorian virtue, will cease to arouse applause. The accumulation of a fortune, the dearest Victorian ambition, will no longer command respect.[28]

In his second article O'Brien examined the White Paper produced by the British government in response to the Beveridge Plan. He noted that Sean Lemass had commended the British document (*Full Employment in a Free Society*) to members of the Dáil as a useful guide to dealing with Irish conditions.[29] His third promoted F.A. Hayek's *The Road to Serfdom* as an antidote to its likely excesses.[30] O'Brien's attempt to Catholicise Hayek suggested profound ambivalence towards social democracy even if he was convinced as an economist of the need for a stronger state role. In 'New Views on Unemployment' (1945) O'Brien summarised the thesis of Keynes's *General Theory of Employment*, the theory underpinning the Beveridge Report. O'Brien had long championed Keynes. The *General Theory* argued, amongst other things that free trade could no longer be trusted to maximise the volume of production. There was then a *prima facie* case for state intervention in the economy. The state, Keynes argued and Beveridge accepted, could alleviate chronic unemployment by stimulating demand through state expenditure. That is, it could break past cycles where high unemployment and high saving co-existed. By spending more than its current revenue, it could add to the total expenditure of the community. It could add directly to consumption – that is, stimulate economic demand by subsidising goods through schemes of public investment or by redistributing income from the rich to the poor.[31] O'Brien endorsed the validity of Keynes's paradigm and, for all his reservations, Beveridge's proposals based upon it. In subsequent articles on the welfare state, clerics invoked Hayek just as economists had routinely cited papal encyclicals in their contributions to *Studies*. What Lynch successfully proposed in 1953 was to shift this conservative consensus towards accepting greater levels of state activism.

The 1956 IRA border campaign prompted some soul searching about the notion of a united Ireland, a hitherto taken-for-granted aspiration of constitutional nationalists writing in *Studies*. Donal Barrington's seminal 'Uniting Ireland' argued that prevalent nationalist thinking was impoverished. It blamed partition on British rule and claimed that what Britain had done it must undo. It must take home its money, its men and its influence, liberate the six occupied counties and re-unite Ireland. The paradox was that nationalists ultimately relied on the British Army to coerce all Irishmen to live together. Partition, he argued, was not forced on Ireland by Britain but necessitated by the conflicting demands of the two parties of Irishmen. It was Ireland's crime against itself rather than England's crime against Ireland.[32] Barrington's article was republished in 1959 as the first pamphlet by Tuairim, a collective of young progressive academics and policy makers.

Barrington was fiercely critical of how de Valera, John A. Costello and particularly Sean MacBride had sought to lever international opinion in favour of southern claims. This, Barrington implied, restated the old demand that the British should impose Irish unity. The scale of southern misunderstanding of the north was huge. Southern efforts (the 'ill-fated Mansion House Committee') sought to fund the campaigns of anti-partition candidates. This met with a backlash in the 1949 general election. It gave the Unionist Party its biggest victory to date and 'wiped out' the Northern Ireland Labour Party. For the first time the latter then came out against partition. At the same time no effort had been made to engage with Unionists.

In his *Memoir*, Conor Cruise O'Brien recalled life as a foreign affairs civil servant under MacBride, who, in 1951, was the minister in charge of such propaganda.[33] O'Brien was tasked to establish an Irish news agency to put out stories comparing the British 'occupation' of the north with Soviet occupation of eastern Europe. O'Brien recalled a pamphlet designed for Irish-American consumption supposedly authored by the American League for an Undivided Ireland but ghost-written by MacBride. MacBride's successor Frank Aiken deemed this policy of 'brandishing the sore thumb all over the world' to be unproductive. In the same issue containing 'Uniting Ireland' O'Brien contributed a seminal article (in terms of his own subsequent political and ideological engagement with Unionists); 'A Sample of Loyalties' (1957) analysed 'the ideas and feelings contained in a batch of essays written towards the end of 1953 by a class of 26 boys, aged 13 to 14 years of age attending a large Protestant secondary school in the Six Counties'. The set topic of the essay was 'Ireland'. The value of the exercise for O'Brien was 'an unguarded candour and clarity' unlikely from 'older or more intellectual members of that community'. Twenty of the essays expressed various degrees of positive feeling towards Ireland as homeland. Many were attached to some sense of Irishness. As put by one boy who professed to like the poetry of Yeats: 'I am sort of a way attracted to its music, its famousness and its green fields. We should be proud of it.' Another wrote: 'Ireland is a good country in spite of their overcrowded towns and their slums and the Roman Catholic inhabitants.' Nine of the twenty-six boys stated a preference for unification. Just one of the boys came out unequivocally against it. Only four went into any specifics about what they meant by re-unification. One concluded it would be good if Northern Ireland and 'Eire' were brought together under the Queen's rule. The second maintained that re-unification should be under the British flag. The third suggested that Ireland should be a separate nation with a king. For the fourth, it required forgetting the seventeenth century.[34]

These responses were far removed from nationalist understandings of what was meant by the unification of Ireland. A degree of religious sectarianism was identifiable but O'Brien cautioned reading too much into some of the misconceptions the boys demonstrated about Catholicism. A similar exercise conducted amongst southern Catholic schoolboys would produce similar howlers. That said, O'Brien left the teacher to whom he owed his article anonymous lest, in the grim words of one of his essayists, he be 'silently disposed of'.

The next major debate on nationalism occurred in the 1966 issue that marked the fiftieth anniversary of the 1916 Rising. Shaw's article on the Rising was refused publication in 1966; the then editor Ronald Burke-Savage SJ considered it too controversial for what was meant to be a commemoration.[35] When it was finally published in 1972 the accompanying editorial by Peter Troddyn SJ described it as a 'tract for the present troubled time'.[36] Weighing in with more than 17,000 words – several times the length of usual contributions to *Studies* – Shaw savaged the account of Irish history mobilised by Pearse and attacked subsequent 'myths' that had grown up around the actual events of 1916. Tone aside (and puns; there was much criticism of Wolfe Tone), Shaw said little that had not been advanced in critiques of Pearse and analyses of Irish history published in *Studies* in 1966. Roland Burke-Savage's 1966 editorial had defended, as did Shaw, the patriotism of Eoin MacNeill, who had opposed the Rising at the last moment.[37] David Thornley emphasised Pearse's obsession with the idea of blood sacrifice. He quoted Pearse from December 1915 as writing about the European war:

> The last sixteen months have been the most glorious in the history of Europe. Heroism has come back to Earth ... The old heart of the earth needed to be warmed with the red wine of the battlefields. Such august homage was never before offered to God as this, the homage of millions of lives given gladly for love of country.[38]

Shaw quoted this also. In the same 1966 issue Augustine Martin picked out another example of Pearse's 'terrifying' rhetoric also cited by Shaw:

> We may make mistakes in the beginning and shoot the wrong people; but bloodshed is a cleansing and a sanctifying thing, and the nation which regards it as the final horror has lost its manhood. There are many things more horrible than bloodshed; and slavery is one of them.[39]

Perhaps the most the most trenchant critique published in *Studies* in its 1966 'commemoration' came from Garret FitzGerald. He admired the courage of the men who died but insisted that they hardly warranted admiration as thinkers:

> This almost mediaeval respect for the letter of what had been written or spoken between 1913 and 1916 by the leaders of the Rising is miscon-ceived. Even if these men had been political or social thinkers of world standing, their thoughts on the Ireland they knew could not have stood

up to such prolonged and unthinking veneration, but they did not regard themselves – nor were they in fact great thinkers.[40]

They had, FitzGerald argued, few clear-cut ideas of political or social philosophy. There had been, for instance, deep differences between Pearse and Connolly over the 1913 strike. But neither went into the GPO with a coherent intellectual, political or social programme; political freedom was an end in itself. To treat then the Proclamation of 1916 as a great source of political or social doctrines was to misunderstand what it meant to those who wrote it. Granted, it contained noble ideals, the wish to secure political freedom expressed in an enduring language, but no clear ideas. It was a mistake for Irish people half a century later to ask themselves of what they might do or say on any issue: 'Their views on modern Ireland would be no more valuable than many of their colleagues still alive, and probably less valuable than many of our contemporaries.' FitzGerald's argument was that Ireland could not be administered on a day-to-day basis by the dead.

The northern conflict came to preoccupy *Studies* to a considerable extent. Debate and analysis in *Studies* emphasised that the need to foster ecumenism and pluralism in the north required reform down south. Here criticism emerged of those very constitutional provisions successfully promoted by the Jesuits in 1937. In 'Constitutional Aspects of Pluralism' (1977), Mary Redmond observed that it was relatively easy to single out various phrases and provisions that might be said to offend against a pluralist society. Her list included the Preamble, where the people of Eire were proclaimed in effect to be a Catholic nationalist people; Articles 2 and 3, which claimed the north; Article 8, which added a proclaimed a Gaelic ethos in addition to the nationalist one; and, of course, Articles 41 to 44, which reflected Catholic teaching.[41] Her remedy included gradual change by referendum. In the same issue, in 'Cultural Pluralism', Liam de Paor argued that time would solve many of the problems rooted in the different origins of the two main communities on the island. English at the end of the day was the common language, the Republic had abandoned the culturally isolationist preoccupations of the post-colonial era, and even in the north there was ample common cultural ground.[42]

In a 1978 piece John Brady SJ argued that citizens of the Republic must emphasise that they did not wish to govern Northern Ireland against the wishes of the majority. In many respects Brady updated Barrington's argument for unification by consent. He maintained that there was a need to modify those aspects of law and public administration that seemed to give the state a markedly Catholic character. These included issues such as divorce and contraception. A carefully framed divorce law would, he argued, be for the common good. The Irish prohibition of the sale of contraceptives in the wake of the 1973 McGee ruling was described as 'bizarre'. Brady argued that to abstain completely from all efforts to influence the decisions of mixed marriages – the abandonment of *Ne Temere* – would be 'an appropriate gesture'. Inter-denominational schooling was needed in the north. Children could be taken to separate classes for religious education but there was a case for pilot work on the ecumenical teaching of religion using the same textbooks for Protestant and Catholics, which would explain divergences in understanding and the existence of a common Christian heritage.[43] In his winter 1985 editorial Brian Lennon SJ also argued that the state should not prohibit divorce.[44]

From the 1960s *Studies* was at the vanguard of progressive social debate. It published articles by members of Tuairim, the new rising generation in Irish public life (Tuairim's charter stipulated that members should be under 40 years of age; Ireland was at the time still run by the 1916-era gerontocracy). In addition to Donal Barrington and Patrick Lynch these included Garret FitzGerald and David Thornley. The new mood found expression within the editorials and articles of Ronald Burke-Savage. In the forward-looking 'Ireland: 1963–1973' he called for a new openness to the disparate intellectual traditions that had shaped Irish society:

> The best of the Protestant Anglo-Irish tradition has much to offer us in its concern for civic responsibilities, for virtues of truthfulness and hard work, and for its concern for the appreciation and cultivation of arts and letters. Our national ideal would be a poor one without these qualities. Thinking in Ireland has been much influenced by English Welfare liberals and socialists. Again many of their ideas must find a place in our national ideal, ideas which often find a firmer foundation and a stronger motive-power in the authentic Christian tradition than in the premises from which their formulators derived them.[45]

Even socialist ideas, Burke-Savage implied, could be claimed for Christian social justice; he referred to the socialist traditions of Methodism and Non-Conformism (which were subsequently much emphasised in the United Kingdom by New Labour). The early 1970s witnessed an alliance between post-Vatican-II clerical advocates of social justice and left anti-poverty activists. This found influential expression in the 1971 Kilkenny Conference of the Council of Social Welfare. The new radical Catholic mood was exemplified by Sr Stanislaus Kennedy's *One Million Poor? The Challenge of Irish Inequality*.[46] In *Studies*, Frank Sammon

SJ published several articles depicting poverty as a structural problem, one resulting from inequality of power and resources, as a problem that could not be solved just by economic growth.[47]

The winter 1982 editorial had proclaimed a 'radical shift' in future editorial policy. 'We aim' it began, 'to be non-academic in future, reacting more to the problems of the day, while maintaining the traditional interest of *Studies* in general Irish culture.' However, such a shift had been building for a number of years. The editorial view from the late 1970s onwards was that *Studies* had misplaced its *raison d'être*.[48] The new emphasis was to be upon the perceived dislocations resulting from social injustices, secularisation and loss of political legitimacy. These were understood as somehow intertwined with the problem of declining Catholic influence in the Republic but also with conflicts in the north. The focus on poverty and inequality was then, to some extent, about reacquiring moral capital. But the new radical emphasis on social justice was also heartfelt. Galvanised by third-world liberation theology Gerry O'Hanlon SJ criticised the preoccupation of northern clergy with doctrinal orthodoxy at the expense of secular welfare. He argued that social justice was a burning issue for northern Catholics whilst the sermons of their clergy tended to focus on matters of personal piety.[49] Down south relevance was equated with radical commitment to addressing social inequalities. With neo-liberalism ascendant, Hayek's *The Road to Serfdom* had many new admirers in the West, but none in *Studies*. Various articles around this time argued that the market was a good servant but a poor master. The state, Kieran Kennedy urged in 1985, should not allow the market to dominate when it produced socially unacceptable results. A 1985 editorial by Brian Lennon SJ urged the Church to position itself to the left of the political mainstream.[50] Now market forces rather than the state were the enemies of social cohesion. In another editorial the same year Lennon professed regret that Irish socialism had been stillborn. Yet another 1985 article (by Emmet Larkin) concluded that the current Irish labour movement had 'produced the most opportunistically conservative Labour Party anywhere in the known world'.[51] This victory of Catholic thought in the early years of *Studies* was now to be regretted.

A 1985 editorial described the reality of Dublin working-class parishes where less than 10 per cent attended Sunday Mass regularly. A 1985 review article by Tom Inglis defined secularisation as 'the decline of traditional religious practices that produce a shared meaning and consciousness amongst members of society'.[52] In the same issue Michael Paul Gallagher SJ argued that 'under the open conditions of Irish modernity' faith could no longer be imposed. The decline of traditional authority meant that it could not be accepted passively. Faith had become, like many other things, a matter of individual choice.[53]

In this context *Studies* promoted anti-authoritarian solidarity rather than a return to obedience. Themed issues such as spring 1983's *Upstairs Downstairs* emphasised the need to challenge social inequality. Autumn 1983's *'Private' Property* emphasised 'the ever widening gap between the managerial class and the Irish worker'.[54] Spring 1984's issue *A Solution to Homelessness* outlined the history of vagrancy laws and their current use against homeless people who had been denied social housing. In a number of articles *Studies* captured the mixture of anger and despair that to some extent characterised the 1980s.

The hallucinogenic despair of the 1980s has more than a little relevance to the Ireland of 2012. Several articles addressed different aspects of social and economic dislocation. In one published in 1983, John Sweeney SJ argued that neo-liberalism had blithely permitted huge levels of social inequality; this he warned would drive disaffected unemployed people into the arms of Sinn Féin. Sweeney argued that the economic success that followed *Economic Development* in 1958 had created an Irish society that was more relatively unequal than before.[55] In a 1984 book review Raymond Crotty lacerated the veneration of Whitaker, 'Ireland's most influential civil servant'. Whitaker in his various roles (first Secretary of the Department of Finance, then Governor of the Central Bank) had, according to Crotty, contributed much to the current economic crisis.[56] The great defining political event of the early 1980s, the 1983 Constitutional Referendum on the Right to Life of the Child, vindicated the influence of Catholic conceptions of human rights, even if religious observance had gone into decline. A 1981 article 'Pessimistic Origins of the Anti-Life Movement' speculated that the prevalence of abortion in wealthy capitalist society was an existential response to materialism born out of secular despair.[57] A 1987 article by Margaret Mac Curtain examined the moving statues phenomenon as a kind of atavistic religion response to social change.[58] *Studies* also published articles criticising economic fatalism, including one by Tom Garvin which emphasised the concrete economic and social gains of the post-1950s era.[59]

The 1990s saw some important debate on the future of Catholicism and the emergence of a neo-conservative critique of social liberalism following what Tony Fahey called in 1994 a post-1960s 'flirtation with liberal thought'. Fahey's sociological analysis of the apparent decline of Catholicism (the main theme of Irish sociology for decades) stood out from the pack by focusing astutely on the options now facing the Irish Church. Simply put, it could dilute itself by spreading itself thinly across the whole of Irish society, for example by continuing to run most of the primary and secondary school system, or it could choose to focus on the needs of a smaller devout population: quality, so to speak, over quantity.[60]

Studies remained to the left of the political mainstream when it came to the pursuit of social inclusion for marginal groups. But it also developed a critique of the impact of social liberalism on Irish society. *Studies* remained, as always, preoccupied with Christian ideas and religion. In keeping with its longstanding pluralist ethos it published in 2004 an article on the political influence of Protestant theological ideas on Unionist politics.[61] The very first issue of *Studies* in 1912 had contained an article on Islam.

In the early twenty-first century some new fields of debate stand out alongside the many other articles that continue to be published on various aforementioned themes. There has been a recurring focus on the crisis of accountability in Irish life. Many articles have addressed topics such as the institutional abuse of children and other vulnerable persons in Irish society. Finola Kennedy's 2000 article on the suppression of the 1931 Carrigan Report depicts a long history of state institutional failure in protecting children from abuse.[62] As Arthur Cleary suggested in 1915 the exploitation (and abuse) of children was most likely where they were rendered powerless and there was no obligation to be accountable for how they were treated.

In June 1994 Father Brendan Smyth was convicted on seventeen counts of sexual abuse of children over a period of thirty years. Smyth, according to Harry Ferguson, in an article called 'The Paedophile Priest', perpetrated appalling acts of violence against children and deserved to be demonised. Yet Ferguson was preoccupied with the vilification of celibate clerics. His underlying argument was that masculinity and male sexuality needed to be better understood and openly discussed in order to separate out the causes of sexual abuse from the moral panic that surrounded it.[63] An accompanying article in the same 1995 issue argued that some Church leaders, in their arrogance and hubris, had chosen to deny the seriousness of what was taking place and did not take steps to stop the behaviour of paedophile clerics.[64] There was, Noel Barber SJ argued in his editorial, too much concern about the 'good name' of the Church and too little concern for victims.[65] The winter 2005 issue contained several articles criticising responses by the institutional Church to the scandal of abuse. A 2010 essay, 'No Cheap Grace' by Seamus Murphy SJ, published in response to the Ryan and Murphy reports on child sexual abuse, bluntly started with 'three simple facts': a large number of priests had sexually assaulted children during the last forty years; their superiors made no serious effort to punish or prevent them; if it were not for media exposé, it would still be going on.[66]

The twenty-first century saw the emergence of immigration as a social and political issue in the Republic of Ireland. My own involvement with the journal (as a member of the editorial board from 2002 to 2012) came about when a suggestion I made to the editor Fergus O'Donoghue SJ to publish a special issue on the topic was warmly received. Since then *Studies* has published articles on human trafficking, the treatment of asylum seekers, the participation of immigrants in politics, critiques of multiculturalism and analyses of immigration policy. It has similarly addressed a range of other contemporary social issues.

Notes

This chapter is abridged from Bryan Fanning, 'Introduction: Studies 1912–2012', in Bryan Fanning (ed.), *An Irish Century: Studies 1912–2012* (Dublin: University College Dublin Press, 2012).

1 John Cooney, *John Charles McQuaid: Ruler of Catholic Ireland* (Dublin: O'Brien, 1999), p. 43.
2 Louis McRedmond, *To the Greater Glory: A History of the Irish Jesuits* (Dublin: Gill and Macmillan, 1991), pp. 236–237.
3 Peter McBrien, 'Poets of the Insurrection III: Joseph Plunkett', *Studies*, 5.18 (1916), 536–547.
4 Padric Gregory, 'Poets of the Insurrection IV: John F. MacEntee', *Studies*, 6.21 (1917), 70–79.
5 Patrick Pearse, 'Some Aspects of Irish Literature', *Studies*, 2.5 (1913), 810–822.
6 Arthur Cleary, 'Votes for Youth', *Studies*, 4.14 (1915), 279–285.
7 Lambert McKenna SJ, 'The Housing Problem in Dublin', *Studies*, 8.30 (1919), 279–295, p. 281.
8 A.E. Cleary, 'Thomas Kettle', *Studies*, 5.20 (1916), 503–515, p. 504.
9 Denis Gwynn, 'Thomas M. Kettle 1890–1916', *Studies*, 55.220 (1966), 384–391.
10 Jane Leonard, 'The Twinge of Memory: Armistice Day and Remembrance Sunday in Dublin since 1919', in G. Walker and R. English (eds), *Unionism in Modern Ireland* (Dublin: Gill and Macmillan, 1996), pp. 107–109.
11 Daniel Corkery, 'Terence MacSwiney: Lord Mayor of Cork', *Studies*, 9.36 (1920), 512–520.
12 AE, 'Lessons of Revolution', *Studies*, 12.45 (1923), 1–6.
13 A.J. O'Rahilly, 'The Meaning of Evolution', *Studies*, 1.1 (1912), pp. 32–51.
14 A.J. O'Rahilly, 'The Gospel of the Superman', *Studies*, 3.12 (1914), pp. 381–403.
15 Virginia M. Crawford, 'The Rise of Fascism and What it Stands For', *Studies*, 12.48 (1923), 539–552, p. 547.

16 A.J. O'Rahilly, 'The Constitution and the Senate', *Studies*, 25.97 (1936), 1–19, p. 8.

17 Daniel A. Binchy, 'Adolf Hitler', *Studies*, 22.85 (1933), 9–47.

18 Rev. Prof. Denis O'Keeffe, 'The Nazi Movement in Germany', *Studies*, 27.105 (1938), 1–12, p. 5.

19 Violet Connolly, 'Two Months in Soviet Russia', *Studies*, 17.68 (1926), 637–648.

20 Peter Somerville, 'Reflections After Visiting Russia', *Studies*, 18.72 (1929), 556–568, p. 561.

21 John Busteed, 'Soviet Russia', *Studies*, 21.84 (1932), 531–548.

22 C.H. Oldham, 'After the Fiscal Inquiry Report', *Studies*, 13.49 (1924), 1–13, p. 1.

23 John Busteed, 'Foreign Trade and National Policy', *Studies*, 16.61 (1927), 69–85, p. 85.

24 John Maynard Keynes, 'National Self Sufficiency', *Studies*, 22.86 (1933), 177–193.

25 Robert Skidelsky, *John Maynard Keynes The Economist as Saviour 1920–1937* (London: Macmillan, 1992), p. 479.

26 Patrick Lynch, 'The Economist and Public Policy', *Studies*, 42.167 (1953), 241–274.

27 Patrick Lynch, 'Escape From Stagnation', *Studies*, 52.206 (1963), 136–163, p. 136.

28 George O'Brien, 'Capitalism in Transition', *Studies*, 33.129 (1944), 37–44, p. 38.

29 George O'Brien, 'Stability of Employment: Its Possibility as a Post-War Aim', *Studies*, 33.131 (1944), 304–315, p. 312.

30 George O'Brien, 'A Challenge to the Planners', *Studies*, 33.130 (1945), 210–218, p. 218.

31 George O'Brien, 'New Views on Unemployment', *Studies*, 34.133 (1945), 52–64, pp. 57–58.

32 Donal Barrington, 'Uniting Ireland', *Studies*, 46.184 (1957), 379–402.

33 Conor Cruise O'Brien, *Memoir: My Life and Themes* (London: Profile, 1998), p. 160.

34 Conor Cruise O'Brien, 'A Sample of Loyalties', *Studies*, 46.184 (1957), 403–410.

35 Francis Shaw SJ, 'The Canon of Irish History: A Challenge', *Studies*, 61.242 (1972), 113–153.

36 Peter M. Troddyn SJ, 'Editorial', *Studies*, 61.242 (1972), 113–114, p. 114.

37 Ronald Burke-Savage SJ, 'Current Comment', *Studies*, 55.217 (1966), 1–6.

38 Patrick Pearse, *Peace and the Gael*, December 1915 cited in David Thornley, 'Patrick Pearse', *Studies*, 55.217 (1966), 10–28.

39 Augustine Martin, 'To Make a Right Rose Tree: Reflections on the Poetry of 1916', *Studies*, 55.217 (1966), 38–50, p. 40.

40 Garret FitzGerald, 'The Significance of 1916', *Studies*, 55.217 (1966), 29–37.

41 Mary Redmond, 'Constitutional Aspects of Pluralism', *Studies*, 67.265 (1978), 39–59.

42 Liam de Paor, 'Cultural Pluralism', *Studies*, 67.265 (1978), 77–87, p. 86.

43 John Brady SJ, 'Pluralism and Northern Ireland', *Studies*, 67.265 (1978), 88–99.

44 Brian Lennon SJ, 'Editorial: Church and State', *Studies*, 74.296 (1985), 369–372, p. 369.

45 Ronald Burke-Savage, 'Ireland: 1963–1973', *Studies*, 52.206 (1963), 117–118.

46 Sr Stanislaus Kennedy (ed.), *One Million Poor? The Challenge of Irish Inequality* (Dublin: Turoe Press, 1981).

47 Frank Sammon SJ, 'The Problem of Poverty in Ireland', *Studies*, 71.281 (1982), 1–13, p. 3.

48 Brian P. Kennedy, 'Seventy-Five Years of *Studies*', *Studies*, 75.300 (1986), 361–374, p. 369.

49 Gerry O'Hanlon SJ, 'Images of God: Northern Ireland and Theology', *Studies*, 73.292 (1984), 291–299, p. 292.

50 Kieran Kennedy, 'The Role of the State in Economic Affairs', *Studies*, 74.294 (1985), 130–144.

51 Emmet Larkin, 'Socialism and Catholicism in Ireland 1910–1914', *Studies*, 74.293 (1985), 66–92, p. 88.

52 Tom Inglis, 'Sacred and Secular in Catholic Ireland: A Review Article of *Irish Values and Attitudes: The Irish Report of the European Value Systems* Study by Michael Fogarty, Liam Ryan and Joseph Lee (Dublin: Dominican Publications, 1984)', *Studies*, 73.293 (1984), 38–46, pp. 40–41.

53 Michael Paul Gallagher SJ, 'Secularisation and New Forms of Faith', *Studies*, 74.296 (1985), 9–25, p. 16.

54 Brian Lennon SJ, 'Front Material', *Studies*, 72.287 (1983), 207–208, p. 207.

55 John Sweeney, 'Upstairs Downstairs: The Challenge of Social Inequality', *Studies*, 72.285 (1983), pp. 6–19.

56 Raymond Crotty, 'Turning Point or on Course?', *Studies*, 73.291 (1984), pp. 233–239.

57 Raymond Dennehy, 'Pessimistic Origins of the Anti-Life Movement', *Studies*, 70.277 (1981), 5–12.

58 Margaret Mac Curtain, 'Moving Statues and Irishwomen', *Studies*, 76.302 (1987), 139–147.

59 Tom Garvin, 'Wealth, Poverty and Development: Reflections on Current Discontents', *Studies*, 78.311 (1989), 211–235.

60 Tony Fahey, 'The Church and Culture: Growth and Decline of Churchly Religion', *Studies*, 83.332 (1994), 367–375.

61 Neil Southern, 'Paisleyism: A Theological Inquiry', *Studies*, 93.371 (2004), 349–361.

62 Finola Kennedy, 'The Suppression of the Carrigan Report: A Historical Perspective on Child Abuse', *Studies*, 89.356 (2000), 354–363.

63 Harry Ferguson, 'The Paedophile Priest', *Studies*, 84.335 (1995), 247–256.

64 Peadar Kirby, 'The Death of Innocence: Whither Now?', *Studies*, 84.335 (1995), 257–335.
65 Noel Barber SJ, 'Editorial', *Studies*, 84.335 (1995), 237–238.
66 Seamus Murphy SJ, 'No Cheap Grace: Reforming the Irish Church', *Studies*, 99.395 (2010), 303–316.

7

The limits of cultural nationalism

In 1933 Daniel Binchy, a professor of legal history and jurisprudence at University College Dublin (UCD), published an astute article in *Studies* on Adolf Hitler.[1] He had represented the Saorstát government as a diplomat in Berlin from 1929 to 1932. Binchy had first heard Hitler speak in Munich in 1921, and at the time he described Hitler to a friend as 'a harmless lunatic with the gift of oratory'. The friend retorted: 'No lunatic with the gift of oratory is harmless.'[2] His article on Hitler appeared when Ireland was in the midst of, as he put it in his book *Church and State in Fascist Italy*, 'its brief flirtation with fascism under the catastrophic leadership of General O'Duffy'.[3] Binchy's 1933 article unpicked Nazi presumptions about racial purity. Hitler may have possibly believed in the existence of an Aryan master race; his more intelligent followers, Binchy was certain, did not. They merely used it as a cloak to cover their crude anti-Semitism, and Hitler used both to promote extreme nationalism. The destruction of great empires and civilisations, Hitler insisted, could always be traced to some contamination of the ruling race with inferior foreign blood. But Hitler's efforts to distinguish a Nordic *Herrenvolk* from the lesser breeds which surrounded it and from corruption within were incoherent. Hitler, Binchy explained, would extend sterilisation policies to those who were either corporally or mentally unfitted to have vigorous offspring.[4] Aryan, Binchy explained, was a term made fashionable by nineteenth-century pseudo-ethnologists. Races as Hitler understood these did not exist and, as such, their purity could hardly be defended by eugenics or anti-Semitism.[5]

A number of subsequent articles on Nazi Germany published in *Studies* took their tone and analysis from Binchy. One in 1938 by the Rev. Denis O'Keeffe, then Professor of Ethics and Politics at UCD, rubbished Nazi racial theories and argued that their real importance was as psychological tools of nation-building:

> It is a natural tendency for nations to seek an escape from the inadequacies of the present in a mythical past. This is a common experience in all countries. But it requires a portentous absence of humour to accept the theory in the form given to it in Nazi literature – in this form it is altogether pathological. A certain minimum of self-esteem is, no doubt, necessary for the nation as for the individual. And unsuccessful peoples, in moments of stress, may have difficulty in reaching it. This is the purpose of mass-propaganda. It aims at restoring self-respect to a defeated people. In moderation racial feeling may be at the worst an amiable weakness, at best a proper pride. The Greek, with much justice, thought himself superior to the barbarian. And in a negative way we have all heard, nearer home, of 'lesser breeds without the law' and of the 'wild hysterics of the Celt'.[6]

In addition to Binchy's 1933 demolition of racial theory and other articles in a similar vein *Studies* published many other analyses of cultural and essentialist nationalism. Irish writers of the time hardly took seriously the concept of race as it was portrayed by Hitler. But some were intensely preoccupied with ideals of Gaelic cultural purity. The 1930s witnessed a number of intellectual skirmishes between cultural nationalists such as Daniel Corkery and his former protégé turned liberal nemesis Sean O'Faoláin. Corkery's *The Hidden Ireland*, an account of pre-Enlightenment Gaelic culture, and *King of the Beggars*, a biography of Daniel O'Connell by O'Faoláin that challenged the authenticity and viability of this Gaelic culture, were proxies for wider post-independence ideological conflicts.[7]

A 1938 symposium in *Studies*, whereby a number of writers including Binchy responded to an article by Michael Tierney on *King of the Beggars*, adroitly captured the underlying intellectual politics. Tierney was a leading Fine Gael intellectual and Professor of Greek at UCD. His piece was an attack on O'Connell's utilitarian and liberal legacy. Echoing an earlier essay, Tierney professed the primacy of culture to democracy, the argument being that ideas of political freedom since the Enlightenment had worked to undermine Irish cultural integrity. His 1934 essay, written against the backdrop of Blueshirt efforts to replicate fascist politics in Ireland, described democracy as a 'flower of delicate nature and brief duration', difficult to maintain in a context where autocracy has been the historical norm.[8] The version of democracy that he advocated would require a Christian-inspired rejection of 'the superficial mysticism of the French Revolution, the visionary mysticism of the English liberal school and the confused and inadequate mechanisms which revolutionaries and radicals have imposed upon older political theories and systems', the defective doctrine of Tom Paine's *The Rights of Man* and *On Liberty* and 'the inverted Hegelian dialectic of Marx'. Paine, for Tierney, represented 'the visionary Jacobin deification of the state which had triumphed over the equally visionary individualism of the English radicals'.[9] In his 1938 article Tierney championed a Catholic cultural 'restoration' that would turn back the clock on nineteenth-century utilitarianism and liberalism and other 'great heresies' of the last three hundred years.

In this context, cultural nationalists and Catholic conservatives found common cause against the foreign ideas that, from their various perspectives, subordinated a pre-Enlightenment Gaelic Ireland to an imported modernity. In its crudest form the conflict was one between isolationists who sought to protect Ireland's authentic culture, however understood, from outside contamination and their intellectual opponents. The politics of cultural nationalism since the death of O'Connell had presented the Gaelic revival as a cultural restoration. But Tierney on one side and O'Faoláin on the other acknowledged that what had been attempted was a 'fake' restoration, a reconstruction based on an idealised-but-now-dead culture. Both had different views on the merits and costs of such a project, with Binchy siding with O'Faoláin.

A modern Irish culture, Tierney argued, could be built on the old Gaelic culture but a viable political system could not. The nation-state, he explained, was a nineteenth-century invention that 'coincided with the decay and gradual disappearance of the native ways of thought, life, and expression'. Tierney drew a parallel between the then-disjuncture between Irish culture and politics and what occurred when the Normans became Gaelicised, when cultural absorption coincided with a calamitous failure to create or even conceive of a Gaelic state. O'Connell's contribution to the modern Irish nation was, Tierney argued, a philosophically utilitarian one that readily discarded this legacy. Tierney's thesis was that the Irish revolution had politically internalised that which it supposedly stood against. Implicit in Tierney's critique of how alien ideas filtered into Ireland was the absence of native political intellectual tradition. The nation-building foundations laid down by O'Connell – the roots of Irish democracy from Catholic emancipation through later extensions of suffrage – were ones that had filled an indigenous vacuum. O'Connell's Benthamite ideas justified the abandonment of Gaelic for the 'superior utility of the English tongue'.

This did not validate, Tierney insisted, a rejection of the linguistic revival even if irritation with some of the crude measures for reviving the Gaelic language was justifiable. That O'Connell's democratic nation-building occurred alongside Gaelic cultural decline was to be regretted. As Tierney put it, 'Democracy is no substitute for culture.' This held even if the culture being revived was inauthentic. Many successful civilisations were built, Tierney explained, on attempts to 'recover literary, linguistic and artistic traditions that were not always genuinely ancestral to them'. The vanished Gaelic past then, however unreal, was a necessary ideological bulwark against the cultural void of individualism and utilitarianism. Gaelic League platforms, he agreed with O'Faoláin, were built on 'faked tradition' but this did not, he argued, warrant a denunciation of the older Gaelic society that preceded the political Irish nation. The foundations of modern Ireland laid down by O'Connell were ones built on an indigenous cultural vacuum.

Tierney, like Corkery, favoured a cultural restoration even though he accepted that whatever might be restored would not be authentic. But Tierney also acknowledged that such cultural restorations did not fulfil the institutional needs of a nation-state. The invocation of a mythic past sometimes worked as symbolic politics but not as a basis of policy making.

Binchy defended O'Faoláin's account of O'Connell as a modernising influence. Like Tierney he criticised O'Connell's argument that the abandonment of the Irish language was utilitarian. But he also criticised the unrealism of revivalists and called for a 'sane and honest policy in regard to Irish'. Ireland, for better or worse, was remained in substance what O'Connell made her: and continues to move along lines which he had laid down for her:

> He bade her speak the English tongue, and the victorious progress of that tongue is even to-day overwhelming the last feeble strongholds of the older language. He bade her think in terms of political and economic nationalism, and she has obeyed him but too well. No better instance could be found than the career of the movement for the revival of Irish, which, in its origins a reaction against O'Connell's neglect of cultural nationalism, has eventually become political in the worst sense of the word, operating entirely with the weapons and the methods of political agitation. The very measure of the success which Professor Tierney ascribes to the Gaelic League in revolutionary politics is the measure of its abject failure to achieve the purpose for which it was called into being. It was far less trouble to create a revolution than to restore Irish, and so a stream which should have been kept aloof from and uncontaminated by political strife was mingled almost from its source with the turbid waters of Irish political nationalism. We know the result.[10]

Binchy, like Tierney, had no quarrel with O'Faoláin's account of the genesis of the modern Irish nation.

The theory that the latter has some kind of continuity with the so-called 'Gaelic state' may be a useful fiction for political and Gaelic League plat-forms; historically it is nonsense, and Mr. O'Faoláin is perfectly justified in calling it a 'faked tradition'. But one can completely accept his view on this point without joining in his denunciation of the older Gaelic order of society.[11]

He also accepted O'Faoláin's criticisms of political and social conditions under the Gaelic order. This had sinned chiefly by refusing to move with the times; in a changing world it remained fossilised, parochial and inef-fective. Moreover, much of this Gaelic order was not 'Gaelic' in origin at all. Their so-called 'Gaelic state' was in reality a curious amalgam of old native law and Norman feudal customs which had never been properly studied, least of all by those who clamoured for its 'restoration'.

Whereas Tierney imagined a dichotomy between culture and democracy – preferring the former – Binchy was preoccupied by one between culture and nationalism. The modern Irish nation was a politi-cal invention that once realised as a nation-state had no particular use for the Gaelic language:

The traditional social order was doomed even before O'Connell's day, and Mr. O'Faoláin has no doubts of his wisdom in cutting the new Ireland away from the moribund past. But would it not have been possible for him at least to save the Irish language from the wreckage and to insert it in his new creation. After all, most countries have managed to assimilate the theory and practice of English utilitarian democracy without jettisoning their native speech ... But to O'Connell as to all educated Irish Catholics, lay and clerical, of his day Irish represented merely the annoying relic of a dead order from which his countrymen must free themselves in order to live; accordingly, far from encouraging it, he hailed the signs of its dis-solution with satisfaction. Mr. O'Faoláin applauds his decision. I deplore it (perhaps because I have less use for political nationalism than he has). But we both recognise its irrevocable effects. They may be summarized in one sentence. English becomes henceforward the 'national language' of the political Irish nation, the language in which its gospel is preached and its concepts formulated, and a thousand latter-day Constitutions (or even 'original' *Bunreachta*) cannot alter that stark reality.

But, he insisted, the modern Irish state had been preceded for centuries by a common culture which transcended the boundaries and the bicker-ings of all the petty sovereignties. Upon that culture, whilst neither great nor significant as a contribution to the common stock of humanity, depended all claims to any distinct Irish identity. The emphasis should be on supporting Gaelic culture insofar as it still existed rather than upon a state-driven artificially imposed faked tradition:

Even still it would be possible to keep future generations in touch with that beauty, with the real as opposed to the sham Gaelic spirit, if only our educational authorities would have the courage to abandon the 'faked tradition' for the English-speaking seven-eighths of the country, and if our political authorities would concentrate their attention on the rapidly dwindling areas where Irish is in fact and not in 'fake' – the native language of the people. But a sane and honest policy in regard to Irish is in our day an even more fantastic dream than was the hankering of the poets in the eighteenth century after the vanished Ireland of their fathers.

Binchy's writings in *Studies* on both Nazi racial theory and the intellectual politics of Irish cultural nationalism variously challenged beliefs in racial, national and cultural purity. If races were ethnological fictions mobilised by nation-states so too were official national cultures. Fake traditions were useful fictions according to Tierney but ones that could best be done without according to Binchy.

Notes

This chapter was previously published as Bryan Fanning, 'Daniel Binchy and the Limits of Cultural Nationalism', *Studies*, 102.407 (2013), 297–303.

1 Daniel A. Binchy, 'Adolf Hitler', *Studies*, 22.85 (1933), 29–47.
2 Binchy, 'Adolf Hitler', p. 29.
3 Daniel Binchy, *Church and State in Fascist Italy* (Oxford: Oxford University Press, 1941), p. 724.
4 Binchy, *Church and State in Fascist Italy*, p. 41.
5 Binchy, *Church and State in Fascist Italy*, pp. 37–38.
6 Rev. Prof. Denis O'Keeffe, 'The Nazi Movement in Germany', *Studies*, 27.105 (1938), 1–12, p. 6.
7 Daniel Corkery, *The Hidden Ireland: A Study of Gaelic Munster in the Eighteenth Century* [1924] (Dublin: Gill and Macmillan, 1970), and Sean O'Faoláin, *King of the Beggars: A Life of Daniel O'Connell, the Irish Liberator* (Dublin: Poolbeg, 1980).
8 Michael Tierney, 'Ireland and the Reform of Democracy', *Studies*, 23.85 (1934), 369–382, p. 369.
9 Tierney, 'Ireland and the Reform of Democracy', pp. 372–374.
10 Quoted in Michael Tierney, 'Daniel O'Connell and the Gaelic Past: Symposium with Responses by Daniel Binchy, Gerard Murphy, John Ryan and Sean O'Faoláin', *Studies*, 27.107 (1938), 353–380, p. 370.
11 Quoted in Tierney, 'Daniel O'Connell', p. 364.

8

Hidden Irelands, silent Irelands

Douglas Hyde's inaugural speech as President of the newly organised National Literacy Society in 1892 was entitled 'The Necessity for De-Anglicising Ireland'. Hyde's call for an Irish-Ireland cultural nationalism became to some extent institutionalised in the new state after independence. As put by Tom Garvin: 'From the 1890s to 1960s, nationalist and nativist themes were used to erect ideological and organisational defences against the cultural and political assaults seen to be emanating from the Anglo-Saxon world and elsewhere.'[1] Collateral damage proved inevitable. The isolationism of the new state affected, even shaped, Irish writers such as Frank O'Connor and Sean O'Faoláin. Much of their work was banned but, as is the way with these things, their reputations in Ireland were bolstered by international success. For O'Faoláin censorship was not the problem *per se* but was a symptom of a wider cultural and intellectual malaise that made it difficult to discuss Irish society realistically. Irish social problems were, he argued, obscured by the ideological mist of romantic nationalism. This, he maintained, was epitomised by Daniel Corkery's *The Hidden Ireland*, a hugely influential text he saw as legitimising cultural isolationism and censorship.

The hidden Ireland that preoccupied O'Faoláin was the silent Ireland of the 1940s.[2] In 1940 he founded *The Bell*, a journal aimed at nurturing sceptic scholarship and factual enquiry.[3] In this endeavour he was supported by Frank O'Connor. During the 1930s both had criticised Corkery in literary journals such as *Dublin Magazine* and *Ireland Today*. The Irish nationalist tradition contained an ideology of cultural defence, centred upon a notion of Irish racial purity that needed to be defended against outside corruption. Their shared concern was that Corkery had helped to popularise this myth of Irish purity that lent false credibility to the 'immunization' work of the Censorship Board.[4]

Both subsequently challenged Corkery on his own ground. O'Faoláin's argument was developed in *King of the Beggars*, his 1938 life of Daniel O'Connell, and in *The Great O'Neill*, a history of destructive conflicts between the Irish nobility of the late sixteenth century.[5] The essence of this thesis was that Corkery's reading of Irish history was fanciful and that the Munster poetic tradition celebrated by Corkery was detached from the real lives and experiences of Irish peasantry. O'Connor was less concerned with the epistemology of Irish historical culture than with the sectarianism of Corkery's poetic canon. Specifically, he attacked Corkery's critique of the Irish poet Brian Merriman, a Clare man and a Protestant.

The Ireland revealed in *The Bell* included prisons, illegitimacy, poverty, TB, slums and pawn shops. Such uncomfortable realities were, for O'Faoláin, obscured by a dominant romantic idealism incapable of examining the real conditions facing Irish people. As he put it in a 1942 editorial: 'Most of our inherited ideas about ourselves are born of patriotism and propaganda, and most of our pictures of life are pictures either drawn from the outside, or about a period and conditions now past.' Ireland, he argued, was choked with 'ideas and idealisms; mainly anachronistic, and almost wholly unadaptable to life as it is lived'.[6] In 1969 he elaborated on this argument:

> Nowadays I sometimes say, to tease my fellows, 'You are all men of the twenties.' Their eyes glow, recalling our glorious twenties. 'I mean,' I add, 'of the eighteen-twenties' – as Yeats (Shelley and all that) was unto his dying day. Not that, with one proviso, there is anything wrong with being a romantic, as Yeats proved. The proviso is whether the world about us will play ball with our romanticism. Otherwise it is like playing tennis with a ghost. Yeats was so lucky! He had the Irish folk world, now taken over by tourism and TV; Irish mythology and hagiography, now and none too soon, in the hands of sceptic scholars...[7]

The Hidden Ireland exemplified the sort of thinking he had in his gun-sights. The young O'Faoláin had been Corkery's protégé, the 'best friend' who was allowed to look at a copy of *Ulysses* which Corkery kept in a locked drawer.[8] O'Faoláin objected to Corkery's idealisation of an uneducated peasant culture in *The Hidden Ireland* as a model for independent Ireland. He argued that real Ireland had its own cosmopolitan European tradition and a place in world literature to build upon.[9] O'Faoláin credited Daniel O'Connell with moulding the 'craven helot peasants' of the early nineteenth century into individuals capable of advancing democracy in Ireland. In essence, the thesis of his O'Connell biography was that the peasantry found their revelation in the Enlightenment, as interpreted by their leaders, rather than the old Gaelic order: 'The literature of the French Revolution, the English radicals, Godwin, Tom Paine, the French Deists, Adam Smith, Mary Wollstonecraft – these assimilated and adapted by O'Connell, put into words of one syllable, were what really interested the poor people of Ireland.'[10]

Corkery's book promoted a rediscovery of the Gaelic poetry tradition as an antidote to an Irish language revival he depicted as tainted by colonialism: 'What pains one' he wrote, 'is to come upon an Irishman who cannot speak either of the Irish language or Irish literature or Gaelic history except in some such terms as the Ascendancy in Ireland have taught him. In his case the Ascendancy have succeeded; the have created in him the slave-mind.'[11] Corkery's project was one of cultural nationalism, to unearth what he believed to be the nobility of Gaelic culture, to challenge pervasive English language accounts of the Irish past in novels, travelogues and histories.[12]

The actual conditions of the peasantry that these described were not rejected by Corkery. Indeed, his descriptions of peasant poverty would not have been out of place in *The Bell*. For instance, 'Every hut had its dung pit in front of the door', 'House and dress were so miserable that food was almost the only expense', or 'Seldom was there a lease, either on house or land; and to improve either led to an increase in rent, perhaps an eviction.'[13] The result, according to Corkery, was that civic life and institutions that might find a place for art had been wiped out.[14] Yet, Corkery argued, the nobility of the Munster Gaelic tradition, exemplified in its poetry, survived under the emaciated conditions of the Penal Law. The eighteenth-century peasant poets were the lineal descendants of the old bardic line, the proud possessors of an aristocratic tradition of literature. This, he maintained, was proof of an indomitable Irishness.

O'Faoláin did not disagree with a lot of what Corkery had to say about the persistence of the Gaelic bardic tradition in this impoverished setting. However, he vehemently objected to the way Corkery depicted the erstwhile Gaelic aristocracy that had sustained the bards through their patronage. These Gaelic houses, according to Corkery, were in some ways similar to Planter ones yet possessed certain characteristics of their own: 'freer contact with Europe, a culture over and above that which they shared with their neighbours, a sense of historic continuity, a closeness to the land, to the very pulse of it, that those Planter houses could not even dream about.'[15] Corkery proclaimed the native superiority of the bardic schools to the European type of university, where the main study was of the Roman law – 'the relic of a dead empire' – and the literature of dead languages. By contrast, the history that was taught in the bardic schools was 'that of Ireland, namely the Brehon Law system; the language was that of Ireland, the literature that of Ireland – and through the medium of the native language were all subjects taught'.[16] O'Faoláin disagreed. In *The Great O'Neill* he argued that the Gaelic past was never so neat and tidy. The claims about Gaelic aristocratic cultural purity advanced by Corkery did not hold up.[17]

O'Faoláin also argued in *King of the Beggars* that the bardic tradition of the eighteenth century was intensely anti-realistic. Their poetic convention was one of exaggerated effusive praise of their own patrons, their 'palaces' and the gifts they bestowed. It was never for things like pennies or bacon, which the poets would be lucky to get, but for 'silks, wines, jewels, steeds, cloaks, gold in abundance, silver and arms for heroes'. Later it was reduced to a convention that bewailed the loss of patronage. The dramatis personae of these poems, O'Faoláin emphasised, were the bards themselves and the aristocrats they identified with but 'never once a peasant'.[18] The bards praised by Corkery were, at best, hapless men out of tune with their times.[19]

At their worst, they were a craven lot and fantasists to boot. Whilst his people starved in windowless hovels the poet O'Rahilly listed over and over the glories of once-great houses, 'glories in which we do not find one homely detail, a thing we could take for fact, one item to make us feel that we are not being taken by the hand into a complete dream-world'.[20] The literary value of such poetry was beside the point, because it had nothing to say about the actual culture within which it was produced:

> It means either that these semi-popular poets had nothing to say to the people that was related to their real political and social condition; or else it means that the people were themselves living in a conventional attitude of mind, asked for and desired no realistic songs, had no wish for a faithful image of their appalling conditions – were, in one word sleep-walking.[21]

O'Faoláin used this argument in *King of the Beggars* to emphasise the scale of Daniel O'Connell's achievement. In O'Faoláin's version the peasants of *The Hidden Ireland* were badly in need of a true political leader but hardly ready for the one that they actually got in O'Connell.[22] His analysis of the poets as translated and cited by Corkery is convincing for the most part. The few exceptions were amongst the 'minor poets' rounded up in one of the later chapters of *The Hidden Ireland*. There, just one poem cited by Corkery, which addressed the treatment of tenants by a landlord, might, barely, have passed O'Faoláin's test. This 'Jacobite poem' by Sean Clarach MacDomhnaill said of one Colonel Dawson of Aherlow, 'He hitched Hunger to the people / forcing them to obey.'[23] More generally, what realism there was focused on the reduced circumstances of impoverished poets forsaken by patrons. The now destitute last official poet of one family wrote:

> My craft being withered with
> change of law in Ireland,
> O grief that I must henceforth
> take to brewing!

Another replied:

> O Tadgh, understanding that you
> are for the brewing,
> I for a space will go skimming the milk.[24]

O'Faoláin looked at such poems from the perspective of a political historian. He argued that *The Hidden Ireland* 'sinned from over softness and romanticism' but acknowledged that his own *King of the Beggars* 'sins, perhaps, from harshness, or impatience, due to a deliberate insistence on political realism'.[25] The criticisms he applied to Corkery's Munster bards were applied subsequently to W.B. Yeats. In *The Irish* he identified in Yeats a weakness which came between him and his immediate Irish successors. These were mostly writers of novels and stories, all observation, all eyes, avid for realism (even if they were never to achieve it), preoccupied with what Stendhal called 'the little actual facts' – those details and precisions which accumulate as well-imaged reality. In their sense, Yeats did not have an observing eye. 'He could evoke like a magician; he could not draw a picture.'[26]

O'Faoláin and Corkery, inevitably, had different tastes in Gaelic poetry. *The Hidden Ireland* gave a chapter over to the work of the Clare poet Brian Merriman whose one great poem, *Cuairt an Mheadhon Oidche* (The Midnight Court) was a fantastical bawdy satire on peasant society, its priests and its cuckolds. Corkery lambasted Merriman's lack of bardic refinement. 'It had no luxuriance in it, nothing flowing, sinuous, gentle or efflorescent. Its accent is, rather boorish, abrupt, snappy' even if it was 'taut and well-articulated'.[27] For Corkery, its distance from the Munster bardic tradition he admired (which he called the living Court of Poetry) was exemplified by 'its description of the peasant's hut or the implicit contrast it makes between the fanciful Midnight Court and the court the people had to do business with'.[28]

Corkery maintained that *The Midnight Court* lacked a true lyricism capable of dealing with nature. This line of criticism missed the point of Merriman's work. His main topics – sex, marriage, inheritance and women's rights – were advanced through satire. Corkery judged Merriman's much praised opening descriptions of east Clare to be commonplace: 'we get no passage of any length sustained in that high style'.[29] This is less than fair to the wonderful animistic vista executed by Merriman at the beginning of the poem. Consider the following two translations, the first by Frank O'Connor first published in 1945:

> When I looked at Lough Graney my heart grew bright,
> Ploughed Lands and green in the morning light,
> Mountains in ranks with crimson borders
> Peering about their neighbour's shoulders.[30]

the second, as rendered in J.N. Fahey's 1998 translation:

> My heart would brighten Loch Graney to spy,
> And the country around it, to the edge of the sky.
> The serried mountains were a delight to the beholder
> Thrusting their heads over each other's shoulder.[31]

O'Connor took huge issue with Corkery's 'sneer' at Merriman as 'a coarse jester'.[32] He depicted him instead as an independent intellectual who drew on contemporary English verse to produce an authentic piece of Gaelic literature rooted in the society he came from:

> His language – that is its principal glory – is also a complete break with literary Irish. It is the spoken Irish of Clare ... What Merriman aimed at was something that had never been guessed at in Gaelic Ireland; a perfectly proportioned work of art on a contemporary subject, with every detail subordinated to the central theme.[33]

Yet Merriman, 'the intellectual Protestant' and schoolteacher-farmer who somehow 'knew as much about Lawrence and Gide as he knew of Savage, Swift, Goldsmith and most of all Rousseau', had no influence on Irish life or Irish thought. This was evident, according to O'Connor, in the demise of the sensuous eighteenth-century society that Merriman lamented in its passing and its replacement by Catholic Puritanism. O'Connor felt constrained when translating *The Midnight Court*; he sought to evoke rather than directly translate Merriman's 'perfect crescendo of frustrated sexual passion'.[34] There are less inhibited translations, yet the tremendous physicality of *The Midnight Court* is evident in O'Connor's:

> Down with marriage! Tis out of date,
> It exhausts the stock and cripples the state.
> The priest has failed with whip and blinker,

> Now give a chance to Tom the Tinker,
> And mix and mash in nature's can
> The tinker and the gentleman;
> Let lovers in every lane extended,
> Follow their whim as God intended,
> And in their pleasure bring to birth
> The morning glory of the earth;[35]

The twentieth-century secret Ireland – where frank translations of Gaelic poems might be censored alongside literary depictions of modern society – was, O'Faoláin argued, obscured by the orthodoxies promoted by *The Hidden Ireland*. O'Faoláin and O'Connor, like many Irish writers of their generation, enthused about the Irish language, peasant lore and country tradition. *The Bell*, for instance, published a series of extracts from Tim Buckley's *The Tailor and Ansty*, an irreverent account of country life. These stories of the actual people of Gougane Barra, where O'Faoláin, O'Connor and Corkery had gone to study the Irish language, fell foul of the censor.

O'Faoláin and O'Connor understood and responded to the problem of censorship differently. Both chose differently from the options of exit (or exile as Irish writers would have it), voice and loyalty. Both spoke out. O'Faoláin's loyalty took to the form of a longstanding practical and patriotic engagement with the realities of Irish life. With *The Bell* he sought to overcome what he saw as indifference to such realities. In 1953 he became the founder President of the Irish Council for Civil Liberties. O'Connor, never an organisation man, was more disposed towards exit. He identified in Merriman a profound sense of intellectual isolation. In writing of the Clare poet's dilemmas he touched on his own alienation. Merriman, he noted, moved eventually to Limerick most probably 'because what Professor Corkery sneers at as "his-much enlightened soul" longed for some sort of intellectual society which in twentieth century Clare it might still long for. To say the man was 150 years before his time would be mere optimism – think of Professor Corkery.'[36] The isolationism both associated with Corkery had run its course by the 1950s. The silent Irelands made up of what could not be discussed in the face of prevailing communal orthodoxies persisted.

Notes

This chapter was previously published as Bryan Fanning, 'Hidden Ireland, Silent Irelands: Sean O'Faoláin and Frank O'Connor versus Daniel Corkery', *Studies*, 95.379 (2006), 251–260.

1 Tom Garvin, 'Patriots and Republicans', in W. Crotty and D.E. Schmitt (eds), *Ireland and the Politics of Change* (London: Longman, 1998), p. 146.
2 Sean O'Faoláin, 'The Silent Ireland', *The Bell*, 6.6 (1943).
3 Sean O'Faoláin, 'On Editing a Magazine', *The Bell*, 9.2 (1944).
4 Richard Bonaccorso, *Sean O'Faolain's Irish Vision* (New York: State of New York Academic Press, 1987), p. 51.
5 Sean O'Faoláin, *King of the Beggars: A Life of Daniel O'Connell, the Irish Liberator* (Dublin: Poolbeg, 1980); Sean O'Faoláin, *The Great O'Neill: A Biography of Hugh O'Neill Earl of Tyrone, 1550–1616* (Dublin: Mercier, 1970).
6 Sean O'Faoláin, 'Why Don't We See It', *The Bell*, 5.3 (1942).
7 Sean O'Faoláin, *The Irish* (London: Penguin, 1969), p. 141.
8 Maurice Harmon, *Sean O'Faoláin: A Life* (London: Constable, 1994), p. 66.
9 *Irish Statesman*, 5 September 1925.
10 O'Faoláin, *King of the Beggars*, p. 39.
11 Daniel Corkery, *The Hidden Ireland: A Study of Gaelic Munster in the Eighteenth Century* (Dublin: Gill and MacMillan, [1924] 1970), p. 10.
12 Corkery, *The Hidden Ireland*, pp. 25–27.
13 Corkery, *The Hidden Ireland*, p. 29.
14 Corkery, *The Hidden Ireland*, p. 36.
15 Corkery, *The Hidden Ireland*, p. 67.
16 Corkery, *The Hidden Ireland*, p. 80.
17 O'Faoláin, *The Great O'Neill*, pp. v–vi.
18 O'Faoláin, *King of the Beggars*, p. 25.
19 O'Faoláin, *King of the Beggars*, p. 26.
20 O'Faoláin, *King of the Beggars*, p. 27.
21 O'Faoláin, *King of the Beggars*, p. 25.
22 O'Faoláin, *King of the Beggars*, p. 139.
23 Quoted in Corkery, *The Hidden Ireland*, p. 242.
24 Quoted in Corkery, *The Hidden Ireland*, p. 110.
25 O'Faoláin, *King of the Beggars*, p. 36.
26 O'Faoláin, *The Irish*, pp. 138–139.
27 Corkery, *The Hidden Ireland*, p. 229.
28 Corkery, *The Hidden Ireland*, p. 239.
29 Corkery, *The Hidden Ireland*, p. 238.
30 Brian Merriman, *The Midnight Court*, trans. Frank O'Connor (Dublin: O'Brien Press, 2000).
31 Brian Merriman, *The Midnight Court*, trans. J.N. Fahey, available online at http://midnight-court.com.
32 Frank O'Connor, 'Preface' to Merriman, *The Midnight Court*, trans. O'Connor, p. 12.
33 O'Connor, 'Preface' to *The Midnight Court*, trans. O'Connor, pp. 12–13.
34 O'Connor, 'Preface' to *The Midnight Court*, trans. O'Connor, p. 14.
35 Merriman, *The Midnight Court*, trans. O'Connor, p. 49.
36 O'Connor, 'Preface' to *The Midnight Court*, trans. O'Connor, p. 13.

9

Liberalism and *The Bell*

Throughout the 1940s and into the 1950s, *The Bell*, Kelly Mathews concludes in *The Bell Magazine and the Representation of Irish Identity*, 'looked unflinchingly on the realities of contemporary Irish life, whether they corresponded with the official version of "the ideal Ireland" or revealed its cruelties and inconsistencies'.[1] *The Bell* was hardly unflinching throughout its fourteen or so years of existence. It wavered from time to time and shifted somewhat in emphasis under different editors, and there was sometimes a gap between intentions declared in editorial manifestos and the stuff that was published. And not everyone who wrote for *The Bell* wanted the same thing. In a 1945 article Conor Cruise O'Brien disparaged its 'caution, its realism, its profound but ambivalent nationalism, its seizures of stodginess and its bad paper'.[2]

What made *The Bell* stand out was its emphasis on how everyday realities contested then-prevalent cultural nationalist orthodoxies. Within intellectual politics these were exemplified by Daniel Corkery, within political rhetoric by Éamon de Valera. But *The Bell*'s founding editor Sean O'Faoláin had no fight to pick with middle Ireland. As he put it in a 1941 editorial:

> That the vast majority of the people here are Catholic is a matter of mathematics. That the country is in the main Nationalist is equally obvious, and that it has Isolationism in its blood must be evident to anybody who has even heard the words 'Sinn Fein' ... Nationalist, Democratic, and Catholic then: that appears to be the sum of what it is clear in the picture of Life here.[3]

A 1943 editorial noted that when Mussolini resigned and the battle of Sicily was at its height the first item on the Irish radio news concerned the pilgrimage of 10,000 people to Croagh Patrick. The second lead item was an account of a *Muintir Na Tíre* conference in Cork.[4] Such seemed to be the priorities of the Irish people, and O'Faoláin saw no problem as such with this.

The Bell published new fiction and poetry but these, for O'Faoláin, were ancillary to its main intended purpose of documenting life in Irish society. In an early editorial he enjoined future contributors to note how writers in the magazine drew on actual experience. Do not, O'Faoláin begged his contributors, write articles on abstract subjects. The mission of *The Bell* was simple but radical. 'We are', O Faoláin wrote, 'writing about our own people, our own generation, our own institutions' in a 'decent, friendly, possibly hot-tempered, but always polite and constructive way'.[5] The business of describing Irish life honestly and plainly was vital if slavish imitation of other nations was to be avoided: 'When Ireland reveals herself truthfully, and fearlessly, she will be in possession of a solid basis on which to build a superstructure of thought; but not until then.' This, he claimed, had never been attempted before in Ireland: 'There were plenty of other magazines that dealt with abstractions. There should be room for one that concerned itself with facts.'[6] His February 1941 editorial characteristically chided 'Irish thinkers and students' who proffered 'vague woolly articles, all personal opinion and no study' and complained of a shortage of suitable articles on Irish social and political problems:

> We encouraged articles on a great many social and economic questions – Jails, Illegitimacy, Crime, Workhouses, Hospitalisation, Fisheries, Canning, Public Libraries, Jockeys, Mental Defectives, Housemaids, Other People's Incomes, Pawnshops, Flower Shows, T.B., Slums, Turf Cutting and so forth. They did not produce a whimper of comment. Does this mean that the people are eager to respond to any declaration of faith in the uptapped vigour of the nation and unexhausted idealism of the nation but are as yet inarticulate or unstudied when it comes to method and detail? Or does it mean that there is a weight of inertia, some large psychological frustration all over the nation, and that until it is removed the energy cannot be released? More and more I feel driven to that last conclusion.[7]

Many but not all issues of *The Bell* contained non-fiction articles that played by the house rules set down by O'Faoláin. Flann O'Brien of all people contributed straight reportage such as 'The Dance Halls' (1941). His factual account of such venues was marshalled to counter then-prevalent hyperbolic claims about 'vestibules of hell' fuelled by clerical preoccupations with sexual immorality. 'The Dance Halls' distinguished between various types of rural and urban dance events, their organisation and, not without humour, the ways patrons got round the prohibition of alcohol in many venues. O'Brien quoted a number of

court and newspaper accounts of the presumed relationship between
dance halls and the emigration of young women. One Father Devane,
a prominent advocate of censorship, was reported as anxious to know
how far dance halls 'set up a restlessness that causes girls to emigrate'.
Why, he asked, were there so many dance halls in Donegal? Emigration,
a letter to *Irish Press* explained, was not caused by dancing: 'Many
Donegal girls come to Dublin. Some get good wages. But they don't
stay in Dublin though Dublin has dance halls galore. They feel lonely in
Dublin, so they go to Glasgow where hundreds of neighbours have made
their homes.'[8] The article sought to engineer a debate about emigration:
the *Irish Press* letter cited by O'Brien was from the socialist novelist
Peadar O'Donnell, a co-founder of *The Bell* who succeeded O'Faoláin
as editor in 1945.

The topic of emigration was revisited in subsequent issues. A 1942
piece by O'Faoláin lambasted the response to emigration of *An Glór*, a
fortnightly periodical published by the Gaelic League. This he described
as an example of 'sentimental sludge', 'full of the old sentimental rhetoric, but too lazy to make one single constructive proposal of any kind
– beyond calling on the Clan of Gaels to answer the voice of Eire in her
misery with the 'fiercely national spirit'.[9] A 1943 article by O'Donnell
on the conditions experienced by emigrants called for the establishment
of Irish centres in British cities.[10] *The Bell* also published, 'I wanted to
be a nurse', an anonymous account by a 21-year-old Irish woman of
her experiences in British hospitals.[11] It revealed that young emigrant
women had more on the minds than dancing. The author described
caring for dying patients during an air raid.

Each issue of *The Bell* contained fiction and poetry. To some extent
its non-fiction was moulded from the observational template of the
short story. In the early days Frank O'Connor contributed both fiction
and non-fiction. Other non-fiction contributors like Flann O'Brien and
O'Donnell were novelists. Some of the reportage collated by O'Faoláin
had all the art of the short story. O'Faoláin's advice to contributors over-
lapped with advice he gave to would-be fiction writers in a 1942 series of
radio talks. This was repeated in a 1944 article for *The Bell* on the craft
of the short story: 'I think that it is safe to say that unless a story makes
this subtle comment on human nature, on the permanent relationship
between people, their variety, their expectedness and unexpectedness,
it is not a story in any modern sense.'[12] The business of describing life
in Ireland did not have to be a turgid one. *The Bell*, he declared, was
a magazine for people 'more sensitive to the Human Comedy, more
shrewd about character, more responsive to all its vagaries and subtle-
ties, than many far more cultivated people who live in the kind of society

where natural personality has been ruled by convention'. Non-fiction, no less than fiction, needed to look beneath the surface of life.

At its best *The Bell* presented compelling snapshots of Irish society. It grappled with a series of taboo issues such as birth control, freemasonry, the Knights of Columbanus, unmarried mothers, illegitimacy, divorce, homosexuality, mental illness and prostitution.[13] There was a recurring focus on poverty and its consequences. For example, 'Off the Dole' (1941) gave a first person account of a visit to a labour exchange by an unemployed journalist.[14] 'Illegitimate' from the same year observed the treatment of women in court. It described the experiences of women from different social classes and conditions in institutions for unmarried women. 'Will you go back to your people?' the judge asked a woman in the dock:

> 'They don't know about the baby, sir, they wouldn't take me.' Breaking down she pulls the shawl over her face and the half-seen child. The crowd has ceased to shift and whisper and even the shiny-haired pressmen are embarrassed under their all-in-a-day's work composure as a guard leads her once more out of court, placed on remand until further enquires are made.[15]

The widespread institutional abuse of such women remained undiscovered, but shortcomings identified in the five homes examined were described. There was, the author wrote, no use in pretending that they did not badly need improvement, supervision and co-ordination. They were described as miserably comfortless, generally incapable of meeting the long-term needs of unmarried women and, most importantly for the author, unable to prevent a needless level of infant mortality because of the lack of resident doctors.

Kelly Matthews's *The Bell Magazine and the Representation of Irish Identity* is primarily a work of literary criticism. The secondary literature she favours often has little to say about *The Bell*. She draws on the work of post-colonial theorists such as Seamus Deane and Luke Gibbons who intellectually and ideologically are much more in sympathy with Corkery than with O'Faoláin. She suggests that the Irish dilemmas highlighted by O'Faoláin anticipated those written about subsequently by Franz Fanon in his anti-colonial treatise *The Wretched of the Earth*.[16] At one point she implies that O'Faoláin's efforts to encourage Irish writers to write about Ireland as it is – to practise what O'Faoláin called *voir clair* – were attempts to transcend a colonial past, when in fact O'Faoláin was virulently critical of post-colonial shibboleths. It would be difficult to see O'Faoláin having much common ground with much of what has been published within Irish studies from post-colonial perspectives. Conor

Cruise O'Brien far better exemplified O'Faoláin's intellectual vantage point, not least in how both were at once sceptical of nationalism but took it very seriously as a social phenomenon.

From the 1930s onwards, Irish historians fought a battle over the Irish past within which 'revisionists' challenged the earlier greening of Irish history. The first phase of historical revisionism against now-institutionalised romantic nationalist orthodoxies in the journal *Irish Historical Studies* coincided with two major books by O'Faoláin, *King of the Beggars* (in defence of Daniel O'Connell's liberal constitutionalism) and *The Great O'Neill* (on the decline of the old Gaelic order romanticised by cultural nationalists like Corkery), that similarly challenged these. *The Bell* is aptly considered by Matthews as a literary periodical. However, it also had much in common as an intellectual project – epistemologically and ontologically – with *Irish Historical Studies*. O'Faoláin did much to rehabilitate O'Connell's Irish reputation following some eighty years of vilification and sidelining by intellectually influential physical-force nationalists like John Mitchel and Patrick Pearse. Whilst arguments about Irish historiography found no place in *The Bell* the reasons why O'Faoláin insisted that it should focus on ordinary life in Ireland tied in closely with his critique of forms of nationalism that claimed legitimacy from the Irish people in the abstract.

Matthews is at her strongest when documenting *The Bell*'s project of representing Irish culture and Irish identity through a focus on everyday life and homespun artefacts. Alongside articles on life in slums, and the experiences of unemployed people and of emigrants, O'Faoláin was also keen to represent the richness of Irish material culture. This culture was primarily a rural one. A number of articles focused on Irish arts and crafts, on musical instruments, cottage furniture and *súgán* chairs that would not be out of place in *The Tailor and Ansty*, the ribald memoir of country life by Eric Cross that O'Faoláin championed.[17] In a 1941 editorial he argued that one can talk about nationality until one is blue in the face and get no nearer the fact, 'but when somebody makes a chair that is patently an Irish chair, and not a Birmingham chair, that *is* Nationality'.[18] The cultural artefacts he championed were chosen for their ordinariness. New 'Irish' designs, he argued, should be based on such native furniture. An obvious precursor here was William Morris's English Arts and Crafts movement a half a century earlier.

O'Faoláin's taste in literature and poetry ran in the same direction. Abstract poetry and abstract art were no less out of place in *The Bell* than abstract nationalism. Overall *The Bell* opposed modernism in literature and the arts. O'Faoláin tellingly wrote that he would have refused to publish T.S. Eliot's *The Waste Land* had it been submitted to *The*

Bell and that he would have also fought against *Ulysses* and *Finnegan's Wake* if he had been given the editorial opportunity.[19] *The Bell*, then, was self-consciously old-fashioned. For all its deserved reputation as a seminal periodical in accounts of twentieth-century Irish modernisation it was at times progressive with a small 'p', conservative with a small 'c' and liberal with a small 'l'. In this it was true to its time and place, a mostly rural, insular Ireland, a young country still preoccupied with cultural nation-building and still uneasy about defining itself in terms of progress and economic growth.

Notes

This chapter is a review of Kelly Matthews, *The Bell Magazine and the Representation of Irish Identity* (Dublin: Four Courts Press, 2012). Previously published in *Studies*, 102.405 (2013), 95–100.

1 Matthews, *The Bell Magazine*, p. 171.
2 At the time O'Brien wrote under a pen name. See Donat O'Donnell, 'Horizon', *The Bell*, 11.6 (1945), 1030–1038.
3 Sean O'Faoláin, 'Attitudes', *The Bell*, 2.6 (1941), 5–12.
4 Sean O'Faoláin, 'Silent Ireland', *The Bell*, 3.6 (1943), 457–466.
5 Sean O'Faoláin, 'For the Future', *The Bell*, 1.2 (1940), 5–6.
6 Sean O'Faoláin, 'Answer to a Criticism', *The Bell*, 1.3 (1940), 5–6.
7 Sean O'Faoláin, 'A Challenge', *The Bell*, 1.5 (1941), 5–7.
8 Peadar O'Donnell cited by Flann O'Brien, 'The Dance Halls', *The Bell*, 1.5 (1941), 44–53.
9 Sean O'Faoláin, 'The Gaelic League', *The Bell*, 4.2 (1942), 77–86.
10 O'Donnell, 'The Irish in Britain', *The Bell*, 6.5 (1943), 361–370.
11 Probationer, 'I Wanted to Be a Nurse', *The Bell*, 7.2 (1944), 213–225.
12 Sean O'Faoláin, 'The Craft of the Short Story', *The Bell*, 7.4 (1944), 337–343.
13 Bill Kirwin, 'The Social Policy of *The Bell*', *Administration*, 37.2 (1989), 99–118.
14 Unemployed, 'Off the Dole', *The Bell*, 1.2 (1941), 44–46.
15 M.P.R.H., 'Illegitimate', *The Bell*, 2.3 (1941), 78–87.
16 Matthews, *The Bell Magazine*, p. 24.
17 Eric Cross, *The Tailor and Ansty* (Dublin: Mercier, 1970).
18 O'Faoláin, 'Attitudes'.
19 Matthews, *The Bell Magazine*, p. 80.

10

Behind the Erin curtain

In his 1959 science fiction novel *Ossian's Ride* Fred Hoyle imagined a near-future Ireland that has perplexed the outside world.[1] The year is 1970. How could, a young scientist is asked by the British secret service, such an apparently backward country suddenly manifest bewilderingly advanced technology? The answer seems to lie beyond a mysterious cordon that extends from Tarbert on the Shannon Estuary via Kanturk and Macroom to the south Kerry coast. Every nation on earth was directing 95 per cent of its undercover activity to Ireland to no avail. Behind the iron curtain that had descended over Kerry there were signs of perplexing technologies at work under the control of the Industrial Corporation of Eire (ICE) – an organisation that had come into existence in 1958, soon after the real-life Irish government had adopted its First Programme for Economic Expansion.

In Hoyle's 1958 a group of scientists had approached the Irish government for permission to set up an industry that would extract chemicals from turf. They asked for and received a ten-year tax break, after which taxes of up to £5 million would be paid each year. But within eight years they were making hundreds of millions of pounds' profits per annum from the export of contraceptive pills. The Church fulminated to no avail ('Against laughter the Hierarchy fights in vain. Think of it, contraceptives from turf!'). But clearly these were not for Irish use, because the birth rate in Ireland had begun to rise. Ireland had become an immigrant destination. Foreign scientists were recruited by ICE in large numbers. By 1970 Hoyle's Ireland had considerable high-tech industry and a chain of commercial nuclear reactors. The British were nervous. So too were the Americans. If ICE could make reactors it could also produce weapons of mass destruction. Hoyle's scientist hero Sherwood eventually discovered that Ireland's miraculous development was directed by aliens from a dying world.

Science fiction for Hoyle was a sideline; he was one of the best-known British scientists of his time. During the war he had been one of the boffins who developed radar. He was a cosmologist who pioneered the study of nucleosynthesis in stars, calculated the age of the universe and coined the term 'Big Bang' that became the shorthand for a theory of its origin he didn't subscribe to. Hoyle was preoccupied with science and progress. His protagonist eventually joined the aliens and the other scientists living and working behind what one reviewer of *Ossian's Ride* called the Erin curtain. Within their compounds they were cut off from the surrounding peasantry, whose lives, habits and occupations hardly seem changed by the fantastic technology in their midst.

Some contemporaneous assessments of the condition of Ireland examined what they saw as insurmountable barriers to progress. A 1957 article by John Kelleher in *Foreign Affairs* entitled 'Ireland and Where Does She Stand?' declared that its leaders had much success in turning the country into the 'small, remote and damp but sinless nirvana of their elderly dreams'.[2] By 1957 it was in the midst of an economic crisis, but Kelleher argued that the prime causes of emigration were not economic. Ireland emerged from the war period a creditor nation, and in a burst of good sense the government had embarked on large-scale housing and hospital building programmes and on improving social services. Quite a few new schools were built. However indifferently or unimaginatively, a welfare state was created. All these improvements were in train by 1950 – and that was the year emigration reached 40,000. What the Irish people had been offered and had rejected, according to Kelleher, was a stultifying climate of paternalism:

> Long years ago Mr. de Valera was credited with the statement that he had only to look into his own heart to know what the Irish people wanted. Whether he said it or not, it sounds like him ... What Mr. de Valera found in his heart was a burning desire for compulsory Irish in the schools and civil service; a thoroughgoing, or at least hardworking, censorship; efficiency and honesty in local government (achieved by taking all real powers away from the elected county and borough councils and killing such community initiative as there was); and in general a society based upon Catholic and 'Gaelic' principles of 'frugal sufficiency' and geared to the supposed tastes and interests of the small-farmer, the truly representative Irish citizen.

For all that the Irish complained about the colonial oppressions that had held them back, Ireland had enjoyed a relatively lucky recent history. Its civil war was less bloody and destructive than similar conflicts in Europe after the First World War, and it had been spared from the devastation of the Second World War. Ireland, Kelleher insisted, had no right to be sick:

> If she compares her resources with those of other small Western countries, and its population with what those have to support, one can hardly avoid deciding that Irish ills are largely psychosomatic. True, they can all be explained from history; but to explain is not always to excuse, the less so indeed since Irish history records so little energetic common sense and so much casual acceptance of accidental developments. Any conversation on Ireland in Ireland is almost bound to produce some defensive mention of the terrible troubles the Irish have survived and the hard time of it the nation has had generally. Alas, the truth is that Ireland has had an almost fatally easy time of it, at least in this century.[3]

According to Kelleher, de Valera and his successors had left Ireland a duller and, in spirit, a deader place than they found it. Its complacent elites, its politicians, clergymen, professional Gaels and other comfortable bourgeoisie looking into each other's hearts found there, or pretended to find, the same tepid desires.

Another disparaging outside critique, Paul Blanchard's 1954 book *The Irish and Catholic Power*, disparaged Ireland's stultifying conservatism and the voluntary deference of the Irish people to the Church. Ireland's population had been falling since the Famine a century earlier. Whilst economic factors contributed to low rates of marriage it was also the case, Blanchard argued, that Irish priests had exalted celibacy to the point where it was almost a national catastrophe. Young women had less chance of marriage than those of the same age in any other country. Priests he interviewed ruefully admitted Ireland's failure to realise Catholic family life for many of its people. Only two out of every five Irishmen between 30 and 34 years of age were married, the lowest proportion in the world. The 1951 census showed that the percentage of unmarried was 'still the highest in the world'. Blanchard acerbically described the frequent photographs in the Dublin newspapers of 'young' married couples, with their balding grooms and their ageing brides, look like extracts from the albums of the middle-aged. It seemed to him that marriage in Ireland was surrounded with such anxieties, hesitations and fears that only the brave, the foolish and the well-to-do risked it at the age which was common in other countries.

  Blanchard contended that the Irish emigrated in large numbers from a socially dysfunctional society, not just for economic reasons. Emigrant lives could be hard but lives at home were stunted. He argued that Irish young people were leaving their nation 'largely because it is a poor place in which to be happy and free'.[4]

These arguments to some extent reflected the views of Catholic modernisers who from the 1950s articulated a new economic nation-building
project, that came in time to supplant the earlier cultural nation-building
ideals exemplified by de Valera. Retrospective academic analyses of
Ireland's economic development also drew on such perspectives. Most
influentially Joseph Lee concluded his *Ireland 1912–1985 Politics and
Society* with a 176-page essay which evaluated independent Ireland's
'cultural, intellectual and spiritual performance'. Lee set himself the
task of explaining the causes of 'Ireland's social and economic backwardness', 'the mystery of the mediocrity of Irish socio-economic performance', 'the dearth of enterprise' and 'the absence of an adequate
performance ethic in the society'.[5]

Lee attributed the Irish pathology to social practices that were
cemented after the Famine. Possession of land was what counted, not
its improvement. Wealth came about through inheritance rather than
individual economic performance. The nature of Irish farming 'itself fostered scepticism about the relationship between effort and reward'. The
return on cattle and sheep depended variously on haggling skills at the
fair or market and on the 'luck' of British prices. According to Lee, post-
Famine pastoralism rewarded 'strokes' rather than sustained labour.[6] He
argued that post-Famine Ireland witnessed the emergence of a 'zero sum'
mind set whereby people saw the advancement of others as only possible
at their own expense. The cure for such prosperity-blocking fatalism,
Lee argued, was a liberal mind set adept at enterprise. Lee argued that
such begrudgery severely hampered the emergence of meritocracy and of
an 'enterprise culture'. Intense competition within communities focused
on securing advantage over existing sources of wealth, farms and public
sector employment. Intense conflicts within families and communities
led to the exclusion of emigrants and the marginalisation of others who
did not emigrate:

Few peoples anywhere have been so prepared to scatter their children
around the world in order to preserve their own living standards. And the
children themselves left the country to improve their material prospects.
Their letters home are full of references to their material progress, prefer-
ably confirmed by the inclusion of notes and money orders. Those who
remained at home further exhibited their own worship of the golden calf
in their devotion to the primacy of the pocket in marriage arrangements
calculated to the last avaricious farthing, in the milking of bovine TB eradi-
cation schemes, in the finessing of government grants, subsidies and loans,
of medical certificates and insurance claims, in the scrounging for petty
advantage amongst protected business men, in the opportunistic cynicism
with which wage and salary claims, not to mention professional fees, were

rapaciously pursued. The Irish may have been inefficient materialists. That was not due to any lack of concern with material gains. If their values be deemed spiritual, then spirituality must be defined as covetousness tempered by sloth.[7]

The notion that there was something derelict in Irish character had long been a feature of analyses of the condition of Ireland. Visiting political economists during the nineteenth century worried about the unwillingness of the Irish to improve themselves, and whilst often they concluded that discrimination against Catholics explained why this was the case, it hardly justified, after Catholic emancipation in 1828, their indolence. To give just one example, Harriet Martineau, who wrote pre- and post-Famine accounts of Irish society, emphasised how prevailing environmental conditions had fostered 'habits of slovenly cultivation, of dependence on the potato, and of consequent idleness'. In effect, she advocated a shift away from peasant oral culture towards a more rational organisation of agricultural life centred on 'regular and punctual labour' and greater 'observance of hours and rules'.[8] She documented examples of tenants not being permitted to improve lands they rented but was, in the main, exasperated by the unwillingness of Catholic peasants to adopt new techniques of working. She argued that giving peasants legal rights of tenure or land ownership would not improve social conditions.[9] She endorsed emigration and land clearances and argued that 'the best hope for Ireland lies in the settlement of British capitalism', meaning the importation of new (non-Catholic) English settlers as part of a rational reorganisation of Ireland's rural economy.[10] The political economy critique of Ireland ranged from sympathetic analyses that emphasised the legacies of the Penal Laws against Catholics to social Darwinist perspectives that judged the Irish as inferior for not having bettered themselves.

Elements found favour with some Catholic nationalists, most notably Daniel O'Connell, who was in political alliance with the Liberal Party and had argued on utilitarian grounds against the retention of the Gaelic language because it did not prepare people for employment in Ireland or in the countries to where they emigrated. However, post-Famine nationalists such as John Mitchel influentially depicted liberal political economy as an expression of colonialism. Mitchel's *The Last Conquest of Ireland (Perhaps)* argued that this defining ideology of British colonial conquest was responsible for the expulsion of Irish peasants after the Famine:

Reflect one moment on the established idea of there being a 'surplus population' in Ireland; – an idea and phrase which were at that time unquestioned and axiomatic in political circles; while, at the same time, there were four millions of improvable waste-lands; and Ireland was still, this very year, exporting food enough to feed eight millions of people in England. Ireland, perhaps, was the only country in the world which had both surplus produce for export and surplus population for export; – too much food for her people, and too many people for her food.[11]

Mitchel and those he influenced like Patrick Pearse forged a nationalism that railed against the kinds of modernity the British Empire and its industrial revolution were seen to exemplify. Douglas Hyde in his seminal 1892 *The Necessity of De-Anglicising Ireland* strongly advocated the need for cultural isolationism, but his definition of culture implicitly included economic ideas as well as language and literature.[12] Their 'Irish-Ireland' cultural nation-building project, of which de Valera became custodian, trenchantly opposed the kinds of secular modernity and liberal individualism that were part and parcel of economic liberalism. In this context of Catholic power and assertive cultural nationalism, criticisms of the inability of the Irish to improve themselves were not taken lying down. Witness the reception of Horace Plunkett's 1904 manifesto for economic development, *Ireland in New Century*. The book came in for much criticism from Catholics who found his castigation of their non-economic tendencies to be patronising. Plunkett was the founder of the co-operative movement in Ireland, a major figure of his time, but he lost much of his influence in the furore that followed the publication of his book.[13] Much of his argument about Irish character would resurface eight decades later in Lee's analysis of cultural barriers to economic modernisation.[14]

Historians like Lee and Tom Garvin in his *Preventing the Future: Why Was Ireland So Poor for So Long?* place considerable emphasis on the rising 1950s generation of political leaders and civil servants who articulated the need for and put down the institutional foundations of a new developmental nation-building project. Lee, for his part, foregrounded an argument about the need to improve Irish character that seemed to owe a lot to Plunkett specifically and to nineteenth-century political economists in a more general ideological sense.[15] This involved moving beyond claims that there existed some pathology of Irish character to considering the means by which the necessary changes could be bought about. For Garvin a huge part of the challenge was how to dismantle the interlocking interest groups that between them buttressed complacency and blocked innovation.[16] During the 1950s Ireland was still being led by the 1916 generation. Similarities with China's 'long march' gerontocracy come to mind. Sean Lemass, the political leader who enabled the new national-building project to be articulated, was the youngest of the 1916 generation and a founding member of Fianna Fáil.

A 1958 report *Economic Development* written by T.K. Whitaker, then Secretary of the Department of Finance, came to be regarded as the foundation text of the new developmentalism. Whitaker argued that an integrated programme of national development was urgently needed if Ireland was to survive as an economic entity.[17] He cited a 1957 article by an iconoclastic Catholic cleric, Bishop William Philbin, who had argued that the essence of the problem was 'an attitude of mind amongst all groups was inimical to growth'.[18] Philbin in a spring 1962 article on the case for joining the Common Market set himself the task of identifying shortcomings that needed to be addressed.[19] Unlike Fred Hoyle, who considered science and technology as the drivers of progress, Philbin argued that social factors mattered more:

> In the test which now confronts us the decisive element will be neither material equipment nor technical skills. The ultimate power-unit of any achievement is the mentality of individual human beings: everything else is in-between machinery of transmission. The future is enquiring of us not so much what we have as who we are.[20]

Philbin rehearsed the stock criticisms of the Irish, arguing that these were often valid, but he insisted that these were less so of Irish people who had integrated themselves into the life of other countries. The success of Irish people in every department of American life suggested that they did better in other more challenging competitive environments that at home.[21] He maintained that if the appropriate influence from abroad could be imported rather than sought by emigration the same benefit might be obtained. The excuse that Ireland's backwardness was due to past repression had come to the end of its useful life:

> If we are not making the most of our country's assets, if our techniques are behind the times, if many of our products cannot compete on equal terms with those of other nations, if our output us relatively low and if our progress in improving these shortcomings is unsatisfactory, then it is time we tried to discover causes other than historical ones for such general inefficiency. These defects are not facts of nature; they cannot be explained merely in terms of geography or climate or coincidence of mischance; they could be remedied by a people sufficiently determined to remedy them.[22]

Philbin argued that economic development had replaced political and agrarian reform as the basis on which Ireland's future as a nation would be determined. Old forms of 'Messianic' nationalism no longer held the keys to the future. There might be no glory in fighting an adverse trade balance, and nobody would write ballads about it, but the true patriots of the age, he insisted, were those who took risks for and made great exertions for the economic well-being of their country.[23]

Whitaker, in an essay published in 1961, argued that 'the psychological factor' was the most important factor of production in Ireland.[24] Within a few years the call for such psychological change had transmuted into the claim that such change had been the main achievement of economic development policies. In a 1964 essay Garret FitzGerald argued that Whitaker's *Economic Development* and subsequent attempts at planning 'more than anything' provided 'a psychological basis for economic recovery' insofar as it helped change radically the unconscious attitude of many influential people and to make Ireland a growth-orientated community.[25] What was described as psychology was a proxy for ideology and even faith in a new Irish manifest destiny. *Economic Development* was repeatedly invoked in dozens of articles in a manner that recalled how an earlier generation ritualistically referred to papal encyclicals. Around Whitaker and *Economic Development* a new nation-building renaissance myth was propagated, along the lines advocated by Philbin, one less glamorous than the 1916 Rising which had put de Valera's generation of nationalists into power, but effective nevertheless. Whitaker's argument that cultural change was a precondition of economic development evolved into the mantra that a cultural change had precipitated the 1960s boom and a new institutional Irish history that dated progress from 1958. For all that he championed what would now be called evidence-based policy making, Whitaker could at times make improbable claims. In an otherwise dry-as-dust 1966 essay, 'Economic Planning in Ireland', he claimed that it was no coincidence that the psychological stimulus of planning coincided with a strong period of economic growth between 1958 and 1963.[26]

Within Irish intellectual politics the new developmental narrative was part of a wider revisionism that challenged how romantic nationalists had portrayed the Irish past. Yet, from O'Connell's time liberalism had been a main current of Irish intellectual life. It had only ever been partially subordinated by cultural nationalism. Ireland's economic policies remained those of nineteenth-century liberals until Lemass and Whitaker ushered in a belated Keynesian emphasis on using state expenditure to pump-prime economic growth. When the civil service journal *Administration* published an issue to mark the fiftieth anniversary of the 1916 Rising, it made no mention of Pearse, James Connolly or even de Valera. Instead it published four articles on different strands of public administration between 1916 and 1966. One of these noted that the many organisations devoted to various aspects of Irish culture had apparently failed in their objectives. Young people were apparently not as interested 'as they should [be] in either the language or the history of the country.'[27] Another article in the 1916-themed issue was entitled

'Sir Horace Plunkett as an Administrator'.[28] Plunkett was portrayed an apt role model (for heroes were not required) for the new modern Ireland that was to be built from policies and plans.

Beyond such limp institutional narratives it fell mostly to Fianna Fáil political leaders to communicate the new national *Geist* to the Irish people. A 1963 cover story in *Time* magazine, which read like an upbeat sequel to Kelleher's 1957 article, celebrated Lemass as the leader of a new progressive Ireland. His son-in-law and future Taoiseach Charles Haughey exemplified the break with earlier cultural nationalist frugality. Only one businessman ever became Taoiseach. Albert Reynolds played a key role in the Northern Ireland peace process, but his administration was otherwise mired in accusations of business corruption investigated by the so-called Beef Tribunal.

By the time Hoyle wrote *Ossian's Ride* important changes in Irish economic policy had already been mooted. The 1960s witnessed the expansion of secondary education, increased urbanisation and the beginnings of secularisation. In 1961 Ireland applied to join the Common Market and was admitted twelve years later. Irish economic development owed much to investment by multi-national companies. The task of attracting these fell to the Industrial Development Authority (IDA), an earthly equivalent of the ICE that operated in Hoyle's fictional 1970. Kerry never got an alien-run contraceptive factory, but Ringaskiddy down the coast in County Cork acquired something similar. Pfizer first built a chemical plant there in 1969 and went on to manufacture most of the world's supply of Viagra.

In a sense the developmental nation-building narrative that placed Whitaker at its centre was also a kind of fiction. *Economic Development* did not emerge in isolation from the trials and errors of a whole generation of previous effort.[29] It did not introduce fundamentally new ideas to the Irish scene. There had long been an interplay between economic liberalism and cultural nationalism but from the 1950s the balance shifted away from the later. Compared to the 1916 Rising and the literature of the Gaelic Revival, *Economic Development* was thin gruel on which to nourish a new nation-building mythos. The kind of economic patriotism advocated by Philbin was hardly as glamorous as that of the heroes of 1916. The challenge for advocates of the new nation-building project, and here we should include the historians who wrote about its importance, was to canonise a second greatest generation. But perhaps what also happened was that Irish people mostly forgot the founding heroes of Irish independence or remembered them differently.

Notes

This chapter was previously published in the *Dublin Review of Books*, November 2014.

1 Fred Hoyle, *Ossian's Ride* (New York: Harper, 1959).
2 John Kelleher, 'Ireland and Where Does She Stand?', *Foreign Affairs*, 35 (April 1957), 485–495, p. 491.
3 Kelleher, 'Ireland and Where Does She Stand?', pp. 491–492.
4 Paul Blanchard, *The Irish and Catholic Power: An American Interpretation* (Boston: Beacon Press, 1954).
5 J.J. Lee, *Ireland 1912–1985: Politics and Society* (Cambridge: Cambridge University Press, 1989), p. 528.
6 Lee, *Ireland 1912–1985*, p. 392.
7 Lee, *Ireland 1912–1985*, p. 522.
8 Brian Conway and Michael R. Hill, 'Harriet Martineau and Ireland', in Séamus Ó Síocháin (eds), *Social Thought on Ireland in the Nineteenth Century* (Dublin: University College Dublin Press, 2009), p. 62.
9 Harriet Martineau, *Letters from Ireland* (Dublin: Irish Academic Press, 2001), p. 53.
10 Martineau, *Letters from Ireland*, pp. 109–114.
11 John Mitchel, *The Last Conquest of Ireland (Perhaps)* (Dublin: University College of Dublin Press [1861] 2005), p. 82.
12 Douglas Hyde, *The Necessity of De-Anglicising Ireland* (Dublin, 1892).
13 See Trevor West, 'Foreword' to Horace Plunkett, *Ireland in the New Century* (New York: Kennikat Press, [1904] 1970), pp. i–iii; Bryan Fanning and Tom Garvin, *The Books that Define Ireland* (Dublin: Merrion, 2014), p. 73.
14 For example see Plunkett, *Ireland in the New Century*, pp. 21–24.
15 For example see Plunkett, *Ireland in the New Century*, pp. 21–24.
16 Tom Garvin, *Preventing the Future: Why Was Ireland So Poor for So Long?* (Dublin: Gill and Macmillan, 2004), pp. 74–77.
17 Set out in a memorandum to government published as an appendix to the report. T.K. Whitaker, *Economic Development* (Dublin: Stationery Office, 1958).
18 William J. Philbin, 'A City on the Hill', *Studies*, 46.2 (1957), 167–259. Cited in Whitaker, *Economic Development*, p. 9.
19 William J. Philbin, 'The Irish and the New Europe', *Studies*, 51.1 (1962), 27–49, p. 29.
20 Philbin, 'Irish and the New Europe', p. 29.
21 Philbin, 'Irish and the New Europe', p. 30.
22 Philbin, 'Irish and the New Europe', p. 32.
23 Philbin, 'Irish and the New Europe', p. 39.
24 T.K. Whitaker, 'The Civil Service and Development', *Administration*, 9.2 (1961), 83–87, p. 86.
25 Garret FitzGerald, 'Second Programme for Economic Expansion: Reflections', *Studies*, 53.211 (1964), 233–252, p. 250.

26 T.K. Whitaker, 'Economic Planning in Ireland', *Administration*, 14.4 (1966), 277–285, p. 284.
27 S. O'Riain, 'Public Affairs 1916–1966: Government as a Whole', *Administration*, 14.3 (1966), 215–226, p. 225.
28 P.J. Meghan, 'Sir Horace Plunkett as an Administrator', *Administration*, 14.3 (1966), 227–245.
29 Michael Fogarty, 'Age of Miracles', *Administration*, 24.1 (1976), 107–111, p. 110.

11

The new young Irelanders

Sprightly venerable former Chief Justice Barrington, at the launch of Tomás Finn's book on Tuairim, described how the organisation which he co-founded fifty-nine years previously was envisaged as a cross between the Young Irelander movement of the 1840s and the Fabian Society. He recounted how at a Tuairim study weekend on emigration a Swedish woman enquired who amongst the participants was sleeping with whom. Nobody was sleeping with anyone, Barrington recalled. When it came to sex Tuairim members were either more innocent or much more circumspect than the Fabians. Tuairim is the Irish for opinion. Tuairim's agenda was one of political, social, economic and educational reform. The age-clause signalled an effort to intellectually break free of the 1916 gerontocracy which had become the political Establishment just as the Young Irelanders in the 1840s challenged Daniel O'Connell's by then-sclerotic domination of Catholic nationalist politics.

The reading of the 1950s and 1960s as a transformative phase in modern Irish history has become ingrained through various histories that valorised some modernising civil servants and politicians, most notably T.K. Whitaker and Sean Lemass. These described how a post-independence conservative and isolationist nation-building project focused on Catholicism and the Irish language gave way to a new focus on economic modernisation. Tomás Finn's account of Tuairim does not break with this. Joe Lee in his 1989 book *Ireland 1912–1985* included a long essay which celebrated the rise of a liberal mind set as a cure for the prosperity-blocking fatalism of the Irish people.[1] The title of Tom Garvin's 2004 book *Preventing the Future: Why Was Ireland So Poor for So Long?* suggested a high-concept thesis (more nuanced in the book itself) that the blockers of progress were swept away by the force of liberal ideas and a generation of intrepid reformers.[2]

Finn's cast of Tuairim characters overlap with the heroes of Lee and Garvin's narratives. The absence of a focus upon ordinary people and their lives within such accounts exemplified a dearth of Irish social history until recently. This had a lot to do with the methodologies of historians who focused on the files of civil servants and the papers of prominent politicians and, because they were writing about the recent past, reverential interviews with key protagonists who often came for the same social milieu. Tomás Finn's monograph on Tuairim is along similar lines and whilst the research is excellent his analysis does little to challenge the hackneyed view that the drivers of Irish progress were senior civil servants, politicians and other Establishment figures.

Tuairim's Constitution stated that the organisation was not connected with any political party, though many of its members were political animals and the organisation encouraged its members to join a political party. Barrington ran unsuccessfully for the Seanad on a Fianna Fáil ticket in 1961. He had married into the Boland political dynasty. David Thornley and Barry Desmond became Labour Party TDs. James Doolon, who became a Professor at National University of Ireland Galway and financial analyst with the World Bank, was the brother-in-law of Fianna Fáil Minister George Colley. Future Fine Gael Taoiseach Garret FitzGerald was also a member. So too were some senior civil servants in the Department of Finance. Several leading members had prominent academic careers, including John Whyte who went on to become Professor of Political Science at University College Dublin (UCD) and Patrick Lynch, an economist who rose through the Department of Finance to become private secretary to Taoiseach John A. Costello in 1948. Lynch left the civil service for academia in 1952 and went on to become a Professor of Economics at UCD. From 1954 to 1975 Lynch was Chairman of Aer Lingus. Other prominent members included Ronan Keane: like Barrington, a future Chief Justice.

The leading figures of Tuairim became part the Republic of Ireland's administrative, political, judicial and educational elite. They promoted pragmatic reform but hardly had a vested interest in dismantling the status quo. From its inaugural meeting on 26 February 1954, Tuairim attracted positive and supportive press coverage. An *Irish Times* article described its manifesto as one of the most sensible its author had ever read. There was no expectation that Tuairim would rock the boat too much.

Tuairim's aim was to shift public opinion and influence government policy. Its methods included study weekends, research groups, pamphlets and articles in newspapers. Its legacy might best be appreciated though its pamphlets. Pamphlets had been a key mechanism of stimulating debates during the eighteenth and nineteenth centuries. But during the twentieth century the main vehicle for sustained intellectual or policy argument was the journal essay. Several Tuairim pamphlets were first published in two prominent Irish journals, *Studies* and *Administration*, which respectively represented intellectual Catholicism comfortable with economic liberalism and public sector technocracy. *Studies* was founded and run by the Jesuits; *Administration* was set up by Lynch in 1953 on behalf of the Association of Higher Civil Servants.

The inaugural Tuairim pamphlet by Barrington in 1978 had first appeared in *Studies* the previous year. Tuairim's 1959 pamphlet *Planning for Economic Development* consisted of two articles by Lynch and C.F. Carter that had been previously published in *Administration*. David Thornely's *Ireland: The End of an Era?* (1965) had also first appeared in *Studies*. What is important to note here is that much of the agenda that Tuairim fostered was also championed in other milieus.

Donal Barrington's classic essay *Uniting Ireland* offered scathing criticism of the capacity of Irish nationalism to transcend religious sectarianism. What he had to say prefigured much that Conor Cruise O'Brien later wrote on the topic. The same 1957 issue of *Studies* that carried *Uniting Ireland* also included an essay by O'Brien that examined the views of Protestant public schoolboys on a united Ireland in essays they had written on the subject.[3] These were far removed from nationalist understandings of what was meant by the unification of Ireland.

Barrington argued that the scale of southern misunderstanding of the north was huge. He blamed the 1956 'Border War' on the ill-considered propaganda effort of successive Irish governments that had used emotionally charged phrases such as 'occupied Ireland' but did little to address the real discrimination and system of 'apartheid' experienced by Catholics in the north. He argued that Unionist bigotry had been stoked by the southern coercive approach to unification. So long as such threats persisted reactionary Orangemen would continue to control the Unionist policy and 'ordinary Protestants' would tolerate discrimination against Catholics in ways that would be impossible were such fears absent. The constant threat from the south had kept alive sectarian bitterness in the north. Barrington's proposed remedy was to formally guarantee the territorial integrity of Northern Ireland in return for effective guarantees, including electoral reform, to protect northern nationalists against the discrimination they now experienced. He also argued for cross-border co-operation in areas such as economic policy, university education and sport.

Tuairim's second pamphlet *Partition Today: A Northern Viewpoint* (1959) by Norman Gibson, an economist at Queen's University Belfast,

similarly argued that the southern government had, by making constitutional claims on the north, exacerbated divisions there between
Protestants and Catholics. Northern governments for their part had
contributed to the alienation of the Catholic minority. To address this
alienation he advocated the establishment of an impartial inquiry into
allegations of discrimination. He suggested that measures be put in
place to allow the Mater Catholic Hospital in Belfast to remain outside
the National Health Service, thus allowing Catholics to safeguard their
medical ethics. He was less sympathetic when it came to supporting a
Catholic school system independent of local authorities. Gibson argued
for the integration of Catholics into the northern state and for economic
contribution with the south. Gibson was optimistic about the future of
the north but subsequently acknowledged that his understanding of the
historical roots of sectarian conflict in the north were poor, putting this
down to an education at the Portora Royal School in Fermanagh that
barely touched on Irish history.

Lynch and C.F. Carter's 1959 two-essay pamphlet *Planning for
Economic Development* was written as a response to T.K. Whitaker's
much-celebrated *Economic Development*, which had been published the
previous year. Whitaker's report signalled a break with previous economic policy. There was nothing remarkable about most of the report,
which focused on agricultural production, but it included as an appendix a memorandum from Whitaker proposing the new policy direction.[4]
In effect the government had not only permitted a civil servant to determine policy but went on to publish the fact to help market that policy
to the public. Whitaker's 'coup' captured the imagination. However,
most of the ideas in *Economic Development* and in Lynch and Carter's
Tuairim pamphlet had been percolating for over a decade in *Studies*. For
example, in 1942 George O'Brien argued that *laissez faire* was a thing
of the past. Ireland like other small nations would, he accepted, have to
develop a planned economy.[5] Within the civil service the key architects
of the new official climate were Whitaker and Lynch. Their double-act
began with their participation as junior finance officials in a debate on
full employment at the Statistical and Social Inquiry Society in April
1945.[6] Within the Department of Finance Lynch instigated the first
capital budget in 1950. His seminal 1953 *Studies* article 'The Economist
and Public Policy' made a specific case for state-directed economic
planning in the Irish case. Professor of Political Economy at Liverpool
University C.F. Carter had been one of Whitaker's key economic advi-
sors. He had served on the Department of Finance Capital Investment
Advisory Committee. Whitaker had him appointed together with Lynch
to the body set up to implement *Economic Development*.

This new nation-building project Whitaker, Lynch and Carter and others championed was exemplified by a belief in technocracy and a new individualistic meritocracy. In what became his half of the 1959 Tuairim pamphlet Carter wrote that the problems of human nature, 'in Irish nature more than most', were ultimately administrative ones. 'Since it is a slow job improving human nature', Carter wrote, 'our first efforts should be devoted to improving this machinery; and since the "machines" are in fact the minds of men, a great deal of the future of Ireland may depend on the quality and training of those found for key positions.'

In 1966 Tuairim's London branch published *Some of Our Children*, a pamphlet on the residential care of deprived children in Ireland. It was written by a research group established in 1964 and had been instigated by Joy Rudd, a member of the London group who had written an article in 1961 on the need for reform of residential care in the branch's *Occasional Bulletin*. The introduction to *Some of Our Children* suggested that its authors benefited from a detachment from Irish affairs that came from living outside the country and that the pamphlet 'was the product of this informed objectivity'.

Some of Our Children opened with a history of reformatory and industrial schools in Ireland and criticisms of the 1908 Children's Act, an anachronism that had been reformed in the United Kingdom but not by the Irish state. The focus was upon the responsibilities of the state rather than religious orders who ran such facilities on its behalf. It then offered descriptions of some of these. St Joseph's School Letterfrack was described as situated in remote but magnificent countryside with large classrooms that been brightly decorated, clean and bright washrooms, and a recreation room equipped for table-tennis, television and films. The boys were described as very well cared for and neatly dressed in bright, casual clothes: coloured and floral shirts, blazers and sports jackets. Letterfrack received a glowing report from Tuairim. Physical abuse was acknowledged in the past tense with none of the horrific detail that characterised subsequent reports on institutional abuse.

Some of Our Children referred to 'accounts from a number of ex-pupils of boy's schools alleging excessive corporal punishment in the past'. The implication was that that this had been 'widespread in Ireland in the past but [was] probably less prevalent today'. The pamphlet noted stories from a number of sources of recent punishments that were excessive or unsuitable, but argued that in the absence of any verification that these took place such accounts they must be treated as hypothetical. In Tomás Finn's analysis the Tuairim research group did not seem to believe what it was told by victims, and was reticent in criticising perpetrators. It argued against corporal punishment for 'sex offences' by boys because such punishment would be more psychologically harmful than the 'sex offence itself'. Nowhere did *Some of Our Children* consider the likelihood of the sexual abuse of children by their custodians.

One of its contributing authors, Peter Tyrell, had been committed to Letterfrack in 1924 at the age of eight along with his two elder brothers. Tyrell wrote a harrowing memoir in 1958 that was eventually published in 2006 as *Founded on Fear*, thirty-nine years after he burned himself to death on Hampstead Heath, having never recovered from the psychological damage caused by the extreme physical abuse he experienced and witnessed as a child at Letterfrack.[7] Although the Tuairim report was critical of the industrial school system it did not include, to Tyrell's distress, any descriptions of such abuse. For all that, *Some of Our Children* made influential proposals for reform it was at once sanitised and anodyne, a contribution to the official reality that victims of abuse had to fight against for decades for recognition. As put by Finn:

> Reluctance to incorporate testimonies such as Tyrell's is likely to have been due to an inability to prove their accuracy and possible fear of legal consequences. Having visited the schools, the group may have genuinely have also believed that such punishment had diminished in severity and frequency. It seems to have been common practice to ensure that the children were well dressed and the premises thoroughly cleaned, often by the children themselves, for visitors. In the end, the research group clearly believed that personal testimony was insufficient as proof ... The fact that even a sympathetic body found it impossible to publish their stories suggests that the London branch felt restricted in what it could say; perhaps partly because of its respectable nature but more by the constraints imposed by contemporary society.

This all seemed, Finn continues, too much for Tyrell, who in April 1967 committed suicide. Even though it barely touched on issues that lay below the surface the report added to a sense of official unease. The Department of Education had long blocked investigation of the industrial school system but some damning accounts of the system were beginning to emerge. These notably included a series of articles by Michael Viney in the *Irish Times* in 1966.

Finn's documentation of the development of Tuairim adds to our understanding of the 1950s and 1960s but misfires when it comes to what he sees as the distinctive contribution of the book: an analysis of the influence of Tuairim ideas and debates. Tuairim was but one vehicle for promulgating ideas about a state role in planning economic development. The main ideas had been championed for more than a decade, and their implementation owed much to the rise of their advocates to key positions – Lemass as Taoiseach, and Whitaker as Secretary of the Department of Finance – and, beyond that, the slow migration into Irish public policy of what were elsewhere longstanding Keynesian economic orthodoxies.

Tuairim was part of a new official Ireland, part of what became the dominant consensus on social and economic modernisation. Its leading members were altruists but incapable of speaking for marginalised groups in Irish society. It remained part of the crowded political centre of Irish politics and perhaps should be viewed not as spearheading the modernisation of Irish society but as exemplifying the often political and social conservatism of this modernisation.

Notes

Review of Tomás Finn, *Tuairim: Intellectual Debate and Policy Formation: Rethinking Ireland, 1954–1975* (Manchester: Manchester University Press, 2012). Previously published in *Studies*, 102.406 (2013), 213–219.

1 J.J. Lee, *Ireland 1912–1985: Politics and Society* (Cambridge: Cambridge University Press, 1989).
2 Tom Garvin, *Preventing the Future: Why Was Ireland So Poor for so Long?* (Dublin: Gill and Macmillan, 2004).
3 Finn, *Tuairim*, p .248; Conor Cruise O'Brien, 'A Sample of Loyalties', *Studies*, 46.184 (1957), 403–410.
4 T.K. Whitaker, *Economic Development* (Dublin: Stationery Office, 1958), pp. 227–229.
5 George O'Brien, 'Economic Visions and Revisions', *Studies*, 31.122 (1942), 211–220, p. 220.
6 T.K. Whitaker, *Interests* (Dublin: Institute of Public Administration, 1983), p. 82.
7 Peter Tyrell, *Founded on Fear* (Dublin: Irish Academic Press, 2006).

12

Women and social policy

The 1951 'Mother and Child' Scheme controversy is usually cited as the defining example of Church interference in the state. However, overt interference was rare. The Catholic Church possessed a 'non-decisional' form of power: it had the capacity to mobilise politically in defence of its interests but rarely needed to do because these could be anticipated and addressed in a 'non-political' and non-contentious manner. As good Catholics, politicians and voters were deeply committed to expressing their faith through the laws and institutions of the country.[1] Before independence, Irish social policy had been shaped by British legislation as well as by Catholicism. The Church sought tight control over education and health, areas seen as crucial to the inter-generational transmission of faith and Catholic morality. The role of the state had expanded from the introduction the Poor Relief Act (1838) to include responsibility for unemployment benefits and old age pensions. Both the Church and the state came to administer demarcated areas of social policy. Catholicism aside, the main ideological influence was a form of economic liberalism which advocated a minimalist state.

The 'Mother and Child' controversy had everything to do with women. The Church objected to an expanded health system that threatened to interfere with the family by directly engaging with women. However, women were little more than idealised chattel within the debate that played out. A letter from the archbishops and bishops of Ireland on 10 October 1950 to the Taoiseach, John A. Costello, suggested that the long-proposed Mother and Child Health Service – it had been set out in a bill in 1948 by the previous Fianna Fáil government led by Éamon de Valera – was contrary to Catholic moral teaching. Ceding the principle of a state role in the control of health care for families might, it argued, open up the way for birth control and abortion. There was no guarantee that state officials would only give gynaecological care in accordance with Catholic principles. The controversy was triggered when Noël Browne, the Minister of Health, appeared to be challenging the status quo. Browne was one of the two Clann na Poblachta members of the 1948–51 inter-party government. He was summonsed to a meeting by Archbishop John Charles McQuaid, where the letter from the hierarchy was read out to him. After the meeting McQuaid depicted Browne as unwilling to compromise his demands for a universal system, which was hardly the case. Browne triggered a political crisis when he published correspondence with McQuaid, which brought down the government.

Posturing around this issue dated back to 1944 when Catholic clergy set out their opposition to the Beveridge Report, which proposed the establishment of a national health service and a welfare state in Britain after the war. Britain's wartime proposals for a welfare state had stimulated widespread debate in Ireland amongst academics, civil servants and clerics. In 1951, in *Studies*, in what was a fairly typical clerical polemic, Edward Coyne SJ citied papal encyclicals to argue against the universal provision of free health services. Coyne described the Mother and Child Scheme as a 'ready-made instrument for future totalitarian aggression'.[2] He offered vivid propaganda to evoke the dangers of giving the state a limited role in social work and public health policy:

> It is a very serious thing when a County Council official has the power by law to walk into any Irishman's home, whether once, twice or oftener in the year, against the will of the parents. It is a very serious thing that this County official should have the legal right to order the children of the family to be brought before him, make these children, boys and girls of 12, 13, 14, 15 and 16, undress and submit to a most intimate medical inspection. It is a very serious thing when such an official has the right to inspect such domestic arrangements as he thinks would militate against the safeguarding of the health of the children: a right to give instructions as to food, exercise and the sleeping arrangements and possibly to bring the habits and directions of the parents in these matters into contempt with the children and so shake all parental authority.[3]

There was, Coyne insisted in a subsequent article, 'something sacred and primary and personally intimate and holy and inviolate in the privileges and duties of paternity: a married man is more than a man, when he shoulders, alone, the proud burden of responsibility for wife, mother and child'. The state with its necessarily 'clumsy, almost sacrilegious methods' should not interfere in this sphere of life.[4] de Valera's 1937 Constitution said as much and similarly parsed papal encyclicals. Under Article 41.1.2 the state guaranteed to protect the authority of the family 'as the necessary basis of social order and as indispensable to the welfare

of the Nation and the State'. Article 41.2.1 stated: 'In particular the
State recognises that by her life within the home, woman gives to the
State a support without which the common good cannot be achieved.'
The Constitution went on to specify how this support to the common
good would be achieved. As put in Article 41.2.2: 'The State shall, there-
fore, endeavour to ensure that mothers shall not be obliged by economic
necessity to engage in labour to the neglect of their duties in the home.'

In April 1932 the newly elected de Valera delivered the eulogy at
Margaret Pearse's funeral that praised her motherly sacrifice in giving
her sons Patrick and Willie for Ireland.[5] That same year a ban on the
employment of married women in the civil service was introduced
and this was extended to one prohibiting the employment of married
women as primary school teachers in 1934, an area where women had
traditionally worked. The Conditions of Employment Act (1936) introduced by Sean Lemass as Minister for Industry and Commerce gave the
state various powers to limit the numbers of women employed in any
branch of industry in order to protect male employment. But the very
first person to hold this portfolio had been a woman. In 1919 Countess
Markievicz became the first MP elected in the British Isles. She was also
the first woman to become a cabinet minister, serving as Minister for
Labour from April 1919 to January 1922. She had also been a founding
member of Fianna Fáil. It was not until 1979 that another woman, Máire
Geoghegan-Quinn, was appointed as an Irish government minister.

Just under half of the unmarried women in the Free State engaged
in paid employment in 1926 (48.6 per cent) and just over half in 1936
(53.3 per cent) but the percentage of married women engaged in paid
employment remained the same at just a little over one in twenty (5.6
per cent) in 1926 and 1936. However, 59 per cent of additional jobs
created in manufacturing industry between 1926 and 1936 (virtually
all those created in that ten-year period) went to women. The overall
percentage of women in manufacturing rose during that period from
26.6 per cent to 31.3 per cent.[6] Partly because it affected relatively few
women the marriage ban did not prompt widespread political opposition from Irishwomen. Restrictions on married women were lifted in
many countries during the 1950s when these began to experience labour
shortages. However, in Ireland these persisted until the 1970s with the
exception of primary teachers, where the marriage bar was lifted in
1957. Discrimination in employment on the basis of gender became
illegal in Ireland in 1973.

Before independence, the National Insurance Act (1911) established
a social insurance system designed to ensure that the male breadwinner
could provide for his family. Women were conceptualised as depend-

ants, entitled to benefits only through their relationships with men as wives or daughters. Even when women engaged in socially insured paid employment they were legally entitled to lesser rates of benefit. These distinctions persisted after the Unemployment Assistance Act (1933). Efforts to address female poverty, such as The Widows and Orphans Pension Act (1935), took the form of developing separate categories of benefit for women rather than addressing such inequalities. The result was a gendered two-tiered system based on a distinction between benefits linked to previous paid employment (Unemployment Assistance, predominantly accessed by men) and means-tested Home Assistance (formally called Poor Relief and accessed by women). Under the Widow and Orphans Pension Act (1935) the entitlements of widows to pensions depended on their dead husband's contributions. If their husbands had sufficient contributions their widows got a widow's pension. If not, they were eligible for Home Assistance.

Although rates of Unemployment Assistance for single men and single women were equalised under the Social Welfare Act (1953) discriminatory practices persisted such as the marriage bar and entitlements for shorter periods of time. Unemployment Assistance was extended to male employees engaged in private domestic service and agriculture in 1953. It was not extended to women in similar occupations until 1966.

In 1955 there were 9,000 women in the civil service. Many of these were better educated and qualified than men within similar jobs, although women were recruited to a segregated lower grade of post, where they also received lower rates of pay and less annual leave.[7] The First Commission on the Status on Women, established in 1970, produced many recommendations around equal pay for women, the introduction of maternity leave, and making women entitled to serve on juries. Women had become entitled to serve on juries before independence under legislation passed in 1919. This entitlement was undermined after independence by a 1924 act that permitted women to exempt themselves from jury duty. A further act introduced by Minister of Justice Kevin O'Higgins in 1927 removed altogether the right of women to serve on juries.[8]

The Employment of Married Women Act (1973) revoked discrimination against married women in the civil service, and The Employment Equality Act (1977) addressed pay inequalities. A number of other acts addressed the benefit entitlements of women. However, insofar as separate benefit categories for women were retained, such as Deserted Wife's Allowance (introduced in 1970), Unmarried Mother's Allowance (1973) and Single Woman's Allowance (1974), the system remained a male-breadwinner one. Many of the benefits introduced during the 1970s envisaged women remaining in the home.

Further reforms during the 1980s and 1990s were driven by the European Union. For example, the EU Equal Treatment Directive (1979) emphasised removing discrimination against married women from social welfare schemes in respect of sickness, accident and unemployment. It envisaged women as ordinarily engaged in paid employment. It emphasised social policies aimed at supporting female as well as male breadwinners. In 1990 the various categories of lone mothers' benefits were reformed as lone parents' benefits. The basis of entitlement to these was reconstituted from the relationship female claimants had/or did not have with men to one based on individual and equal entitlement to benefits as citizens.

The overall participation of women in paid employment remained fairly constant between 1961 (29 per cent) and 1993 (34 per cent). What changed most was the participation of married women. Just 7.1 per cent of these were engaged in paid employment in 1971, but this had risen to 30.9 per cent by 1989 and 47.8 per cent by 2003. From 1990 to 2000 the percentage of married women with young children in paid employment rose from 42.2 per cent to 55.2 per cent.[9] In the 2002 census the highest participation rates of married women in the workforce (75.5 per cent) were found to be for women between the ages of 25 and 34 years – that is, ages when women are most likely to have young children. But overall, women continued to participate in paid employment to a lesser extent than men and spend more time as carers in the home. This detrimentally affected their income levels and their levels of entitlement to employment-related benefits and pensions.

The development of Irish social policy since independence took the form of gradual institutional development and the gradual extension of welfare rights and entitlements. Economic underdevelopment and a lack of resources inhibited this expansion as much if not more than Catholicism. Class politics, which in some other countries influenced the expansion of the welfare state, were moribund in Ireland, partly because of the lack of industrialisation. In the absence of real possibilities for rapid welfare expansion in the post-war era, social policy did not become politicised to the same extent as had occurred in Britain. The 'Mother and Child Scheme' controversy served as a kind of proxy debate about the future of social policy. Catholic social thought in the Irish case proved better at rejecting change than advocating alternatives and became less influential in any case as Ireland become more economically developed and secular.

During the 1990s, on the cusp of the 'Celtic Tiger' era, Irish social policy debates remained preoccupied with the Catholic social values articulated in Article 41 of the Constitution. For example, *Strengthening Families for Life* (1998), the report of the Commission on the Family, expressed concerns that women should not be forced to take up paid employment.[10] Furthermore, the Commission depicted childcare provision outside the home as a minority need.[11] Yet, the presumptions set out within the 1937 Constitution about the role of women in Irish society (as dependants) and the economy (as unpaid carers) have been severely tested by social and economic change. The proposition set out in Article 41.1.2 that 'by her life within the home, woman gives to the State a support without which the common good cannot be achieved' was challenged in the era of the 'Celtic Tiger' by economic and social policy norms that presume that women would ordinarily be engaged in paid employment. Similarly, the presumption under Article 41.2.2 that mothers shall not be obliged by economic necessity to engage in labour to the neglect of their duties in the home was undermined by the economic necessity of dual-income households. The rapid expansion of the economy during the 1990s, measured in terms of an increase in the Gross National Product, has been partially the result of the increasing participation of women in paid employment, and the further expansion of the economy was seen to necessitate further increases in female paid employment. However, the Commission's emphasis on preserving the 'right' of mothers not to engage in paid employment was sidelined by an increased policy on economic individualism.[12] Within this debate a Catholic emphasis on the primacy of the family became to some extent subordinated by a neo-liberal emphasis on the primacy of the market.

Notes

1 Finola Kennedy, *Cottage to Creche: Family Change in Ireland* (Dublin: Institute of Public Administration, 2001), p. 249.
2 Edward J. Coyne SJ, 'The Mother and Child Service', *Studies*, 40.158 (1951), 128–149, p. 139.
3 Coyne, 'Mother and Child Service', pp. 128–138.
4 Edward J. Coyne SJ, 'Health Bill 1952', *Studies*, 42.165 (1953), 1–22, p. 6.
5 See *Irish Press*, 27 April 1932.
6 Mary E. Daly, 'Women in the Irish Free State 1922–39: The Interaction Between Economics and Ideology', *Journal of Women's History*, 6.4, (1995), 99–116, pp. 103–110.
7 Neans De Paor, 'Women in the Civil Service' [1955], in Bryan Fanning and Tony McNamara (eds), *Ireland Develops: Administration and Social Policy: 1953–2003* (Dublin: Institute of Public Administration, 2003), pp. 233–239.

  8 Bryan Fanning, *Histories of the Irish Future* (London: Bloomsbury, 2015), p. 164.
  9 Anthony McCashin, *Social Security in Ireland* (Dublin: Institute of Public Administration, 2004), p. 72.
 10 Department of Children and Family Affairs, *Strengthening Families for Life: Report of The Commission on the Family* (Dublin: Stationery Office, 1998).
 11 Department of Children and Family Affairs, *Strengthening Families for Life*, p. 62.
 12 Gabriel Kiely, 'Individualisation', in Bryan Fanning, Gabriel Kiely, Suzanne Quin and Patricia Kennedy (eds), *Theorising Irish Social Policy* (Dublin: University College Dublin Press, 2004), p. 64.

13

New rules of belonging

Economic Development (1958) – a report written by T.K. Whitaker, then the senior official in the Department of Finance – has been venerated as the foundation text of a new post-1950s nation-building project.[1] The main body of the report was nothing special; it mostly focused on prospects for Irish agriculture. However, *Economic Development* included as an appendix Whitaker's December 1957 memorandum to the cabinet proposing the new policy direction.[2] In time, a focus on making economic growth the defining national project sidelined a longstanding emphasis on cultural nation-building project that had pre-dated independence.

The second canonical text of this new developmental nation-building project was the OECD/Irish Government 1965 report *Investment in Education*. This has been credited with jolting the focus of Irish education from religious formation to one on economic development.[3] Consider the change from earlier official accounts of the purpose of education, such as the following from a 1954 report on the function of primary schools published by the Department of Education:

> The school exists to assist and supplement the work of parents in the rearing of children. Their first duty is to train their children to love and fear God. That duty becomes the first purpose of the primary school. It is fulfilled by the school through the religious and moral training of the child, through the teaching of good habits, through his instruction in the duties of citizenship and in his obligations to his parents and community – in short, through all that tends to the formation of a person of character, strong in his desire to fulfil the end of his creation.[4]

Investment in Education ignored all this. It set out a blueprint for the future that was at odds with the traditional Catholic ethos. It spoke about Ireland's future in an altogether different language. In it and more generally, religious expertise, epitomised by papal encyclicals and episcopal pronouncements, was displaced from the 1960s onwards by World Bank policy, OECD reports, EU funding protocols and whatever was deemed from time to time to constitute 'best practice'.[5] *Investment in Education* steered Irish education policy onto a path that continues to be followed. 'As education is at once a cause and a consequence of economic growth', the report declared, 'economic planning is incomplete without educational planning. Education, as well as having its own intrinsic values, is a necessary element in economic activity.'[6]

The far-less-celebrated *Report of the Commission on Itinerancy* (1963) warrants inclusion in the canon of Irish developmental texts.[7] In advocating the assimilation of what were then called itinerants or tinkers it suggested new modern rules of belonging for all. The economic 'take-off' that began in the late 1950s changed Ireland from a predominantly rural to a predominantly urban society. It also resulted in the displacement of the Travelling People, the name they preferred, from their precarious niche in rural society. The Commission was set up at a time when Travellers had become displaced from the rural economy and were identified as an urban (and suburban) problem by the majority community. The impetus that led to its establishment is captured in the title of Aoife Bhreatnach's *Becoming Conspicuous: Irish Travellers, Society and the State 1922–70.*[8] The terms of reference of the Commission on Itinerancy (1960–63) required it 'to enquire into the problem arising from the presence in the country of itinerants in considerable numbers' and to consider what steps might be taken 'to promote their absorption into the general community', and 'pending such absorption, to reduce to a minimum the disadvantages to themselves and to the community resulting from their itinerant habits'.[9]

The origin of the Travellers is unclear. It seems that their ancestors constituted but one element of a large permanent and seasonally migrant population.[10] Prior to the Famine, the *First Report from His Majesty's Commissioners for Inquiring into the Conditions of the Poorer Classes in Ireland (1835)*, which examined poverty in seventeen Irish counties, depicted a complex rural society, within which there were strong social bonds between sedentary and migratory ways of life.[11] Small tenant farmers were part of a peasantry touched by the need for seasonal migration. They were obliged by customs of hospitality to give alms to those seasonal beggars unable to subsist for the entire year on their own rented smallholding and to various other categories of dispossessed vagrants. For example, there is frequent reference in the 1835 report to the practice of older parents, having made over their land to their children in the expectation of being supported by them, leaving home at times of shortage to go begging, and often not returning.[12]

The Famine, particularly after 1847, devastated this marginal peasantry. In its aftermath rural Irish society changed utterly. What was depicted by visiting anthropologists like Arensberg and Kimball during the 1930s as a traditional rural society was in fact a modern one.[13] New forms of inheritance and moral regulation came to be imposed after the Famine; the rural population declined rapidly, smallholdings were consolidated and, with the success of the agrarian nationalist campaigns of the Land League some decades later, Ireland's surviving peasantry became conservative landowners.

The ancestors of Travellers subsisted as a landless class within rural society. They retained a distinct if marginal economic role within rural society until at least the 1950s, when their skills and trades became obsolete. By the 1960s Travellers had become economically and socially displaced from rural society. The general movement of Travellers to urban centres was part of broader demographic changes in Irish society. When they became a visible presence on the outskirts of towns and cities they became a political problem akin to, if on a much smaller scale, the unwanted rural poor who flocked to the shanty towns and favelas of South American cities.

Oscar Traynor, the Minister of Justice, opposed setting up the Commission on Itinerancy. He expressed concern that if itinerants were forced to settle the end result would be, in the selected areas, permanent colonies of tinkers. 'What about the residents in the neighbourhood', he wondered in a 1959 Dáil debate, 'who will find themselves pestered day in, day out, and whose property will deteriorate in value?'[14] The Taoiseach Sean Lemass gave the job of setting up the Commission to his son-in-law Charles Haughey, who was Traynor's parliamentary secretary. Lemass was as much its architect as he had been the political force behind *Economic Development* and of the shifts in Irish economic policy it set in train.

In a 1962 Dáil debate, Haughey, by then the Minister of Justice, was asked by another member of Fianna Fáil if he was aware that the menace of wandering horses was on the increase in Dublin suburbs. Haughey replied that he was fully aware of the many problems 'posed by the presence of a large number of itinerants in the outskirts of Dublin'.[15] In an address to the inaugural meeting of the Commission, Haughey said that 'there can be no final solution to the problems created by itinerants until they are absorbed into the general community'.[16] In the same address, published in the Commission's 1963 report as an appendix Haughey addressed the inability of the Gardaí, the schools and the courts to control the itinerant population. The offences of itinerants consisted, he said, 'mainly of petty thieving, begging to the point of intimidation, disorderly conduct, trespass with their animals on pastures, crops and gardens, destructions of fences and gates, obstruction to traffic on the public roads and insanitary practices at their encampments'.[17]

Haughey then rehearsed the failure of the Gardaí and the Department of Education to compel itinerant children to attend school. There were some 1,600 itinerant children of compulsory school-going age who were clearly not attending schools. A previous attempt to deal with the children of vagrants, the 1942 School Attendance Bill, had been passed by the Dáil and the Seanad; this required vagrants to register particulars of their families and of the education being received by their children at their local Garda station. The Bill proposed to grant powers to the state to commit children to industrial schools. However, the President refused to sign the bill and it had been, as Haughey put it, considered repugnant by the Supreme Court to the Constitution.[18]

The sort of coercion considered in 1942 resembled somewhat, in its intent, the policy at the time in Australia of forcibly removing aboriginal children from their families. It also was in keeping which how Ireland sequestered its unmarried mothers in Magdelene laundries and its vulnerable children in industrial schools. In 1966 Clare County Council debated a proposal to confine all itinerants living within a twenty- or thirty-mile radius of Limerick city within a regional camp where the children could be educated, in one place, about how the settled way of life was better than a nomadic one. At the meeting it was agreed that Clare County Council – in conjunction with Limerick County Council, Limerick City Corporation and Tipperary North Riding Council – would request the Minister of Defence to make the proposed site, a surplus army barracks at Knockalisheen, available.[19] However, nothing of the sort had been countenanced by the Commission for all that it concluded that that the itinerant way of life was unacceptable in modern Ireland:

> For both social and economic reasons it is clearly undesirable that a section of the population should be isolated and follow a way of life which is harsh, primitive and of low economic value both to those who follow it and to the nation and, most important, which tends to create a closed and separate community which will become increasingly inferior to the rest of the national population and from which it will become increasingly difficult to escape.[20]

The Commission's 1963 report was stronger on diagnosis than on prescriptions. It emphasised that the rules of belonging of Irish society were being changed by 'the ever-rising standards of living of settled people' and the 'static, if not deteriorating, standards of itinerants' would further exclude them from this modernising society. It argued that 'the ever-growing disparity in relative social standards must render more difficult the mental adjustment which will be required of the settled people' to put up the longstanding ways of life of the itinerants: 'The plight of itinerants and their isolation by the settled community, which is becoming progressively worse, is a serious problem and one which has not troubled the public conscience to any degree.'[21] Rising standards of education amongst the 'ordinary population' were deemed likely to increase the social distance between the 'ordinary population' and the mostly illiterate itinerants.[22] Social distance is a sociological concept used to gauge levels of acceptance and intolerance of those perceived to be different from the norm or, to put another way, to gauge how the dominant majority group in a society feels about different minority groups. In a chapter on the 'Attitude of Settled Population to Itinerants' the Commission stated that

> The attitudes of most of the settled people ... is one of hostility often accompanied by fear. In addition in nearly all areas itinerants are despised as inferior beings and are regarded as the dregs of society. Many feel that they would demean themselves by associating with them. Their presence is considered to lower the tone of a neighborhood. ... The majority of the settled population wish to avoid any contact with itinerants in any form and break off any contact that is established as soon as possible.[23]

Aoife Bhreatnach summarised the social contract proposed by the Commission on Itinerancy thus: 'Travellers were asked to surrender nomadism, family economy, self-employment, flexible work patterns, horses and their own homes for dubious pleasures of public housing, full-time school attendance, subsistence on welfare benefits and organised charity.'[24] In return they could expect gain better living conditions and a more regulated existence. However, the Commission was hardly optimistic that what was being proposed would work. A major barrier preventing their settlement and assimilation was prejudice amongst what was referred to as the 'ordinary population':

> The attitude of the settled population in so far as itinerants are concerned is not confined to those on the road. It has been bought to the notice of the Commission that some families of itinerant extraction who managed to settle in different areas are still, often scornfully, known as 'tinkers', even in succeeding generations. This must affect the ability of such families to live a normal life and must be taken into account in estimating the time necessary to achieve complete integration.[25]

Itinerants find it difficult to find many forms of employment because of their background and the unwillingness of some employees to associate with them. The Commission is aware of at least one case where an itinerant girl whose origin was unknown to an employer and for whom she worked very satisfactorily as a waitress in a hotel was dismissed because of an objection of a customer who recognized her.[26]

The remedies proposed by the Commission could not overcome the patterns of prejudice it identified. Efforts to settle Travellers in designated halting sites were blocked by local politicians representing residents of whatever areas were proposed. Much of the schooling provided for Traveller children was segregated and designed so that there would be no contact with settled children. Many families were settled in Council housing, but the population living a simulacrum of the old nomadic existence also rose generation on generation. Overt discrimination in the allocation of social housing as well as attachment to a migratory way of life ensured that some of the grown-up children of those settled lived on the side of the road.[27] In 1982, Haughey who was by then Taoiseach, was asked virtually the same question that had been put to him in the Dáil two decades earlier: What was he going to do about the grave risk to children living on the side of the road in County Dublin? Haughey replied that 'the problem has been with us for some time' and that there was no easy solution to it.[28]

The absence of a final solution to the Traveller problem – the means to compel them to integrate into a society that despised them and that placed insurmountable political obstacles against nearly every effort to settle them – has for decades drip-fuelled further hostility and intolerance within local politics and in the media. To take one 1996 example of the latter (there are so many to choose from), Mary Ellen Synon declared that their way of life was

a life of appetite ungoverned by intellect ... It is a life worse than the life of beasts, for beasts at least are guided by wholesome instinct. Traveller life is without the ennobling intellect of man or the steadying instinct of animals. This tinker 'culture' is without achievement, discipline, reason or intellectual ambition. It is a morass. And one of the surprising things about it is that not every individual bred in this swamp turns out bad. Some individuals among the tinkers find the will not to become evil.[29]

Now this seems to almost a deliberate pastiche of nineteenth-century denigrations of the Irish of the kind examined in *Apes and Angels: The Irishman in Victorian Caricature* (1971) by Liz Curtis.[30] Before the Famine the condition of Ireland attracted considerable scrutiny by English political economists. These variously argued that the Irish poor

were feckless and improvident with some maintaining that the deficien-
cies of Irish character were the result of the Penal Laws that prevented
Catholics from bettering themselves in the professions and commerce,
and that exploitative tenancy conditions that gave smallholders no
impetus to improve their cabins or land. As put by the French liberal
Gustave de Beaumont in 1839:

> 'We are so poor! Is the reply of the Irish peasants, when they are reproached
> with increasing their misery by neglect; and as they continue in the filth
> that chokes their hovels, without the slightest wish to keep them clean.
>
> Irish intemperance and love of whisky, is one of the most deplorable of the
> national vices, arises from the same source. As he believes it impossible over
> to establish any durable accordance between his income and expenses, he
> dissipates without scruple the moderate wages of his temporary employment.
> Scarcely has he received his wages, when he runs to the whisky shop, and for
> a moment at least, drowns his misery in drunkenness and brutalization.
>
> Thus, by the very condition of the people, all the vices usually produced
> by extreme misery are naturally explained. Thus also the secondary vices,
> which are the usual accompaniments of those I have mentioned, may also
> be explained; thus the Irishman, precisely because he does nothing, boasts
> and blusters; as he has a master, he is a flatterer, and full of insolence when
> he is not cringing. These vices, indeed, add to his misery, but they were first
> derived from it. From the same source that his other pernicious inclinations
> flow, is derived that sad habit of falsehood, and that frightful predisposi-
> tion to the most cruel and most iniquitous outrages.
>
> There is no need of a very deep study of the character and habits of the
> Irish people to discover that they are often deficient in the most simple
> notions of good and evil, of right and wrong.[31]

A trawl through the writings by other well-meaning visitors to Ireland –
and I mean no irony; colonial racism was only part of the story – reveals
many such pejorative quotes. Liberal political economists like Beaumont,
Thomas Malthus and Richard Whately, the author of the Report of the
1835 Irish Poor Law Commission, all similarly decried the character of
the Irish whilst opposing laws and rules that apparently hampered the
ability of individuals to improve themselves.[32] Malthus maintained that
due to the Penal Laws the Irish peasant had 'not been subjected to the
ordinary stimulants which produce industrious habits'.[33] Seventeen years
after Catholic emancipation his intellectual enemy Friedrich Engels, in
The Condition of the Working Class in England (1845), portrayed Irish
immigrants as 'rough, intemperate and improvident' and to blame for
degrading the English working classes with their 'brutal habits'. Engels
considered the 'dissolute unsteady drunken Irish' incapable of becoming
mechanics or mill-hands.[34]

Part of the mission of Irish cultural nationalism was to refute colonial stereotypes. The Gaelic revival was to some extent intellectually based, like equivalent romantic nationalisms in other European countries, on the idolisation of the peasantry by literate urban middle-class nationalists. In 1907, there was a well-choreographed riot at the premier of John Millington Synge's *Playboy of the Western World*. Behind the spectacle of a rowdy urban audience protesting at peasants being portrayed as unruly lay some of the core contradictions of Irish nationalism. Cultural nationalists were themselves modernisers who reinvented and sometimes sanitised the past in putting forward their ideals of the kind of society they wished to bring about. A comic play that told the story of a young man who claimed to have killed his father in a fight seemed to play into the worst kind of anti-Irish stereotypes. In response to his Irish critics Synge replied: 'Anybody who has lived in real intimacy with the Irish peasantry will know that the wildest sayings and ideas in this play are tame indeed, compared with the fancies one may hear in any little hillside cabin in Geesala, or Carraroe, or Dingle Bay.'[35] There are few degrees of separation between the denigration of the supposedly improvident nineteenth-century poorer classes and antipathy towards of Travellers more than a century later. This antipathy owes much to the internalisation of liberal ideals of improvement and social hygiene over a longer period of time. But it was only with the emergence of a developmental nation-building project in the second half of the twentieth century that Travellers became the subject of scrutiny by the Irish state as unwelcome ghosts of a former kind of existence and as a darkness on the edge of Irish towns.

Notes

1 J.J. Lee, *Ireland 1912–1985: Politics and Society* (Cambridge: Cambridge University Press, 1989), p. 341.
2 T.K. Whitaker, *Economic Development* (Dublin: Stationery Office, 1958), pp. 227–229.
3 Tom Garvin, *Preventing the Future: Why Was Ireland So Poor for So Long?* (Dublin: Gill and Macmillan, 2004), p. 152.
4 Department of Education, *Report of the Council of Education, on (1) The function of the primary school (2) The curriculum to be pursued in the primary school, Pr 2583* (Dublin: Stationery Office, 1954).
5 Denis O'Sullivan, *Cultural Politics and Irish Education since the 1950s: Policy, Paradigms and Power* (Dublin: Institute of Public Administration, 2005), p. 129.
6 Government of Ireland/OECD *Investment in Education* (Dublin: Stationery Office, 1965), p. 350.

7 Commission on Itinerancy, *Report of the Commission on Itinerancy* (Dublin: Stationery Office, 1963).

8 Aoife Bhreatnach, *Becoming Conspicuous: Irish Travellers, Society and the State 1922–70* (Dublin: University College Dublin Press, 2006).

9 *Report of the Commission on Itinerancy*, p. 11.

10 See Jane Helleiner, 'Gypsies, Celts and Tinkers: Colonial Antecedents of Anti-traveller Racism in Ireland', *Ethnic and Racial Studies*, 18.3 (1995), 532–535.

11 Richard Whately, *The Poor Inquiry Ireland: First Report to the King's Most Excellent Majesty* (Dublin, 1835).

12 *First Report from His Majesty's Commissioners for Inquiring into the Conditions of the Poorer Classes in Ireland (1835).*

13 C. Arensberg, and S.T. Kimball, *Family and Community in Ireland* (Cambridge, MA: Harvard University Press, 1940).

14 Oscar Traynor, *Dáil Eireann Debates*, Vol. 174 (21 April 1959).

15 Eugene Timmons and Charles Haughey, *Dáil Eireann Debates*, Vol. 198 (1 December 1962).

16 *Report of the Commission on Itinerancy*, p. 111.

17 *Report of the Commission on Itinerancy*, p. 112.

18 *Report of the Commission on Itinerancy*, p. 112.

19 *Clare Champion*, 18 June 1966.

20 *Report of the Commission on Itinerancy*, p. 104.

21 *Report of the Commission on Itinerancy*, p. 102.

22 *Report of the Commission on Itinerancy*, p. 70.

23 *Report of the Commission on Itinerancy*, p. 102.

24 Bhreatnach, *Becoming Conspicuous*, p. 119.

25 Bhreatnach, *Becoming Conspicuous*, p. 103.

26 Bhreatnach, *Becoming Conspicuous*, p. 102.

27 See Bryan Fanning, *Racism and Social Change in the Republic of Ireland*, 2nd edition (Manchester: Manchester University Press, 2012).

28 Charles Haughey and Jim Mitchell, *Dáil Eireann Debates*, Vol. 328 No.9 (1 December 1962).

29 Mary Ellen Synon, 'Time to Get Touch on Tinker Terror Culture', *Sunday Independent*, 28 January 1996.

30 L.P. Curtis, *Apes and Angels: The Irishman in Victorian Caricature* (New York: New York University Press, 1971).

31 Gustave de Beaumont, *Ireland*, ed. Tom Garvin and Andreas Hess (Cambridge, MA: Harvard University Press, [1829] 2006), p. 196.

32 Bryan Fanning, *Histories of the Irish Future* (London: Bloomsbury, 2015), p. 238.

33 Thomas Malthus, *Principles of Political Economy* (London, [1820] 1968), p. 346.

34 Friedrich Engels, *The Condition of the Working Class in England* (London: Allen and Unwin, [1892] 1943) p. 119.

35 J.M. Synge, 'Preface' to *The Playboy of the Western World* (Dublin: Maunsel, 1907).

14

Partisan reviews

Beyond the need to earn a living there were, George Orwell reckoned in his 1946 essay 'Why I Write', four great motives for writing prose: sheer egoism, aesthetic enthusiasm, the desire to see things as they are and, his own main reason, political purpose.[1] *Periodicals and Journalism in Twentieth-Century Ireland*, edited by Mark O'Brien and Felix Larkin, is the first comprehensive survey of its kind of outlets for Irish public intellectuals and journalists who shared Orwell's reasons for writing. Whilst some of these periodicals championed reportage and were committed to investigative journalism many were explicitly partisan in the doctrines and ideologies they championed. Only one, *The Bell*, edited by Sean O'Faoláin, overlaps with the choices in my own survey of Irish journals, *The Quest for Modern Ireland: The Battle of Ideas 1912–1986*.[2] My focus was upon Irish journals which were influential or representative of prominent ideological perspectives, where academics and intellectuals set out their stalls. The focus here is on specialist periodicals and magazines. These, according to O'Brien and Larkin, provided outlets for journalists writing against the flow of mainstream Irish society and a space for the diversity of opinion that was not available in the national newspapers or in the provincial press.

The list of periodicals covered includes *The United Irishman* edited by Arthur Griffith, *An Claidheamh Soluis* edited by Patrick Pearse, *The Leader* edited by D.P. Moran, the suffragist *Irish Citizen* edited by Francis Sheehy-Skeffington, James Connolly's *The Worker*, *The Irish Statesman* edited by George Russell (AE) along with more recent seminal magazines including *Magill*. Articles focus on context and the controversies these became embroiled in. In the cases of some long-running periodicals the focus is on a seminal phase or particular editor. A common thread is a focus on the often-domineering editors who set the tone and were often player-managers responsible for much of the content. Taken together these periodicals covered the main fringes of political and intellectual life in the Republic of Ireland. Most were highly partisan advocates of some or other ideological position and explicitly engaged in propaganda. Others, whilst still partisan, contained fine journalism and reportage. There is no focus on Northern Irish periodicals, and only one aimed at women is examined.

Griffith ran and wrote most of *The United Irishman* from 1899 to 1906. In it he serialised his blueprint for an independent Ireland, *The Resurrection of Hungary* (1904).[3] The elephant in the room, necessarily addressed by Colum Kenny's chapter, is Griffith's anti-Semitism.[4] Michael Laffan in the *Dictionary of Irish Biography* has described this as 'the habits or prejudices of his youth', referring to outbursts in 1904 that coincided with what has been called the Limerick 'pogrom', with the pithy qualification that 'with occasional lapses, he outgrew them'. Kenny implies that Griffith's declared hostility towards Jews in Ireland was contradicted by his support for Zionism and by some genuine friendships with individual Jews. In the same 23 April 1904 article in the *United Irishman* that denigrated nine-tenths of Irish Jews as 'usurers and parasites', Griffith praised those honest and patriotic Jews who desired to re-establish the Hebrew nation of Palestine. Intellectually, this was consistent with the case for self-determination proposed in *The Resurrection of Hungary* and with the claims of European romantic nationalism that nationality was one of the great truths of human nature and that people could only realise themselves fully by sticking to their own as members of an identifiable culture demarcated by language and tradition.

An Claidheamh Soluis (The Sword of Light) grew out of the short-lived Gaelic League periodical *Fáinne an Lae* (Dawn of the Day) founded by Eoin MacNeill in 1898. It incubated an 'Irish-Ireland' nation-building project that became institutionalised in the state after independence. Pearse was its editor from 1903 to 1909 and in his first editorial declared that: 'Our ideal is to place in the hands of the Irish speaker in Glenties or Aran a newspaper giving him, in vivid idiomatic Irish, a consecutive and adequate record of the home and foreign history of the week.'[5] Gaelic-speaking rural areas were idealised. There was nothing in the *Gaeltacht*, according to one March 1914 article, 'like the cringing poverty and stunting misery of the city'. The English language, this article continued, had 'bought no wealth to the 75 per cent of Dublin families that live in tenements'. How a Gaelic revival might lift Dublin's slums out of poverty was not explained. In style and tone the debates rehearsed in *An Claidheamh Soluis* were, according to Regina Uí Chollatáin, those of 'a middle-class urban elite movement'.[6] Furthermore, the case for the Irish language, by necessity, had to be put in English. More than 300 editorials by Pearse were published in both languages.

One of the standout chapters is Patrick Maume's 'Irish-Ireland and Catholic Whiggery: D.P. Moran' on *The Leader*. Moran viewed separatist nationalist rhetoric as a self-deception that reinforced Irish unionism. Under Moran's editorship *The Leader* advocated clerical nationalism and a pragmatic approach to Anglo-Irish relations aimed at securing Catholic influence over Irish administration. Maume argues that: '*The Leader* is best understood as the product of the relative quiescence of political nationalism between the Parnell split of 1890 and the revival of home rule as an immediate political prospect from 1910.'[7]

In Moran's analysis, three elements were needed to secure Irish independence. He endorsed a nationalism that insisted that to be Irish was, firstly and secondly, to be Gaelic and to be Gaelic was, with a few honourable exceptions, to be Catholic. Thirdly, Moran emphasised economic development as a means to self-determination. Its then-leading advocates were Horace Plunkett, the Protestant moderate Unionist founder of the Irish co-operative movement and, amongst Catholics, Fr Tomas Finlay, a Jesuit, who with Plunkett and George Russell (AE) had been the driving force behind *The Irish Homestead*, the co-operative movement weekly. Initial capital to launch *The Leader* was secured by Finlay, who was a serial founder of Catholic magazines and periodicals.

Moran endorsed Plunkett against nationalist parliamentary candidates in 1900 and 1901. He later turned against him following the publication of Plunkett's book *Ireland in the New Century* (1904).[8] This alienated Catholics by claiming that their faith, unlike Protestantism, constituted a barrier to economic development; its repression of individuality seemed calculated to check the qualities of initiative and self-reliance that Max Weber emphasised in *The Protestant Ethic and the Spirit of Capitalism*, which was published around the same time.[9] *The Leader* serialised an anti-Plunkett polemic by Fr Michael Riordan that was published in book form as *Catholicity and Progress in Ireland* (1905).[10] *The Leader* under Moran campaigned against discrimination against Catholics within the civil service and in Protestant-dominated firms, notably the banks and the railways, which as public companies with many Catholic shareholders and reliance on state charters were more vulnerable to criticism than family-owned firms. Between 1902 and 1904 Moran supported efforts by the Jesuit-run Catholic Association, again sponsored by Finlay, to expose anti-Catholic discrimination and promote Catholic interests in business and the professions.

At the same time Moran denounced 'Cawtholic' secondary schools like Clongowes, Castleknock and Blackrock for playing foreign games, slighting the Irish language and turning pupils into 'pseudo-aristocratic West British snobs who sneered at trade and industry and gravitated into overstocked and underpaid white-collar professions at home and abroad'. He believed Catholic power and a Gaelic revival would not be enough to make Ireland independent. The problem was finding Catholic advocates of economic development or ways of promoting this that did not seem anti-Catholic.

At the beginning of the second decade of the twentieth century, with John Redmond's home rule movement in full swing, socialists and suffragists published historically significant if not necessarily politically influential periodicals. *The Irish Citizen* was the official organ of the Irish Women's Franchise League (IWFL), a suffragette organisation modelled to a considerable extent on Christabel Pankhurst's Women's Social and Political Union (WSPU). The IWFL was founded by Hanna Sheehy-Skeffington and Margaret Cousins. It was, however, edited by their husbands, Francis Sheehy-Skeffington and James Cousins. In 1913 Margaret and James Cousins emigrated, leaving the Sheehy-Skeffington's in charge. The Irish Parliamentary Party (IPP) saw the suffrage question as a threat to home rule, which depended on its alliance with the Liberal Party. Fearing that if Asquith's government fell home rule would also fall by the wayside; male fellow travellers of the IWFL such as Tom Kettle toed the IPP line. Not one IPP Member of Parliament supported the 1912 suffrage bill, not even those who were on the cross-party committee that drafted it.

The Irish Citizen was modelled on the WSPU's *Votes For Women* just as the IWFL's activism was inspired by the WSPU. But in 1914 Pankhurst echoed Redmond's gambit of supporting the war and setting aside their respective demands for its duration. The Irish Women's Suffrage Federation also decided to suspend active suffrage propaganda once war was declared, a policy that drove some members to resign – most notably Mary MacSwiney, who argued in *The Irish Citizen* that most in the league were 'Brits first, suffragists second and Irishwomen perhaps a bad third'.[11] The focus on much of the writing on early Irish feminism tends to focus, as it does here in Sonja Tiernan's chapter, on a small group of notable Republican women.[12] It is not often emphasised that the vast majority of Irish suffragists were Unionists. Some 228,991 women, over ten thousand more, signed a similarly worded declaration to the Ulster Covenant signed by 218,806 men.[13] More emphasis could have been given to pioneering journalism and opinion pieces in *The Irish Citizen*, such as those on how the courts and all-male juries dealt with rape cases, wife beating and concealed illegitimate pregnancies. For example, a July 1914 article – part of a campaign to monitor court cases involving sexual offences against young girls – emphasised the need to hear the woman's point of view in courts where judges saw 'the natural and irresistible impulses animating the man' as mitigating circumstances in their rulings.[14] *The Irish Citizen* also made the case for female barristers and judges.

The focus of James Curry's chapter, '*The Worker*: James Connolly's "Organ of the Irish Working Class"', is on a short-lived 1914–25 small-circulation periodical edited by Connolly after much more widely circulated predecessor *The Irish Worker* had been banned.[15] *The Irish Worker* was founded in 1911 as the organ of the Irish Transport and General Workers Union, It ran for 189 issues over a three-and-a-half-year period and at its peak racked up sales of about 20,000. It was suppressed in December 1914 for opposing Britain's involvement in the Great War. For example, in a November 1914 article in *The Irish Worker* Connolly made an anti-conscription case for revolution in Ireland. No rebellion, he argued, could conceivably lead to such slaughter of Irish manhood as would result from John Redmond's call to Home Rulers to enlist in the British Army.[16]

The debut issue of *The Worker* was published on 26 December 1914. It had a limited circulation and was, Connolly wrote in January 1915, but a shadow of its predecessor. It relied a lot for content on reprints of articles that had appeared elsewhere. These included an interview with James Larkin first published in New York and extracts from an article by George Bernard Shaw that had first appeared in the *New Statesman*. It was printed in Glasgow and one of its issues was intercepted by the Dublin Metropolitan Police. All copies were destroyed except ten kept 'for official purposes'.[17] *The Worker* was replaced in turn by *The Worker's Republic*, a title Connolly had first used in 1898, which ran until his death in the 1916 Rising.

The Irish Bulletin (1919–21) was conceived of as a daily news bulletin to foreign correspondents on behalf of Dáil Éireann as part of a £500 budget for propaganda measures, including entertainment of friendly journalists. Just thirty copies of the first issue were printed. It had five main themes: exposing the violent repression instituted by crown forces in Ireland; highlighting what it considered to be the disastrous policies of the British government; demonstrating that Dáil Éireann and its attendant counter-state was the legitimate and effective expression of the will of the Irish people; showing the national unity of the Irish people in the face of British aggression; and defending the activities of the IRA and their attacks on crown forces as a war against illegal forces of occupation. It came to be regarded, Ian Kenneally argues, 'as an untrammelled success, a powerful influence on press opinion'.[18]

Ian d'Alton describes *The Irish Statesman* as a 'pivotal publication, melding the best of the intellectual Anglo-Irish literary tradition with a coming to terms by an elite that, perhaps naïvely, had hoped for a freer Free State'.[19] George Russell edited *The Irish Statesman* for seven years from 1923 to 1930. His final elegiac editorial described it as belonging to a movement that began in the late nineteenth century and 'which has by now almost spent its force'. Funding to set it up was brokered by Horace Plunkett, who was also a contributor; both had been involved in *The Irish Homestead*. By its very existence *The Irish Statesman* challenged the 'Irish-Ireland' orthodoxies of the Free State. Most articles were in English, a few in French, but *The Irish Statesman* never published any Gaelic content. Illustrative titles include 'Cricket in Ireland', 'Jazz' and 'The Mystical Aspect of the Revolution'. According to d'Alton, the general tone – Ireland as part of Europe and the Empire, with something to offer to both – owed much to Plunkett. Its audience was an elite one; 'it is probably true to say', d'Alton writes, 'that a subscription to the *Statesman* would enable an Irish lady or gentleman to hold their own at dinner-parties in London or Dublin'.[20] It covered the arts and music as well as international current affairs. It was derided in *The Catholic Bulletin* as 'the weekly of the New Ascendancy' and 'Plunkett's House Journal' and, with a degree of humour, the subsidised organ of 'The AEsthetes'. Under AE's editorship *The Irish Statesman* sought to promote a 'humane, politically engaged and broadly literate' intellectual climate. What killed it in the end was the Wall Street Crash that impoverished its American backers.

To a certain extent its successor was *The Bell* which, under O'Faoláin's editorship, professed similar liberal goals, was born out of 'searing frustration' with 'the conservatism – or counter-revolution – that had followed Irish independence' and targeted 'an intelligent selective readership'.[21] *The Bell* included a focus on documentary journalism as well one on literature and intellectual topics. Seminal articles on prisons, illegitimacy, workhouses, slums and pawnshops were commissioned. O'Faoláin's editorials used the term *voir clair* to mean pretty much what Orwell referred to in 'Why I Write': the desire to see things as they are. O'Faoláin contrasted this aspiration with the prevailing abstract idealism of Irish society. Here *The Bell* differed from many if not most Irish periodicals before and of its time.

Dublin Opinion was a monthly miscellany of cartoons and humorous short articles that ran from 1922 to 1968. It held on to a readership of about 40,000 for most of its existence. Its first cover featured a cartoon of Arthur Griffith and Éamon de Valera smoking pipes of peace with 'unity blend' tobacco. Its first editorial ('Pull together') expressed hope that all would unify in a spirit of friendliness and goodwill. Its political manifesto, set out in November 1922 during the civil war declared:

> Our politics – we have none. It is our duty to support the Free State, because it is here, for good or ill, by the wish of the people. Against the principle of the Republicans there is nothing to be said. Principle is written in letters of gold, proof against the acids of logic and sophistry. And so, if in these pages we poke a little fun or make a weak jest at the expense of men of various political views, we mean it in the spirit that will be theirs again – the spirit of camaraderie – the spirit that is so necessary, particularly between men who have been comrades in arms.

Dublin Opinion, as the title suggested, represented an urban Ireland, in contrast to the 'Irish-Ireland' idealisation of ruralism and Gaelic nationalist periodicals such as *The Leader*. But by the 1960s this kind of nationalism had lost ground. As put by Felix Larkin 'The politicians whom it had learned to lampoon so brilliantly were growing old and passing from the scene, and it simply did not have the measure of the next generation then emerging to claim power.'[22] Its successor was perhaps the television programme *Halls Pictorial Weekly*, which ran from 1971 to 1980 and starred Frank Kelly, who was the son of Charles E. Kelly, one of the founding editors of and main contributors to *Dublin Opinion*. Charles E. Kelly also held down a 'conspiciously successful' parallel career as a civil servant. This included a period, from 1948 to 1952, as director of broadcasting for Radio Éireann, which was at the time part of the Department of Posts and Telegraphs.

Hibernia had been established in 1937 by the Knights of Columbanus. It was run from the same premises as *The Leader*. In 1968 the title was sold on John Mulcahy and under his editorship established a reputation for critical anti-establishment commentary on politics on and business. *Hibernia* focused on stories about bad planning, illegal property development and local government corruption. Its coverage of the Northern Ireland conflict repeatedly went 'where other media would not' in, for example, exposing the mistreatment of prisoners by the Royal Ulster Constabulary or factional conflicts within the Republican movement.[23] When *Hibernia* closed in 1980 Vincent Browne offered the following assessment:

> [*Hibernia*] acquired a liberal and sometimes radical aura. The paper maintained a consistently liberal line on the North, repression, prisons, women's liberation and industrial relations ... Whilst maintaining a courageous line as editor [Mulcahy's] concept of journalism as an intelligent summation of the known facts, mingled with informed opinion, and usually conducted almost entirely by phone from the office, results in a style that may lack the investigative edge required by a serious paper.[24]

Magill was founded in 1977 by Browne with an explicit remit for such well-researched investigative reportage. In its first incarnation, under his editorship, it has been the most important and influential periodical in recent decades. Browne identified five themes for the magazine and these dominated its editorial pages – civil liberties, Northern Ireland, women's rights, the redistribution of wealth and, most prominently, the issue of accountability. As argued by Browne in the January 1985 issue: 'The whole purpose of journalism is to enforce accountability on the part not just of public bodies but on the part of all institutions of power in society. Thus journalism is concerned not just with Governments but also with police forces, bureaucrats, courts, big business, trade unions, churches, even newspapers themselves.' *Magill*'s forte was investigative journalism, whether on the arms crisis, the trial of Joanne Hayes (which came to be known as the Kerry Babies case) or the treatment of patients in mental hospitals. An article on the latter by Hellen Connolly was the result of a six-month investigation. Gene Kerrigan's Kerry Babies article weighed in at more than 15,000 words.[25]

The chronological structure of *Periodicals and Journalism in Twentieth-Century Ireland* provides a fascinating overview of the development of critiques of Irish society from the margins as well as insights into the main ideological shifts across the period it covers. In our own time, where much of the focus of critical commentary is upon accountability, the chasm emphasised by O'Faoláin between ideology and polemics on one hand and non-fiction investigation on the other remains pertinent. Many of the chapters in this book have precious little to say about the actual contents of the periodicals under discussion and focus instead, to good effect, on ideological positions and editorial politics. A number of fringe periodicals are mostly interesting for the doctrines they espoused. Much of the writing that appears in many of these is too much in thrall to in-house doctrinal orthodoxy to stand on its own merits. That John Horgan (one of the contributors here) does not include pieces from most of these in his 2013 anthology *Great Irish Reportage* says a lot.[26] Horgan concludes that much of the best Irish journalism appeared in mainstream newspapers, though a number of his selections first appeared in *Magill*.

Notes

Review of Mark O'Brien and Felix M. Larkin (eds), *Periodicals and Journalism in Twentieth-Century Ireland* (Dublin: Four Courts Press, 2014). Previously published in the *Dublin Review of Books*, January 2015.

1 George Orwell, *Why I Write* (London: Penguin, 2004).
2 Bryan Fanning, *The Quest for Modern Ireland: The Battle of Ideas 1912–1986* (Dublin: Irish Academic Press, 2008).
3 Arthur Griffith, *The Resurrection of Hungary* (Dublin: University College Dublin Press, [1904] 2003).
4 Colum Kenny, '"An Extraordinary Clever Journalist": Arthur Griffith's Editorships, 1899–1919', in O'Brien and Larkin (eds), *Periodicals and Journalism*, pp. 16–30.
5 Patrick Pearse, 'Editorial', *An Claidheamh Soluis*, 6 June 1903.
6 Regina Uí Chollatáin, 'An Claidheamh Soluis agus Fáinne an Lae: The Turning of the Tide', in O'Brien and Larkin (eds), *Periodicals and Journalism*, pp. 31–46.
7 Patrick Maume, 'Irish-Ireland and Catholic Whiggery: D.P. Moran and *The Leader*', in O'Brien and Larkin (eds), *Periodicals and Journalism*, pp. 47–60.
8 Horace Plunkett, *Ireland in the New Century* (New York: Kennikat Press, [1904] 1970).
9 Max Weber, *The Protestant Ethic and the Spirit of Capitalism*, trans. Talcott Parsons (London: Unwin, 1930), first published 1904–05 in *Archiv für Sozialwissenschaft und Sozialpolitik*, 20–21.
10 Michael O'Riordan, *Catholicity and Progress in Ireland* (London: Trench, Trubner and Co, 1905).
11 Mary MacSwiney, Untitled, *The Irish Citizen*, 21 November 1914.
12 Sonja Tiernan, '"Challenging the Headship of Man": Militant Suffragism and the *Irish Citizen*', in O'Brien and Larkin (eds), *Periodicals and Journalism*, pp. 61–74.
13 Marcus Tanner, *Ireland's Holy Wars: The Struggle for a Nation's Soul 1500–2000* (New Haven: Yale University Press, 2001), p. 275.
14 M.E. Duggan, 'In the Courts', *Irish Citizen*, 11 July 1914.
15 James Curry, '*The Worker*: James Connolly's "Organ of the Irish Working Class"', in O'Brien and Larkin (eds), *Periodicals and Journalism*, pp. 75–88.
16 James Connolly, *Irish Worker*, 21 November 1914.
17 Curry, '*The Worker*', p. 86.
18 Ian Kenneally, '"A Tainted Source"? The *Irish Bulletin*, 1919–21', in O'Brien and Larkin (eds), *Periodicals and Journalism*, pp. 89–101.
19 Ian d'Alton, 'In "a Comity of Cultures": The Rise and Fall of the Irish Statesman 1919–30', in O'Brien and Larkin (eds), *Periodicals and Journalism*, pp. 102–122.
20 D'Alton, 'In "a Comity of Cultures"', p. 113.
21 Mark O'Brien, 'Other Voices: *The Bell* and Documentary Journalism', in O'Brien and Larkin (eds), *Periodicals and Journalism*, pp. 158–172.
22 Felix M. Larkin, '"Humour is the Safety Valve of a Nation": *Dublin Opinion*, 1922–68', in O'Brien and Larkin (eds), *Periodicals and Journalism*, pp. 123–142.
23 Brian Trench, '*Hibernia*: Voices of Dissent, 1968–80', in O'Brien and Larkin (eds), *Periodicals and Journalism*, pp. 187–202.
24 Vincent Browne, *Sunday Independent*, 31 October 1980.

25 Kevin Rafter, '"The Passion of Particularity": *Magill*, 1977–90', in O'Brien and Larkin (eds), *Periodicals and Journalism*, pp. 219–233.
26 John Horgan (ed.), *Great Irish Reportage* (Dublin: Penguin Ireland, 2013).

15

Tales of two tigers

The term 'Celtic Tiger' was first coined on 31 August 1994 by the author of an article in the newsletter of the American investment bank Morgan Stanley that suggested comparisons with the East Asian tiger economies.[1] It was quickly adopted by Irish financial journalists and economists and soon became ubiquitous within media and political debates. In *Inside the Celtic Tiger: The Irish Economy and the Asian Model* (1998) Denis O'Hearn argued that the few widely agreed characteristics of tiger economies were largely descriptive and superficial. The harder one looked at particular cases the more disparate these 'tigers' appeared to become and the greater the differences how and why particular countries achieved their economic success seemed to be. Yet, the original four East Asian 'tigers' shared some core economic characteristics. Each had maintained average annual economic growth rates of more than 8 per cent from the 1960s until the 1990s.[2] Between 1960 and 1990 Taiwan's GDP rose by an average of 9.3 per cent per annum. Such growth rates were very high compared to European averages of 2 per cent across the same period. During the same period Ireland's GDP expanded at almost twice the European rate (averaging 3.9 per cent per annum) but also at about half the rate of those East Asian countries to which it was being likened.[3] Whilst Irish growth rates stood out compared to the rest of the European Union these were modest compared to Taiwan and the other East Asian economic tigers. But by the early 1990s Irish growth had begun to accelerate for reasons that suggested that comparisons with East Asian economic development were valid. During the 1970s productivity per capita was only half as in the United Kingdom. By 1996 it had exceeded British levels.[4]

Ireland and Taiwan were still poor, peripheral and technologically backward societies in 1950. By the end of the 1960s, state-led industrial-development policies had emerged in both countries, which rapidly expanded levels of indigenous human capital between 1960 and 1980.[5] In both cases the state actively promoted economic development. There are some similarities in how they went about this. Both countries introduced duty-free export processing zones – at Shannon Airport in Ireland in 1961 and near Kaolsuing in Taiwan in 1964 – aimed at encouraging foreign manufacturers to establish factories. Ireland attracted a mixture of European and American-owned companies, Taiwan attracted predominantly Japanese firms. Both have sought to attract multi-national companies (MNCs) and pressure these to source a significant percentage of their components locally.[6]

There were some broad similarities between the development trajectories of the Irish and Asian tiger economies. All benefited from large-scale inward investment from MNCs, and each developed strong niche sectors in high-tech production – computers in all cases and also pharmaceuticals in the Irish case. However, the nature of MNC investment differed in the Irish case from that experienced in East Asia. Inward investment into Europe and Ireland predominantly came from the United States. American MNCs typically established US-owned subsidiaries, whereas in East Asian cases inward investment was predominantly from Japan – and Japanese MNCs had tended to established joint-owned enterprises. Partly, this came about because Japanese MNCs favoured subcontracting over direct investment in subsidiaries. Its domestic labour supply was small compared to that of the United States, and labour shortages precipitated the shift of productive capacity to other countries. This encouraged the growth of domestic industrial sectors in countries where they invested. It involved the downward shedding of technologies and was met in host countries by concerted efforts to upgrade their technological capacity. For example, Taiwan built steelworks to supply Japanese industry and then used the steel to build a machine-tool industry.[7]

There were also some crucial differences. Since the late 1960s Ireland has focused mainly on industrial-development policies based in direct foreign investment. In Taiwan the Kuomintang (KMT) dictatorship mistrusted large-scale private industry, so the state took on a larger role in fostering industrial innovation, for example through state-led research agencies. In Ireland the role of the state in co-ordinating industrial development was more hands-off: the state actively solicited inward investment and provided through its Industrial Development Authority (IDA) advance factory sites and other facilities to attract inward development. But the nature and extent of state co-ordination in these cases came to differ. Taiwan had a Japanese-style state bureaucracy where civil servants and even politicians tended to have specialist skills – for example, qualifications in engineering. Ireland inherited an English-style bureaucracy dominated by non-specialist civil servants. This contributed to a less-direct management of industry by the state in the Irish case.

Both states successfully attracted foreign-owned computer industries. Unlike Ireland, Taiwan then pushed these to procure an increasing number of components locally and to transfer production expertise to local suppliers. The state also promoted the use of Taiwanese venture capital to expand the information technology sector.[8] Taiwan developed a viable computer manufacturing industry that included internationally successful brands as ACER. In the Irish case, the state neither prioritised capital investment into computer manufacturing nor sought to compel foreign-owned companies to foster Irish supply chains. Partly for these reasons computer manufacturing faltered. American MNCs characteristically shared technology with and purchased components from their own subsidiaries. More sustainable successes were achieved in software design where human capital was a key factor of production.

Different models of inward investment were met by somewhat different state-led developmental policies. Comparative analyses have emphasised differences between the East Asian Bureaucratic Developmental State (BDS) model and what emerged in the Irish developmental state approach. The BDS model adopted from Japan combined elements of protectionism and state enterprise that differed considerably from what pertained in the West. East Asian developmental states articulated projects of economic nationalism by means of state control over finance and the labour market. These blurred distinctions between public and private ownership and, more generally, ones between the state and the market.[9] Characteristically the state intervened directly in the economy, for example by controlling wage levels and promoting indigenous capital formation.[10]

Academic comparative analyses of the Celtic and East Asian tigers have identified much stronger state controls over the factors of production than were evident in the Irish case. During the 1980s the Irish state put in place a system of developmental corporatism or 'social partnership' that negotiated national development plans, and wage agreements with employers and trade unions fell considerably short of the degree of state control and co-ordination of economic activity found in the East Asian tiger countries.[11] In Ireland, through semi-state agencies like the IDA, the state gave grants and subsidies to MNCs. It expanded the education system to provide skilled workforces. However, it also removed all protectionisms against foreign capital in 1964. It introduced low rates of corporation tax that succeeded in attracting to Ireland disproportionate levels of the inward investment coming into the European Union. Between 1988 and 1998 Ireland attracted 40 per cent of the American electronics investment into Europe. A similar but smaller agglomeration of pharmaceutical companies occurred during the same period.[12]

Taiwan's BDS approach to economic modernisation emerged through top-down directives within a system of authoritarian capitalism. During the period of martial law between 1948 and 1988 strikes were illegal and labour was organised into a government-controlled union.[13] The policy-making processes of the ruling Kuomintang party and the state were effectively indistinguishable.[14] Later, during the 1980s and 1990s, social movements and civil society emerged to open out political decision-making: an opposition party, the Democratic Progressive Party (DPP), was founded in 1986, and martial law was lifted in 1987 after thirty-eight years. Democratic elections to the National Assembly were held in 1991 and to the Legislative Yuan in 1992. In 1994 the Constitution was amended to allow presidential elections. In 2000 the DPP won the presidential election for the first time.

In the Irish case, according to Sean O'Riain, a 'flexible-developmental state' emerged whereby the state encouraged (rather than coerced) corporatist planning alongside neo-liberal responses to globalisation.[15] Unlike Taiwan, Ireland was a multi-party democracy where the state had a limited capacity to command the economy and direct the productive capacities of society. Free-market neo-liberal responses to globalisation were managed through a system of 'social partnership' agreements between the state, employers and trade unions. Under Ireland's 'competitive corporatist' or 'competition state' model the role of government was to facilitate the free movement of capital, goods, services and labour.[16] In articulating these neo-liberal goals Irish politicians and media used terms such as *Ireland Inc* or *Ireland PLC*. Between 2001 and 2004 Ireland was ranked as the most globalised country in the world according to the AT Kearney/*Foreign Policy Magazine* index. During the same period Taiwan was ranked as considerably less globalised. It ranked 32nd in 2002, 34th in 2003 and 36th in 2004. The index measures four kinds of global integration. The first 'economic integration' index (where Ireland ranked highest) combined data on trade, foreign direct investment (FDI), capital flows and investment income payments and receipts. Taiwan ranked 27th on this measure in 2004. In 2002 an AT Kearney/ *Foreign Policy Magazine* report noted that Ireland attracted an FDI inflow of 24.7 billion US dollars. Ireland ranked second for 2004 on the second 'personal contact' index. This compared international, tourism and cross-border remittances. By comparison Taiwan ranked 32nd. On the third 'technological connectivity' index Ireland ranked 14th and

Taiwan ranked 17th. On the fourth 'political integration' index, which tracked state membership of international organisations and ratification of international treaties, Ireland ranked 11th and Taiwan ranked as the lowest of all 62 countries included in the index. That Singapore ranked 2nd on the composite index for 2004 (high on economic integration, low on political and personal integration) suggests the need for caution about grouping all East Asian 'tigers' together.[17] However, comparisons between Ireland and Taiwan reveal that Ireland the Irish economy is considerably more open and that the Taiwanese economy is considerably more protected. This suggests considerable underlying differences in the nature of state developmental approaches in both cases.

Cultural contexts of economic development

Taiwan's experiences of state formation and ethnic politics clearly differ from any norm. In 1896 Taiwan was ceded to the Japanese Empire and remained under colonial rule until after the Second World War. The dominant sense of ethnic nationality in Taiwan – The Republic of China (ROC) – has developed in complex symmetry with that of the mainland People's Republic of China. Both Chinese states came to enshrine ethnic conceptions of nationality whilst at the same time they have been contesting each other's legitimacy since 1948. The arrival of over a million migrants from mainland China in the aftermath of Chiang Kai-Shek's defeat by the People's Liberation Army, in essence China's old government and army in exile, profoundly changed Taiwan's ethnic and culture composition. Before 1949 mainlanders made up just one-quarter of Taiwan's population. By the early 1950s two million refugees from the mainland were claimed to live in Taiwan, forming one-third of a total population of 6 million. Excepting only small minorities of aboriginal peoples and a minority Japanese settler population most of the rest of the Taiwanese population consisted two Han Chinese ethnic groups (Minnanre and Hakka) descendent from waves of migration from the mainland in earlier centuries. Prior to 1945 Taiwan had been under Japanese colonial control.

After 1949 the ROC based in Taiwan retained a government structure that claimed sovereignty over all thirty-five provinces of China as well as layers of 'local' government. By the 1950s, the exile of the ROC in Taiwan looked increasingly long term, and a new state-led modernisation project emerged. The population of Taipei rose from 200,000 in 1949 to more than one million by the mid-1960s. By 2005, Taiwan had a population of 23 million. Of these, mainlanders and their children made up 13 per cent.[18]

The cultural politics of post-1949 Taiwan encompassed a period of de-Japanisation followed by a pronounced 'Sinic Revival' during the 1960s. In reaction to Mao's 1966 'cultural revolution' on the mainland, Chinese culture was strongly promoted by the ROC in school curricula and other areas. As put by Cheng-yi Lin and Wen-cheng Lin:

> Through politically-screened teachers and deliberate design of the school curriculum, the ROC government promoted China as the motherland as well as a Chinese national identity among Taiwanese. Mandarin was stipulated as the sole language, and other dialects were banned at schools, in the military, and at all levels of the government. TV and radio programming in dialects was kept to a minimum. To an extent, political socialisation in Taiwan was successful during the first four decades of KMT rule. The majority of the people in Taiwan identified themselves as Chinese and supported Taiwan's unification with China in 1989.[19]

In effect, the post-1949 period witnessed the growing dominance of Chinese culture. Firstly, a period of 'cultural re-unification' (1945–67) saw an emphasis on reconsolidating Chinese culture, purging Japanese influences and suppressing local Taiwanese cultural expression. This included imposing Standard Mandarin as the official language and banning Taiwanese and Japanese from the mass media. Secondly, a 'cultural renaissances' period witnessed a systematic attempt 'to cultivate a large-scale societal consciousness' of traditional Chinese culture. Here the ROC deployed some of the classic nation-building techniques described by Benedict Anderson and Ernest Gellner (see Chapter 1). As put by Alan Chun: 'By invoking "tradition", the authorities appeared to resuscitate elements of the past, but they were clearly inventing tradition (by virtue of their selectivity). The government in effect played an active role (as author) in writing the culture.'[20] However, this did not result in an uncontested 'Chinese' national identity.

Ireland achieved independence in 1922 and before that had been, since 1801, part of the United Kingdom. Its post-independence politics were preoccupied with cultural nationalism and de-colonisation. Its education system prioritised the inter-generational reproduction of Catholicism and cultural identity (the Irish language) over the expansion of human capital. Cultural protectionism was paralleled after 1932 by economic protectionism that included a prohibition on the investment of foreign capital. Its politics were preoccupied, to a considerable extent, with the ideal of a 32-county united Ireland, the incorporation of Northern Ireland into the 26-county Irish Free State that in 1948 was declared the Republic of Ireland.

In many respects Ireland was a typical European *Kulturnation* built upon the foundations of nineteenth-century romantic nationalism to create a dominant shared sense of ethnic shared identity made possible by mass literacy, education and other aspects of modernity. This Irish-Ireland nationalism came symbolically to dominate the new state from the 1920s to at least the 1960s. After independence Irish-Ireland cultural nationalism served to promote both cultural and economic isolationism. In 1932 a Fianna Fáil government was elected on a platform of economic isolationism. Éamon de Valera, the dominant political figure for the next two decades, preached a doctrine of economic self-sufficiency, preventing imports, discouraging foreign capital and promoting import substitute manufacturing. Once elected in 1932 he introduced the Control of Manufactures Act. This required that most of the capital in Irish companies should be Irish-owned. The aim was to undermine British dominance within Irish industry. de Valera also imposed tariff barriers aimed at fostering import substitution. It precipitated the so-called 'economic war' with the United Kingdom, of mutual tariff barriers that lasted until 1938 when the British removed restrictions on imports for Ireland.[21]

To some extent the economic development policies of the post-1932 period resembled those of the KMT. In addition to restrictions on foreign capital these centred on the formation of semi-state companies to produce electricity (ESB), harvest turf for use as fuel (Bord na Móna), process sugar beet (Comhlucht Siucra Éireann) or develop air travel (Aer Lingus). This predominance of state-led capital investment in the Irish economy coincided with a de-colonising period of pronounced cultural nationalism.

From the 1950s the 'Irish-Ireland' nation-building project became contested by a developmental modernising one, which came to emphasise economic and human capital reproduction as utilitarian nation-building goals. Protectionism unravelled during the 1950s when import substitution policies proved unable to sustain employment.[22] The emergence of a new developmental paradigm was signalised by the high-profile publication in 1958 of a report entitled *Economic Development*. Its significance was that it institutionalised the perspective that protectionism did not work. Key landmarks in the liberalisation of trade included the removal of restrictions on foreign capital investment in 1964, the Anglo-Irish Free Trade Agreement in 1965 and EEC membership in 1973.[23] In an example of developmental realpolitik a 1976 report from the National Economic and Social Council argued that if the foreign investment needed to provide new jobs were discouraged Irish people would still have to work for foreign capital, but would be doing so outside of Ireland rather than at home.[24] The Irish developmental settlement occurred partly due to the co-option of erstwhile blocking coalitions within a competitive corporatist system of social partnership. Trade unions and employers repeatedly signed up for the pursuit of economic growth as a national project.[25] Symbolic political preoccupations with a united Ireland seemed unfeasible. Urbanisation and the expansion of education fostered secularism. Economists achieved an influence once held by clerics. In sociological terms a modernisation of belonging occurred that prioritised human capital over forms of cultural capital. In the language of sociologists the pursuit of economic growth became a hegemonic neo-liberal 'competitive corporatist' national project. 'Social partnership' agreements negotiated by the Irish state with employers and unions were in effect national plans for economic development.

In summary, in Taiwan cultural nation-building co-existed with economic nation-building whilst in the Irish case the main phase of cultural nation-building preceded developmentalism. Having abandoned all forms of protectionism by the mid-1960s, Ireland was open to a neo-liberal development project that resulted in its economy becoming the most globalised in the world. The underlying political acceptance of such openness – exemplified by various social partnership agreements – contrasted with a resistance to some forms of globalisation in Taiwan. Clearly the uneasy relationship between the ROC and the PRC has kept the politics of nationality in the foreground, whereas there has been little emphasis on cultural nation-building for several decades in the Irish case. Simply put, the goal of economic development came to subordinate other political goals in the Irish case more than it appears to be the case in Taiwan.

Notes

This chapter is abridged from Bryan Fanning, 'Developmental Immigration in the Republic of Ireland and Taiwan', *Taiwan in Comparative Perspective*, 4.1 (2012), 8–29.

1 Kevin Gardiner, 'The Irish Economy: A Celtic Tiger', in *Ireland: Challenging for Promotion*, Morgan Stanley Euroletter (31 August 1994), pp. 9–21.
2 Denis O'Hearn, *Inside the Celtic Tiger: The Irish Economy and the Asian Model* (London: Pluto Press, 1998), pp. 3–5.
3 O'Hearn, *Inside the Celtic Tiger*, p. 61.
4 O'Hearn, *Inside the Celtic Tiger*, p. 65.
5 Dan Breznitz, *Innovation and the State: Political Choice and Strategies for Growth in Israel, Taiwan and Ireland* (New Haven: Yale University Press, 2007), p. 7.
6 Breznitz, *Innovation and the State*, p. 194.

7 O'Hearn, *Inside the Celtic Tiger*, p. 22.
8 Dan Breznitz, 'Innovation and the State: Development Strategies for High Technology Industries in a World of Fragmented Production: Israel, Ireland and Taiwan', *Enterprise and Society*, 7.4 (2006), 675–685, p. 684.
9 M. Woo-Cummings, *The Developmental State* (New York: Cornell University Press, 1999), p. 21.
10 W.G. Huff, 'What is the Singapore Model of Economic Development?', *Cambridge Journal of Economics*, 19.6 (1995), 735–759.
11 Sean O'Riain, 'The Flexible Developmental State: Globalization, Information Technology, and the "Celtic Tiger"', *Policy and Politics*, 28.2 (2000), 157–193, p. 158.
12 O'Hearn, *Inside the Celtic Tiger*, p. 75.
13 L. Cheng, 'Transnational Labor, Citizenship and the Taiwan State', in Arthur Rosett, Lucie Cheng and Margaret Woo (eds), *East Asian Law: Universal Norms and Local Culture* (New York: Routledge Curzon, 2002), p. 95.
14 Fang-Mei Lin, 'Women's Organizations and the Changing State/Society Relationship: Resistance, Co-option by the State or Partnership?', *Taiwan in Comparative Perspective*, 2.1 (2008), 47–64, p. 53.
15 Sean O'Riain, 'Social Partnership as a Mode of Governance', *The Economic and Social Review*, 37.3 (2006), 311–318.
16 W.K. Roche and T. Cradden, 'Neo-corporatism and Social Partnership', in M. Adshead and M. Millar (eds), *Public Administration and Public Policy in Ireland: Theory and Practice* (London: Routledge, 2003), p. 73.
17 A. Hesham, 'Measurement of a Multidimensional Index of Globalisation', *Global Economy Journal*, 6.2 (2006), 1–28, p. 8.
18 Cheng-yi Lin and Wen-cheng Lin, 'Democracy, Divided National Identity and Taiwan's National Security, *Taiwan Journal of Democracy*, 1.2 (2005), 69–87, p. 70.
19 Lin and Lin, 'Democracy', p. 72.
20 Alan Chun, 'Discoveries of Identity in the Changing Spaces of Public Culture in Taiwan, Hong Kong and Singapore', *Theory, Culture and Society*, 13.1 (1996), 51–75, p. 56.
21 Tom Garvin, *Preventing the Future: Why Was Ireland So Poor for So Long?* (Dublin: Gill and Macmillan, 2004), p. 113.
22 Cormac O'Grada and Kevin O'Rourke, 'Economic Growth since 1945', in N. Crafts and G. Toniolo (eds), *Economic Growth in Europe since 1945* (Cambridge: Cambridge University Press, 1996), p. 141.
23 John Fitzgerald, *Ireland's Failure and Belated Convergence*, ESRI Working Paper No 133 (Dublin: Economic and Social Research Institute, 2000), p. 3.
24 National Economic and Social Council, *Prelude to Planning* (Dublin: Stationery Office, 1976), 20.
25 O'Riain, 'Social Partnership', p. 213.

16

The sociology of boom and bust

The Republic of Ireland's post-Celtic-Tiger collapse has become the focus of a considerable body of literature, much of this focused on the institutional failure of the Irish state to regulate the banks and property markets, on the failures of Irish political culture and on a crisis of public morality. Sean O'Riain's *The Rise and Fall of Ireland's Celtic Tiger: Liberalism, Boom and Bust* offers a sociological analysis that is very much focused on the role of institutions. It challenges arguments made most prominently by Fintan O'Toole in *Ship of Fools: How Stupidity and Corruption Sunk the Celtic Tiger* (2009) that bad political culture and bad public morality were to blame.[1] Such narratives, O'Riain argues, really tell us little: the standard account they present tends to reduce Irish political and economic failures to the greed, opportunism and incompetence of individuals. Neither does he think that blaming neo-liberalism – a term that O'Riain for the most part avoids – somehow explains the Irish case.[2]

Instead he focuses on the characteristics of Ireland's political economy and its often dysfunctional interplay of liberalism, clientelism and corporatism. Many of the elements that made the banking crisis possible, he notes, 'were intrinsic elements of market liberalism'. These included the limiting of public regulation, the rejection of political guidance of the economy, the indifference of private regulation to securing the common good and the structural importance and discursive privileging of markets and particularly finance.[3] Such malign liberalism, he argues, combined with clientelism during the 2000s to destabilise a creative corporatism that had done much during the previous decade to enable the Irish economy to escape from its long-term underdevelopment.

Whether the label sociology fits this book better than political economy is debatable, but political economy and sociology are by no means mutually exclusive. Political economy was what economics used to be called when it focused on the social context of economic decision-making as well as upon market forces. Specific political economies are also sociological entities for all the language and metaphors of economics came to dominate public discourse. It is not unusual to hear politicians and even trade unionists on Irish radio describing the Republic of Ireland as 'Ireland PLC'. Horace Plunkett wrote at the beginning of the twentieth century that Ireland's political economy was characterised by a big 'P' and a small 'e'. Since the middle of that century the Republic of Ireland has been pursuing an explicit developmental nation-building project aimed at growing the 'e'.

Governance is what one is left with when the running of things is apparently depoliticised, where politics is reduced to a small 'p'. O'Riain's emphasis on the role of institutions is focused on their capacities to lever economic development and to regulate the economy. *The Rise and Fall of Ireland's Celtic Tiger* is preoccupied with disentangling varieties of Irish liberalism, seeing these as integral to understanding the sociology of Ireland's boom and bust and that of almost half a century of earlier developmental nation-building. He examines Ireland as a case of liberal political economy, 'an economy where market activity was taken to be the dominant and legitimate way of allocating resources and making economic decisions'. Specifically he argues that developmental and corporatist institutions were critical in promoting rapid economic growth during the 1990s but that their positive influence was derailed by the property bubble of the 2000s fuelled by market liberalism and state boosterism.[4]

Ireland's liberal political economy pre-dates independence. The list of other liberal political economies also included the UK and its English-speaking former colonies – Australia, Canada, New Zealand and the United States. In his 1871 book *The Last Conquest of Ireland (Perhaps)* John Mitchel described the domination of political and economic liberalism over post-Famine Ireland as more insidious (more hegemonic, as Antonio Gramsci would later put it) than any military domination. His account of how liberalism as a colonising ideal had penetrated constitutional nationalism in the era of Daniel O'Connell came to heavily influence subsequent generations of revolutionary nationalists.[5] Liberal understandings of the market mechanism and property ownership drew variously on natural rights doctrines, Whiggism, classical political economy, utilitarianism, evangelical Christianity and evolutionary biology.[6] Nineteenth-century liberalism became a component of the ideological, social and institutional processes of Irish nation-building as much as did Catholicism.[7] It provided the ideological lens through which early visiting sociologists such as Harriet Martineau and Gustave de Beaumont studied the condition of Ireland and set the ideological tone of the subsequent modernisation of Irish society. In 1932 University College Dublin economist George O'Brien invited John Maynard Keynes to give the first memorial Finlay lecture, named for a Professor of Political Economy. The lecture was attended by Éamon de Valera and his incoming cabinet, including Sean Lemass, as well as by W.T. Cosgrave and members of the former Cumann na nGaedheal government. Keynes, when later recalling his visit to Dublin, described Cosgrave as 'such a nineteenth century liberal' whose views on economics recalled those of his own father.[8] So when during the 1950s Lemass and his civil servant T.K. Whitaker presided over a new economic nation-building project the underlying assumptions as to what was needed – the expansion of education, human capital, the end of protectionism, industrial expansion and a spirit of enterprise – did little more than echo arguments by nineteenth-century political economists like Bishop Richard Whately and Tomas Malthus that improvement of the condition of Ireland required firstly the improvement of the Irish themselves.

An awful lot has been written about the pernicious effects of neo-liberalism by Irish sociologists. By and large sociologists, professing an academic discipline that deals in theories of social structure and socio-structural inequalities, are drawn to the Left. They are necessarily sceptical of paeans to individualism and human agency. But all too often terms like neo-liberalism are thrown down without much concrete explanation. Readers are invited to understand the world in Manichean terms, with neo-liberalism as the dark side of the force. Neo-liberalism is in the main implicitly used to refer to an ideology that, through steps that are not explained, fosters more and more exploitative forms of free-market capitalism that work to undermine social cohesion. The leap from ideology in general to specific structural influences on society is rarely disentangled in detail.

Perhaps the most influential critique of neo-liberalism as an ideology in the Irish case has been Kieran Allen's *The Celtic Tiger: The Myth of Social Partnership in Ireland* (2000). He defined an ideology as a set of ideas shared by a large number of people which forms some kind of coherent related system and is connected to the maintenance of power and economic privilege. Dominant ideologies, he argued, typically work by masking conflicts of interest and by presenting their outlook as the most practical, rational and feasible. In such terms he described the concept of social partnership as an ideology that masked a process whereby resources were transferred to the wealthier sections of Irish society. Likewise social partnership institutions were disparaged as a means of securing the complicity of those being exploited.[9] O'Riain, on the other hand, defends the achievements of 1990s social partnership. Rather than seeing it as a mechanism for the creation of some kind of false consciousness or merely as a vehicle for competitive corporatism – a mechanism for driving down wage costs and public expenditure – he emphasises its real achievements. He describes the Irish system during the 1990s as a form of creative corporatism. It fostered support for active Labour market policy and research and development to levels close to those provided by European social market economies.[10] O'Riain classified 1990s Ireland as a Developmental Network State.

The Rise and Fall of the Celtic Tiger places little emphasis on ideology. The term does not even feature in the bibliography. Nor does the term 'neo-liberalism' (although it is used sparingly). Not so his previous book *The Politics of High-Tech Growth*, which argued that a new form of state developmentalism emerged in Ireland and elsewhere 'from within a neoliberal order' in the form of a network of 'global regions' – a new information economy – linked by transnational corporate, scientific and occupational ties. In the 1990s, he wrote in *The Politics of High-Tech Growth*, the 'Celtic Tiger' appeared to be a shining star of neo-liberal orthodoxy.[11] Yet, beneath the 'neo-liberal veneer' there was a richer story of state–society alliances, state involvement in industrial develop-ment, a system of institutions that sought to adjust to neo-liberalism and to protect themselves from it.

Irish developmentalism, as an explicitly articled nation-building project, can be traced to T.K. Whitaker's seminal report *Economic Development* (1958) and the *First Programme of Economic Expansion* published in the same year. Accounts of Irish economic modernisation also highlight the joint OECD/Irish Government report *Investment in Education* (1965), which prefigured a rapid expansion of the secondary school system and a skilling up of the Irish workforce. The removal of all forms of economic protectionism by the 1960s was accompanied by low taxes and subsidies for external investment. The Irish economy became radically open to foreign capital. As put by O'Riain: 'Contemporary globalization appears to have found Ireland well before it found the rest of the globe. From the late 1950s forward, Ireland pursued an uninterrupted strategy of increasing integration in the global economy – actively pursuing foreign investment and becoming one of the most open economies in the world.' Ireland became the harbinger of a new form of developmentalism in a world 'where national restrictions on foreign investment [became] increasingly difficult to sustain'.[12]

From the 1950s the state became the key actor in attracting foreign direct investment. Protectionism had ended completely by 1964. During the 1960s foreign investment grew rapidly. By 1973 foreign firms accounted for 15.9 per cent of gross output, rising from 2.3 per cent in 1960. But the percentage of government revenue from taxes on capital and corporations declined from 2.3 per cent of GDP in 1965 to 1.2 per cent in 1985. The Industrial Development Authority, as O'Riain put it in his 2004 book, took on the role of 'hunter gatherer' of foreign direct investment and became unusually powerful within the national state system. Yet by the 1980s Ireland was the sick man of Europe. The gains of foreign investment were often expropriated. Keynesian economics worked poorly in the Irish case. High state spending contrbuted to a huge national debt but the benefits of this expenditure – what economists call the multiplier effect, when spending circulates and recirculates within the economy – were poor. The Irish case, like those of South American countries and Europe's southern periphery, was seen to exemplify underdevelopment theory for all that none of these possessed a liberal political economy. In early 1980s sociology classes I was taught that underdevelopment theory best fitted the Irish case. Multi-nationals might site themselves in Ireland, but would only bring their low-skilled activities and would expropriate their profits to metropolitan core economies. On a 1984 student placement with the Shannon Free Airport Regional Development Authority it was drilled into me that the Shannon region was not in competition with Tipperary or Dublin but with regions in the Philippines and elsewhere around the world that might compete for investment by multi-nationals. Shannon Development bought in foreign companies but also pursued backward economic linkages supplying services to these within the regional economy. The new university in Limerick where I studied had been created as part of this infrastructure.

During the 1990s, Ireland cut taxes, attracted huge amounts of foreign investment and underwent an economic boom that leapfrogged it towards the top of the European income league. There was much more here, according to O'Riain in *The Politics of High Tech Growth*, than a simple story of neo-liberal globalisation. For all that foreign investors paid little tax and expropriated their profits elsewhere, such investment had grown enormously by the 1990s when being in English-speaking low corporation tax Ireland granted access to the Single European Market. Also, such investment was no longer limited to low-skilled production but increasingly involved high-tech industries that could draw on a well-educated population, state-fostered industrial innovation with some focus on research and wage restraint brokered by social partnership. Supply chain clusters of indigenous firms developed around Irish-based pharmaceutical and software companies but also within financial services. But foreign investment was only part of the story. From the 1980s the political centre of gravity of the Irish developmental project was a system of corporatist partnership. The Celtic Tiger also grew out of an expanded public sector and a dense network of institutions of 'social partnership' extending across almost all spheres of the political economy and integrating local actors, state agencies and European Union programmes.

The thesis of *The Rise and Fall of Ireland's Celtic Tiger* is that economic growth during the 1990s was not due to a convergence on market-led orthodoxy, but a partial move towards a European-style combination of industrial policy, social investment and social partnership. In the 2000s this dynamic was derailed by the financialisation of the economy, which was facilitated by economic and monetary union and the financial liberalisation of Europe. National political compromises built this 'financialisation' into the structure of public finances. The term refers to the growing accumulation of power and percentage of profits within the economy accruing to the banks and other financial institutions as distinct from producers of goods and other kinds of services.

What the growing financialisation of the Irish economy meant in sociological terms according to O'Riain, drawing on the work of Karl Polanyi, was dominance of financial markets over the social structures within which these were embedded. It was not just that investment in commercial and residential real estate became detached from economic demand for such property. A new 'rationality' prevailed where it appeared reasonable for banks to borrow from other banks to invest in the property bubble. On top of this the financialisation of the European economy resulted from the creation of the euro and EU-wide capital market integration. Irish banks collapsed owing money to German banks whose lending was predicated on the same rationality.

The property and credit bubble was already deflating from 2007 onwards, but the international crisis of 2008 produced a particularly dramatic crash in Ireland's economy. The financial crisis resulted from an unholy combination of property speculation by developers, reckless lending by bankers and a lack of governmental oversight and regulation. This created a property and banking bubble that brought the Irish economy to its knees when the international financial system ran into trouble in 2008. The liabilities of the banks were guaranteed by the Irish State in 2008 and developer loans and assets were taken under state management. A fiscal crisis mushroomed as the public finances were burdened with the cost of bailing out failing banks, but also with a growing deficit as tax revenues associated with the bubble collapsed.

By relying so heavily on property taxes the state had a vested interest in property market inflation. The collapse of state revenues triggered austerity policies. On top of this an economic crisis was triggered when investment and domestic demand collapsed. This in turn fuelled a social crisis of negative equity and mortgage arrears, cutbacks in public services, a huge rise in unemployment and the return of large-scale emigration. And on top of this again Ireland experienced a reputational crisis, evident in the reluctance of international lenders to finance the government debt culminating in an EU–IMF bailout in November 2010.

O'Riain's broad analysis of Irish underdevelopment, the boom period and the subsequent bust focuses throughout on the structure of institutions and the shifting liberal, corporatist and clientelist political contexts within which these operated. Ireland's historic underdevelopment had been underpinned, he argues, by liberal post-colonial institutions that did not prove up to the task of promoting economic development but also by the influence of clientelist politics. During the 1990s, corporatism appeared to offer a way forward 'as much for its institutional innovations as in its economics'. O'Riain argues that institutional innovation during that decade was genuine for all that these institutions subsequently failed to provide the necessary accountability when: 'the 2000s saw the resurgence of the combination of liberalism and clientelism in a new form'. In this context the 'property and banking "growth machine" drove many of the key economic decisions while corporatism was hollowed out in part to become a narrow form of political exchange in an increasingly speculative economy'.[13]

Notes

Review of Sean O'Riain, *The Rise and Fall of Ireland's Celtic Tiger: Liberalism, Boom and Bust* (Cambridge: Cambridge University Press, 2014). Previously published in *The Irish Journal of Sociology*, 22.1 (2014), 159–164.

1 Fintan O'Toole, *Ship of Fools: How Stupidity and Corruption Sunk the Celtic Tiger* (London: Faber and Faber, 2009).
2 O'Riain, *Rise and Fall*, p. 171.
3 O'Riain, *Rise and Fall*, p. 114.
4 O'Riain, *Rise and Fall*, pp. 9–10.
5 John Mitchel, *The Last Conquest of Ireland (Perhaps)* (Dublin: University College Dublin Press, [1871] 2005).
6 Richard Bellamy, *Victorian Liberalism: Nineteenth Century Political Thought and Practice* (London: Routledge, 1990), p. 2.
7 John Breuilly, *Labour and Liberalism in Nineteenth-Century Europe: Essays in Comparative History* (Manchester: Manchester University Press, 1994), p. 234.

8 Robert Skidelsky, *John Maynard Keynes: The Economist As Saviour 1920–1937* (London: Macmillan, 1992), p. 479.
9 Kieran Allen, *The Celtic Tiger: The Myth of Social Partnership in Ireland* (Manchester: Manchester University Press, 2000), p. 59.
10 O'Riain, *Rise and Fall*, p. 233.
11 Sean O'Riain, *The Politics of High-Tech Growth: Developmental Network States in the Global Economy* (Cambridge: Cambridge University Press, 2004), p. 5.
12 O'Riain, *Politics of High-Tech Growth*, p. 39.
13 O'Riain, *Rise and Fall*, p. 233.

17

Immigration, the Celtic Tiger and the economic crisis

One of the legacies of the Celtic Tiger period of rapid economic growth has been the transformation of the Republic of Ireland (hereafter Ireland) into a multi-ethnic society with a large permanent immigrant population. The 2006 census identified 419,733 non-Irish citizens as living in the country. By 2011, when the next census was taken, this number had risen to 544,357. Ireland's immigrant population seemed to have increased during the economic crisis. In fact it peaked in 2008 at over 575,000, or 12.8 per cent of the total population. It then declined a little during the economic crisis to 550,400 in 2010 but rose to 564,300 by 2014. Some 259,900 migrants arrived in Ireland during the years 2007 and 2008, but from 2009 the number of newcomers went into steep decline. This bottomed out in 2010 at around 41,000 and rose somewhat in the years that followed. Unemployment levels during the boom averaged at around 4 per cent. By July 2008 the unemployment level had risen to 6.5 per cent, by July 2012 to 14.8 per cent. Then 2009 witnessed a huge rise in emigration. Out of a total of 72,000 almost three-quarters (73.3 per cent) were migrants, and of those who left Ireland in 2009 just over a quarter (26.7 per cent) were Irish citizens. This ratio soon changed; of the 69,200 who left in 2009 some 41.8 per cent were Irish. In both 2011 and 2012 more than half of those who emigrated (52.1 per cent and 53.4 per cent) were Irish citizens. In all some 358,100 departed from Ireland between 2008 and 2012. Of these around 149,700 were Irish, 20,900 of those who left had come from outside the EU and about 187,500 came from EU member states.[1] Migration trends were much more complex than this brief summary suggests. For example, some of the Irish who 'emigrated' did so on short-term work holiday visas to Australia. Immigration figures included returning Irish citizens but also new non-Irish citizen immigrants.[2]

Political responses to Ireland's economic crisis included a change of government, sweeping austerity measures and, for a period of time, an inchoate sense that Ireland faced some kind of existential crisis. This was variously expressed as national self-excoriation, numbed quiescence and, as austerity measures bit, through anti-establishment protest politics. What became perhaps the dominant critique was captured by Fintan O'Toole in his 2009 bestseller polemic *Ship of Fools: How Stupidity and Corruption Sank the Celtic Tiger*.[3] According to the standard mantra, Ireland had experienced a banking crisis, a crisis in the public finances, an economic crisis, a social crisis caused by mass unemployment and a reputational crisis. Fianna Fáil was blamed by voters for the economic crisis and lost most of its parliamentary seats in the 2011 election. The subsequent Fine Gael and Labour Party coalition government continued the austerity measures of the previous government. All sorts of institutional reforms were promised before the 2011 election but these commitments were mostly abandoned. The economic crisis triggered huge increases in unemployment and emigration, the collapse of house prices and the spectre of repossessions for those who fell behind in their mortgage payments, tax increases and pay cuts for those still employed, swinging cuts to public services like education and healthcare and incalculable feelings of anxiety, trauma and anger.

Irish politics displayed little of the anti-immigrant populism that played out in the political mainstream of some other European Union countries. Ireland had no history of anti-immigrant political parties akin to France's Front Nationale. Despite Ireland's loss of economic sovereignty under the International Monetary Fund (IMF) / European Union(EU) / European Central Bank troika, efforts to launch a similar political party in Ireland were belated and unsuccessful. The manifesto of the so-called National Independence Party (NIP) included a commitment to leave the euro and turn away economic migrants. A February 2014 interview in *Metro Éireann*, the main immigrant newspaper, with its founder saw no cause for alarm. It was published under a subheading which read: 'One thing is for sure: Peter O'Loughlin is no Nigel Farage.' There was little to indicate, according to Piaras Mac Éinrí, a migration expert at University College Cork, that the NIP would not go the same way as the Immigration Control Platform, which had been set up more than a decade earlier and was still 'very little more than a website'. The main headline of the article was 'New anti-immigrant party hopes to tap into general malaise', to which might be added: 'and fails to do so'.[4]

However, attitudes towards immigrants were possibly more negative in 2008 compared to previous years and by 2010 had become more negative still. In 2002 around 5 per cent of the population opposed immigration of any kind. By 2010, according to the same European Social Survey data sources, the percentage had risen, depending on the question asked, to just under 20 per cent (opposition to any immigration by ethnically different migrants) or just over 20 per cent (opposition to any immigration from poorer non-EU countries).[5] Different surveys asking such questions have produced quite different results, but all of these suggest that there were more than enough anti-immigrant Irish to sustain some kind of anti-immigrant political movement or to tempt some mainstream politicians into making some anti-immigrant populist gestures. *Hidden Messages, Overt Agendas*, a 2010 NGO analysis of political responses to immigration during the first two years of the economic crisis, found no smoking gun. It would be fair to say that a keep-calm-and-carry-on political correctness prevailed within mainstream political discourse, at least on the surface.[6] Cack-handed attempts at dog whistle politics by a few minor figures were censured or widely criticised. Immigration remained off the political radar for the most part during the post-2008 economic crisis.

Immigrants and the Celtic Tiger

During the late 1990s, during Ireland's one and only immigration crisis, at least in terms of how this was portrayed, some media accounts claimed that Ireland was being 'swamped' by asylum seekers. No newspaper headlines proclaimed anything of the kind in response to the subsequent arrival of far greater numbers of labour migrants. In Ireland as elsewhere in Fortress Europe, a raft of legislation did much to criminalise and make dangerous the act of seeking asylum. Behind the scenes the Department of Justice sought to undermine and then remove the constitutional right of the Irish-born children of immigrants to citizenship, interpreted by the High Court from 1987 as a right to remain in the state with their families. The 1987 ruling had allowed for the regularisation of a significant number of asylum seekers and other immigrants with Irish-born children. A policy decision was made to begin to refuse residency status to asylum-seeker families with Irish-born children in the knowledge that this would trigger a further test case in the Supreme Court.[7] In April 2002 the 1987 ruling was overturned in the High Court (*Lobe v. Minister of Justice*). On 23 January 2003 the Supreme Court upheld this ruling, in essence holding that the Irish citizen child of non-citizens could be deported with its parents unless the non-citizen parent agreed to be deported without their child. This ruling was effectively superseded by the outcome of the June 2004 Referendum on Citizenship that removed the existing birthright to citizenship from the Irish-born children of non-citizens.

There were three elements to Ireland's 2004 immigration policy settlement: the Citizenship Referendum, the removal of visa criteria from migrants from the new EU member states and the introduction of legislation that prohibited both migrants and returning Irish citizens from claiming social-security benefits on arrival. The Citizenship Referendum was unusual in that there had been no earlier political demand for one, not from any political party or interest group. Most referenda in Ireland were held only after protracted campaigns in support of these were acceded to by the government of the day, and these have often tended to be close-run things. The government's campaign for 'common-sense citizenship' was stoked by claims made by the then Minister of Justice Michael McDowell that African women were exploiting the maternity hospitals.[8] How and to what extent this influenced the 79.8 per cent who voted yes in the 2004 Referendum was unclear.[9] European Social Survey data for 2002 suggested that just 5 per cent of the population were very strongly opposed to immigration.[10] Irish National Election Survey data put this percentage far higher. Surveys from 2004 found that 33.2 per cent 'strongly agreed' with the statement 'there should be very strong limits to the numbers of immigrants coming to Ireland'.[11] What is clear is that the cognitive 'us' versus 'them' distinctions between Irish nationals and so-called 'non-nationals' emphasised by the 'common-sense citizenship' camp struck a chord with voters. A greater percentage of the Irish electorate voted to remove the citizenship birthright than voted against the government that had led Ireland into the crash.

For all that, the nationalism that objected to Irish-born children of immigrants automatically becoming Irish citizens was a kind that appeared to be lightly worn. According to Sinisa Malesevic, Irish nationalism is significantly more dominant and influential now than it was in those insular post-independence decades when nationalist rhetoric appeared more blatant. Just because it shouted louder did not mean this earlier form of nationalism was stronger.[12]

So how then might Irish nationalism be stronger now? The argument turns on the concept of 'banal nationalism' coined by Michael Billig to refer to the ways in which we are reminded on a daily basis, often subliminally, that we belong to some or other nation. It refers to everyday expressions of nationalism in national sports like hurling in the Irish case, or in Irish rugby teams which, when they participate in international tournaments, sing a specially composed song, 'Ireland's Call' beforehand. Other examples include distinctions made by the national media between domestic and international news and weather reports that focus mostly on the territory of the Irish nation-state.[13] Beyond this, according to Malesevic, the infrastructure of the Irish state has dramatically thickened over time in areas such as education and social policy. All of this facilitates a deeper ideological penetration of nationalist ideas and practices.[14] A combination of banal nationalism and statist nation-building infrastructure has arguably worked to reinforce a sense of what Anderson calls a 'deep horizontal comradeship' amongst the citizens of the Irish state.[15] Voters in the Referendum inevitably drew on their own strong preconceptions of what it was to be Irish.[16] They did not need to reach for actual blood and soil justifications for their beliefs in national distinctiveness in order to draw such conclusions. Almost 80 per cent of those who voted in the Referendum apparently declared to immigrants: 'we're Irish; you are not'.

Yet also in 2004, in what turned out to be a radical act of social engineering, Ireland (alongside the UK and Sweden) became one of just three countries that did not impose any restrictions upon the free movement of workers from the new East European EU member states. The UK counted 290,000 arrivals between May 2004 and September 2005. Ireland, with less than one tenth of its population, issued about 160,000 new social-security numbers between May 2004 and November 2005: some 86,900 to Polish migrants, 29,500 to Lithuanians, 14,600 to Latvians and 29,900 to those from other new EU member states. The 2006 census identified some 610,000 people, or 14.7 per cent of the total population (4,239,848), as born outside the state and approximately 10 per cent of the total population as 'non-Irish nationals'. Simultaneously the 2004 Social Welfare (Miscellaneous Provisions) Act restricted the entitlements of 'non-nationals' but also Irish citizens who had lived outside the state by introducing a habitual residency condition. People who moved to Ireland, including Irish citizens who had lived abroad, were prevented from claiming certain state benefits on arrival. Again, there had been no political pressure to introduce such legislation. Under the terms of the 2004 settlement Ireland unequivocally welcomed large-scale labour immigration but sought to control membership of the Irish nation.

Post-2004 political rhetoric and policy debates talked up the economic benefits of immigration. Within the latter the national interest and economic growth were portrayed as one and the same. At a time when some other European countries were having tortured deliberations about migrant integration and national identity, integration in the Irish case was blithely defined as participation in the labour market. For example, *Managing Migration*, a 2006 report by the National Economic and Social Council, a social partnership forum that represented the trade unions, employers and the state, credited the persistence of economic growth to ongoing immigration.[17] It described the incoming flow of immigrants as the fuel that kept the Celtic Tiger going. It cited data indicating that Ireland came second only to Canada in attracting the best-educated immigrants of all OECD countries.[18] The social partnership consensus was that large-scale immigration was in the national interest and this in turn was to be exclusively defined in terms of economic growth.[19] Similar arguments were made in the sole major report setting out integration policy, *Migration Nation* (2008), published around this time. Here, immigration was presented as a proof that the economic nation-building project instigated by Sean Lemass fifty years earlier had been a success.[20]

Immigration and the economic crisis

Following the 2007 general election, the Fianna Fáil and Green Party government appointed a Minister of State for Integration Policy. The first post-holder, Conor Lenihan, struck a tone of optimistic inclusivity.[21] However, few concrete actions were funded other than already-existing English language teaching posts in primary schools. Immigrants were to be benignly left to their own devices and to the providence of market forces. *Migration Nation* cited off-the-shelf EU common basic principles of integration but was vague when it came to policy commitments. Ireland came to lag behind many countries on many indicators of integration: access to education, rights to family re-unification and even rights to participate fully in the labour market, that sphere where the politicians and bureaucrats in charge of Ireland PLC envisaged integration as taking place, if they thought of it at all. In most of these domains there was, simply put, less political commitment to integration and less resources put in to integration measures than in many other EU countries.[22]

Yet, there was some emphasis on political integration that focused on the pre-existing right of non-Irish citizen residents to vote in local government elections. Two former asylum seekers were elected as town councillors in 2004 in Ennis and Portlaoise. In the run-up to the May 2009 local government election voter campaigns targeted at immigrants received some state funding. By the time of this election the economic crisis was well under way. Yet, several political parties made unprecedented efforts to reach out to prospective immigrant supporters. For example, Fianna Fáil and Fine Gael, then the two largest political parties, hired integration officers (both were Polish) and sought to attract members from immigrant communities, and these and other political parties selected a number candidates of African and East European origin.[23] In the weeks prior to the elections Fianna Fáil government ministers campaigned on behalf of non-citizen immigrant candidates. For example, Brian Lenihan, the beleaguered Minister of Finance, took time out from trying to deal with the economic meltdown to address a public meeting in Mulhuddart on behalf of Fianna Fáil candidate Idowu Olafimihan, who stood unsuccessfully for election in a Dublin West ward.[24]

The aforementioned 2010 report, *Hidden Messages, Overt Agendas*, commissioned by the Migrant Rights Centre Ireland (MRCI) and written by Niall Crowley, former Director of the Equality Authority, described statements by Irish politicians as typically 'politically correct' but argued that this masked an undercurrent of antipathy towards unwanted immigrants.[25] The MRCI was the main NGO advocating on behalf of vulnerable and exploited migrants.[26] Crowley's analysis was that government ministers made statements that were carefully positive about the valuable presence and contribution of migrant workers and their families in Ireland whilst, simultaneously, harsh restrictions on unwanted migrants were being mooted.[27] For example, Conor Lenihan's January 2009 Chinese New Year press release noted that the number of work permits issued to Chinese people had decreased from 1,188 in 2007 to 661 in 2008, adding that: 'While the number of Chinese people coming to our shores has greatly decreased, the Chinese remain a valued part of our society.'[28]

Somewhat similarly an April 2009 speech by Mary Coughlan, Minister for Enterprise, Trade and Employment, announced new regulations that would restrict work permit numbers whilst also declaring that: 'Our immigrant population have and continue to make a significant contribution to our economy and to society as a whole here in Ireland.'[29] Politicians kept up the warm words but implied that colder economic realities held sway. But even as unemployment and emigration rapidly rose, the business case for immigration was still emphasised. According to John Curran, who had replaced Lenihan as integration minister, in a 2009 speech: 'It is important that, despite the economic downturn, we acknowledge that our economy will continue to attract non-Irish national workers.'[30] Some months earlier, in January 2009, British Prime Minister Gordon Brown made a speech promising British jobs for British workers. No major Irish politician made any equivalent speech.

Yet, behind the scenes there was considerable ambivalence towards migrants who had lost their toehold in the economy. Where this seems to have most forcefully found expression was in hostility to certain kinds of long-term residents becoming Irish citizens. Here, to no little extent, the contradictions between the 2004 Referendum result and dominant economic doctrine played out. Notwithstanding a mood of apparent political openness during the 2009 elections and in speeches on immigration the Fianna Fáil / Green Party government simultaneously sanctioned draconian barriers against migrants seeking to become Irish citizens. In 2009 some 47 per cent of all applications for citizenship were turned down under ministerial discretion. By comparison, equivalent rates of refusal of long-term residents seeking naturalisation in the United Kingdom and Australia for the same period were just 9 per cent and in Canada just 3 per cent. *Metro Éireann* reported that the Minister for Justice Dermot Ahern 'had not ruled-out' disqualifying citizenship applicants who had become unemployed or were claiming social welfare despite evidence that discrimination on such grounds was in fact widespread.[31] Even minor driving offences were being cited by Department of Justice officials as reasons for turning down citizenship applications.[32]

The apparent unwillingness to give citizenship to immigrants who had experienced unemployment coincided with rising levels of unemployment in general. Immigrant unemployment levels reached more than 18 per cent compared to more than 14 per cent for the country as a whole. In February 2009, Mary Hanafin, the Fianna Fáil Minister for Social and Family Affairs, acknowledged the need to contest potential resentment towards migrants as unemployment rose: 'We've all heard that they are taking our jobs, that they're all scamming the welfare – it's not true.'[33] From the perspective of NGOs working to support unemployed immigrants the problem was that her department was creatively invoking the habitual residence condition in order to deny some of these who had lived in Ireland for several years access to social protection. Research on the treatment of migrants seeking to claim benefits identified 'adversarial approaches, reliance on speculation and the use of inappropriate, aggressive and racist language' amongst officials who assessed their claims.[34]

However, the economic crisis period also witnessed significant improvements in the residency entitlements of vulnerable and irregular migrants. A number of articles in *Metro Éireann* focused on the plight of an estimated 30,000 undocumented migrants, campaigns by NGOs on their behalf and the relative success of these campaigns. In 2009 the government suggested that it would deport non-EU migrants who had become unemployed but, following a campaign by the MRCI, a proposed three-month leeway period was increased to six months. At the same time new rules granted permanent residency status to non-EU migrants who had lived in Ireland for five years under the work permit system.[35]

Also in 2009 the government introduced a four-month 'bridging visa' for foreign nationals who had become undocumented because of exploitation so that they could seek legitimate employment, or to obtain a work permit if they were already employed. The MRCI's assessment was that the government was 'on the right path towards fixing problems experienced by vulnerable migrants in the work permit system'.[36] The context here was some improvement from a low base. Of thirty-one countries whose integration policies were compared on the Migrant Integration Policy index for 2011, Ireland had the meanest system of family re-unification rights for non-EU migrants on renewable work visas.[37] During the economic crisis government policy towards non-EU migrants had two elements. It became harder for new non-EU migrants to obtain visas to work in Ireland, but the rules became more flexible for those already living in Ireland who had become unemployed. In all, 20,900 non-EU migrants left Ireland between 2008 and 2012. But the overall reduction in the numbers of those with work visas (133,232 in 2010, 128,104 in 2011 and 120,281 in 2012) was small, and the totals may in fact have increased if the numbers of non-EU origin residents who became Irish citizens are taken into account.[38]

In March 2009 the National Consultative Committee on Racism and Interculturalism, the main state agency responsible for monitoring and advising government on racism, was shut down. In May 2010 *Metro Éireann* published an account of an interview with Mary White, the third integration minister in as many years, under the headline 'There's no black or white Ireland', which was an excerpt from the following quotation:

> I want to make sure that this is a comfortable country in which to live and do business, whether you're Irish or new Irish. I've often said in the past couple of weeks that there is no black Ireland or white Ireland – there is Ireland. There is no old Ireland or new Ireland, there is Ireland, our country. And I want to make sure that everyone who is here can experience a sense of freedom, of participating in our communities right around the country.

In response to a follow-up question the minister stated that racism was not a significant problem in Ireland.[39] However, anecdotal evidence suggested a rise of racism during the economic crisis.[40] Research reports documenting harrowing experiences of racism received only fleeting media coverage.[41] A March 2011 article in *Metro Éireann* argued that racism had fallen far off Ireland's political agenda.[42] Media and political debate fixated on the surface discourses only. A few cases where minor politicians made inappropriate comments received considerable media attention. Most notably, in 2011 the Fine Gael Mayor of Naas in County Kildare lost the party whip and was forced to resign after he stated that he would no longer represent (lobby on behalf of) any of his Nigerian constituents. In an email he wrote that he found most Africans who visited his constituency office to be 'very demanding' and 'very quick to play the race card if you disagreed with their point of view'. How matters played out might be gleaned from the following sequence of newspaper headlines: '"Controversy Will not Rest" Until Scully Quits Council Says Critic',[43] 'When Will Fine Gael Expel Cllr Scully?'[44] and '"Racist Remarks" Ex-mayor Loses Job'.[45] Scully resigned, was expelled from Fine Gael and was readmitted to the party two years later. The pageant followed the well-worn contours of the naughty public figure shuffle: outcry, penitence and rehabilitation. None of this meant that racism in Irish society was taken seriously by politicans.

It proved much easier to become an Irish citizen during the economic crisis than during the Celtic Tiger era. Between 1 January 2009 and 31 May 2013, 63,900 applications for naturalisation were approved, most of these following the 2011 change of government. The refusal rate was still high by international standards. During the same period, 14,700 or 18.7 per cent were refused, but it seems most of these refusals pre-dated the 2011 election.[46] Accounts of large naturalisation ceremonies presided over by the Taoiseach or a senior government minister featured regularly in *Metro Éireann*.[47] The positive rhetoric that characterised these ceremonies is worth quoting:

> Addressing some of the 2,250 new Irish citizens from 110 countries who pledged their allegiance to the Irish State over two days at special ceremonies in Dublin recently, Taoiseach Enda Kenny also told them to make Ireland their proud home.
>
> 'As citizens of this country, you are coming "home"', he said. 'Today you begin to write your own chapters of Ireland's history. Your story will become Ireland's story. Since you arrived on these shores, you have enriched your communities, enhanced your workplaces, bringing new light, new depth, a new sense of imagining, to what it means to be a citizen of Ireland in the 21st century.'[48]

A March 2013 article in *Metro Éireann* reported that Ceemex, an immigration law firm which represented African families with Irish-born children, had closed down because business had fallen off. The practice had won a landmark case that led to the granting of residency status to 17,000 parents of Irish-born children under the 2005 Irish Born Child Scheme.[49] Many of these were black Africans who began their lives in Ireland as asylum seekers. For example, 1,204 Nigerians became Irish citizens in 2011, 5,702 in 2012.[50] They had been unwelcome guests of the Irish nation during the Celtic Tiger years. Now in the midst of an economic crisis they were welcomed as never before. An article in *Metro Éireann* calculated that the Irish state received some 50 million euros in fees from naturalisation and long-term residency fees charged from the beginning of 2009 to the end of 2013.[51] And whilst one can be sure that this financial upside was mentioned at some or other high-level meeting, the stark contrast with the previous apparently calculated efforts to turn down as many as possible cannot be denied. Much of the credit was owed to Alan Shatter, the Minister of Justice of the new government – he received the *Africa World* newspaper's man of the year award for 2012 for, in effect, wielding his discretionary power over citizenship applications differently from his predecessors – and to the Immigrant Council of Ireland which had long campaigned for reform in the naturalisation process. In 2013, 24,263 (97.6%) of the applications for naturalisation considered were granted; just 716 (2.4%) were refused. Of those who became Irish citizens that year 5,792 were immigrants from Nigeria, 3,009 were from India, 2,486 were from the Philippines, 1,807 were from Pakistan and 695 were from the Ukraine.[52]

The 'new Irish' and the people of Ireland

Much of the academic writing on immigration and diversity on the Irish case, including some of my own, draws attention to experiences of racism, discrimination and inequality, and to complacency in addressing these.[53] The 2004 Citizenship Referendum seemed to defensively define Irishness according to a nineteenth-century ethno-nationalist formula. No doubt racism and xenophobia might explain some proportion of votes in favour of what the Referendum proposed. The outcome of the Referendum indicates that nationalism still matters hugely. The pastel-coloured posters of the 'common-sense citizenship' campaign did not have to spell out who was Irish and who was not. These drew on an accumulated bank of shared symbolisms and accreted meanings that constitute banal nationalism. A key issue for the future will be how and to what extent Irishness becomes symbolically redefined.

One of the phrases used to describe immigrants in general has been the 'new Irish'. It is perhaps more accurate to describe those who have taken out Irish citizenship as such. These 'new Irish' now constitute a few per cent of Irish citizens. They predominately come from countries outside of the EU. Irish citizenship offers them practical protections that immigrants from EU countries do not need because of treaties that permit them to travel freely, to work without restriction and to access social services on the same basis as citizens. Most of these new Irish are 'black'. There has been no opposition to post-2011 efforts aimed at folding such immigrants into the Irish nation. However, most of Ireland's immigrant population comes from countries that joined the EU in 2004. Very few of these have since sought to become Irish citizens. Of these an estimated 150,000 Poles now constitute Ireland's largest immigrant community. They are not, by any definition, members of the Irish nation but they are members of Irish society.

Ireland in the second decade of the twenty-first century is in the midst of high-profile commemorations of the centenary of the events that led to Irish independence. Irish society has changed utterly, the composition of the Irish nation has changed a bit, but the symbolism of banal nationalism seems not to have changed much yet. Enda Kenny's declaration that new citizens will write new chapters of Irish story is apposite. Ireland's banal nationalism will most probably be partially reconstituted over time. An accretion of stories, symbols and images attesting to the diversity of Ireland will build up over time. But other stories of racism, discrimination and hardship are likely to be only welcomed in comfortable retrospect.

If the Irish state appeared more benign in its responses to immigrants during the economic crisis than during the boom it was also the case that the heavy lifting of installing a coercive apparatus to repel asylum seekers, regulate citizenship and toughen up border controls had been undertaken by previous governments and by the European Union. At the time of writing – in May 2015 – Fortress Europe, in which Ireland is complicit, bears responsibility for unprecedented numbers of refugee deaths in the Mediterranean. There are no guarantees that immigration will not become politicised at some stage in the future if Ireland's current appearance of tolerance is tested to any great extent.

Notes

This chapter was previously published as Bryan Fanning, 'Immigration, the Celtic Tiger and the Economic Crisis', *Irish Studies Review* (2016), available online November 2015. DOI: 10.1080/0970882.2015.1112995

1 For a demographic overview see Mary Gilmartin, *The Changing Landscape of Irish Migration 2000–2012*, NIRSA Working Paper No.69 (Maynooth: NIRSA, 2012), p. 10.
2 Philip J. O'Connell and Corona Joyce, *International Migration in Ireland, 2014* (Dublin: Geary Institute for Public Policy), p. 27.
3 Fintan O'Toole, *Ship of Fools: How Stupidity and Corruption Sank the Celtic Tiger* (London: Faber and Faber, 2009), p. 17.

4 'New Anti-immigrant Party Hopes to Tap into General Malaise', *Metro Éireann*, 1 February 2014.

5 Frances McGinnity, Emma Quinn, Gillian Kingston and Phillip O'Connell, *Annual Monitoring Report on Integration: 2012* (Dublin: Integration Centre/Economic and Social Research Institute, 2012), pp. 65–66.

6 Niall Crowley, *Hidden Messages, Overt Agendas* (Dublin: Migrant Rights Centre Ireland, 2010).

7 Siobhán Mullaly, 'Children, Citizenship and Constitutional Change', in Bryan Fanning (ed.), *Immigration and Social Change in the Republic of Ireland* (Manchester: Manchester University Press, 2007), pp. 31–37.

8 Bryan Fanning and Fidele Mutwarasibo, 'Nationals/Non-nationals: Immigration, Citizenship and Politics in the Republic of Ireland', *Ethnic and Racial Studies*, 30.4 (2007), 439–460, p. 450.

9 See Eoin O'Malley, 'Why Is There No Radical Right Party in Ireland?', *West European Politics*, 31.5 (2008), 960–977, and Steve Garner, 'Ireland and Immigration: Explaining the Absence of the Far Right', *Patterns of Prejudice*, 41.2 (2007), 109–130.

10 McGinnity et al., *Annual Monitoring Report*, pp. 65–66.

11 Michael Marsh and Richard Sinnott, *Irish National Election Survey (INES) 2002–2007: Data Description and Documentation* (Dublin: Trinity College Dublin and University College Dublin, 2009), p. 138 http://issda.ucd.ie/documentation/codebook_26_05_2009.pdf.

12 Sinisa Malesevic, 'Irishness and Nationalisms', in Tom Inglis (ed.), *Are the Irish Different?* (Manchester: Manchester University Press, 2014), p. 17.

13 Michael Billig, *Banal Nationalism* (London: Sage, 1995).

14 Malesevic, 'Irishness and Nationalisms', p. 19.

15 Benedict Anderson, *Imagined Communities: Reflections on the Origins and Spread of Nationalism* (London: Verso, [1983] 2006) quoted in Malesevic, 'Irishness and Nationalisms', p. 19.

16 Andrew Thompson, 'Nations, National Identities and Human Agency: Putting People Back into Nations', *The Sociological Review*, 49.1 (2001), pp. 18–32.

17 National Economic and Social Forum, *Managing Migration in Ireland: A Social and Economic Analysis* (Dublin: Stationery Office, 2006), p. 6.

18 National Economic and Social Forum, *Managing Migration*, p. 96.

19 National Economic and Social Forum, *Managing Migration*, p. 148.

20 Office of the Minister of Integration, *Migration Nation: Statement in Integration Strategy and Diversity Management* (Dublin: Stationery Office, 2008), p. 8.

21 'Lenihan Gets Nigerian Advisor', *Metro Éireann*, 26 June 2008.

22 For a comparative analysis see Thomas Huddleston, Jan Niessen, Eadaoin Ni Chaoimh and Emile White, *Migration Integration Policy Index: 2011* (Brussels: British Council/Migration Policy Group, 2011).

23 Bryan Fanning, Kevin Howard and Neil O'Boyle, 'Immigrant Candidates and Politics in the Republic of Ireland: Racialization, Ethnic Nepotism or Localism?', *Nationalism and Ethnic Politics*, 16.3 (2011), 420–442.

24 Chinedu Onyejelem, 'Iwodu Gets a Boost from FF Minister', *Metro Éireann*, 7 May 2009.

25 Niall Crowley, *Hidden Messages, Overt Agendas* (Dublin: Migrant Rights Centre Ireland, 2010).

26 For case studies on the experiences of vulnerable migrants see reports by the Migrant Rights Centre Ireland www.mrci.ie.

27 Crowley, *Hidden Messages, Overt Agendas*, p. 11.

28 'Little Joy for Chinese Seeking Irish Work Permits', *Metro Éireann*, 29 January 2009.

29 Quoted in Crowley, *Hidden Messages, Overt Agendas*, p. 11.

30 Quoted in Crowley, *Hidden Messages, Overt Agendas*, p. 12.

31 Catherine O'Reilly, 'Citizenship Risk for Jobless Migrants', *Metro Éireann*, 25 June 2009.

32 Catherine O'Reilly, 'Road to Nowhere: Dept Admits Drivers Penalty Points Count Against Citizenship Applications', *Metro Éireann*, 11 November 2009.

33 Quoted in Crowley, *Hidden Messages, Overt Agendas*, p. 11.

34 Catherine Reilly, 'Report Highlights Barriers to Welfare Faced by Immigrants', *Metro Éireann*, 1 March 2012.

35 'New Rules for Redundant Migrants', *Metro Éireann*, 3 September 2009; 'Gov Grants Reprieve for Undocumented Migrants', *Metro Éireann*, 17 September 2009.

36 Chinedu Onyejelem, 'Govt Lifts Work Restrictions on Bulgarian, Romanian Nationals', *Metro Éireann*, 1 August 2012.

37 Mipex, *Migration Integration Policy Index* III (Brussels: MIPEX/British Council, 2011), pp. 106–110.

38 McGinnity et al., *Annual Monitoring Report*, p. 45.

39 Catherine O'Reilly, 'There's No Black or White Ireland', *Metro Éireann*, 27 May 2010.

40 Catherine O'Reilly, 'Racism Growing Nationwide Says Prominent Immigrant', *Metro Éireann*, 15 August 2012.

41 Bryan Fanning, Brian Kiloran and Saorlaith Ní Bhroin, *Taking Racism Seriously: Migrants' Experience of Violence, Harassment and Anti-social Behaviour in the Dublin Area* (Dublin: Immigrant Council of Ireland, 2011).

42 'Racism has Fallen Off Ireland's Political Agenda', *Metro Éireann*, 1 March 2011.

43 '"Controversy Will Not Rest" Until Scully Quits Council Says Critic', *Metro Éireann*, 1 December 2011.

44 Rashid Butt, 'When Will Fine Gael Expel Cllr Scully?', *Metro Éireann*, 15 December 2011.

45 '"Racist Remarks" Ex-mayor Loses FG Party Whip', *Metro Éireann*, 1 March 2012.

46 'Citizenship Stats Show 14,000 Refusals in 4 years', *Metro Éireann*, 1 July 2013.

47 Nicole Antoine, 'New Citizens Express their Delight at Ireland's Largest Oath Ceremony', *Metro Éireann*, 15 July 2013.

48 Chinedu Onyejelem, 'Immigration: Welcomes and Goodbyes – Enda Praises New Citizens', *Metro Éireann*, 15 February 2012.
49 Catherine O'Reilly, 'Ceemex Bows Out After More Than 10 Years at Forefront of Immigration Law', *Metro Éireann*, 6 March 2013.
50 McGinnity et al., *Annual Monitoring Report*, p. 47.
51 Chinedu Onyejelem, 'Govt Nets €50m in 5 Years from Citizenship Fees', *Metro Éireann*, 1 August 2013.
52 Irish Naturalisation and Immigration Service (November 2014). See O'Connell and Joyce, *International Migration in Ireland, 2014*, p. 49.
53 Bryan Fanning, *Racism and Social Change in the Republic of Ireland*, 2nd edition (Manchester: Manchester University Press, 2012).

18

The future of Irish identity

James Joyce had Leopold Bloom, his fictional Irish Jew protagonist of *Ulysses*, define a nation as the same people living in the same place. Thousands of pages have been written since by academics on the ambivalent place of Leopold Bloom within the Irish nation of 1904 when the novel was set. Joseph Stalin in 1913, nine years before *Ulysses* was published, offered the following definition: 'A nation is a historically constituted, stable community of people, formed on the basis of a common language, territory, economic life, and psychological make-up manifested in a common culture.'[1] Stalin concluded that because multilingual Russia did not meet all of these criteria that Russia was not a single nation – unlike Georgia, where he came from. That same year Stephen Brown, a Jesuit, published two essays – 'What is a Nation' and 'The Question of Irish Nationality' – that discussed the extent to which the Irish case fitted criteria for nationhood identified by 'anthropologists and sociologists'.[2] In essence such definitions examined how and in what contexts people might be presumed to share a particular national identity. Brown identified custom, the unwritten and traditional codes which rule the habits of people and 'by long iteration, furrows deep traits in its character' as a 'nation-building force'.[3] In this he drew heavily on Ernest Renan's classic 1882 essay *Qu'est-ce qu'une nation?*, where Renan wrote that any given nation owed its existence to 'the possession in common of a rich legacy of remembrances' and its future to an 'everyday plebiscite'.[4] Brown concluded that a nation consisted of a relatively large group living together in common territory in organised social relations held together by a peculiar kind of spiritual oneness: people who had come to think that they were the same and who lived in the same place, who shared, in effect, a national identity.

There was, Brown insisted, nothing mystic about this sense of oneness. National consciousness consisted, 'of common memories of historic things wrought in common and suffered in common in the past, and secondly the actual consent to carry on that common life, as a distinct people, master of its destinies, shaper of its future'.[5] Such consent was what Renan meant by a daily plebiscite. Along these lines Benedict Anderson has more recently influentially described nations as imagined communities (though not imaginary ones).[6] Michael Billig in *Banal Nationalism* adds that nations are unconsciously imagined as well as being the product-conscious choices or collective acts of the imagination.[7]

Whilst such writings on nationalism and national identity put limited emphasis on linguistic distinctiveness, many Irish cultural nationalists seemed to focus on little else. The early twenty-first-century Ireland that Patrick Pearse imagined in 1906 was one in which the Gaelic revival was an overwhelming all-island success. As things turned out, the Irish language remained symbolically important but it did not thrive as an indoor plant in the care of the Irish state. After independence the language became institutionalised as a compulsory school subject and a validator of Irish distinctiveness. Gaelic did not succeed in defining a distinctive Irish consciousness because not enough people spoke it, wrote in it or read it. A symposium of articles and responses to these in *Studies* in 1923, one year after independence, by champions of the restoration of Irish was blunt about the challenges.[8] 'Now after thirty years of propaganda', Osborn Bergin, one of the most eminent scholars of Gaelic, wrote, 'public opinion, the schools and the government are all on its side, yet the position of the spoken language is precarious in the extreme'.[9]

Another contributor, an Irish-speaking German Jesuit, wrote that if the language was to be rescued one of two things was needed. First would be the emergence of some literary genius who would do for Irish what Shakespeare and Dante respectively did for English and Italian. However, he noted that literary geniuses were not made to order. He neglected to mention that those at hand, Joyce and W.B. Yeats, wrote in English. The only other way, he reckoned, was through coercion. Gaelic could only be fully restored by 'the will-power of a language dictator'. But this hero or despot would be reviled in the Dáil, caricatured in the newspapers and loftily refuted in university lectures.[10]

All this suggested that wider enthusiasm for the Irish language was limited. Bergin thought that it might be possible for the Irish state to produce a standardised version of Irish out of the various existing dialects and use this in official documents, but that a commonly spoken language could not 'be made to order and suddenly imposed on the nation'.[11] Another contributor argued that the state should see to it that 'in every Irish-speaking district Irish shall be petted and English discouraged'. The petting was to be a financial one: 'parents will speak Irish to their children when Irish spells bread and butter, as English did in the past'.[12] However, he acknowledged that this policy of supporting *Gaeltacht* districts would not reverse the use of English by most of the population.

After independence the Irish language became a compulsory school subject. Since the expansion of secondary education from the late 1960s onwards most children have been taught Irish every day that they have spent at school for fourteen years but many have ended up neither fluent nor as habitual users of the language. In 1989 Údarás na Gaeltachta, the body responsible for economic and cultural development of Irish-speaking areas, claimed in television commercials that one million people spoke Irish. However, the commercials were withdrawn after a complaint about false advertising was lodged with the Advertising Standards Authority for Ireland.[13] More modest assertions predominate with annual *Seachtain na Gaeilge* (Irish-speaking week) media campaigns urging Irish people to make use of their *cúpla focal* (a couple of words), a phrase that some Irish people use self-depreciatingly to describe their lack of fluency. When Joe McHugh was appointed as junior government minister responsible for *Gaeltacht* affairs in 2014 he admitted that he was not fluent in Irish, notwithstanding fourteen years of compulsory education. In a radio interview he suggested that in this he was hardly alone: 'Obviously like a number of people we went to school, we did primary school, we did Leaving Cert and we tried to learn Irish the whole way through.'[14] Likewise, Heather Humphries, the cabinet Minister for Arts, Heritage and the Gaeltacht, to whom McHugh reported and who had overall responsibility for the 2016 centenary commemorations of the 1916 Rising, stated that she studied Irish up to Leaving Certificate standard but, because 'she did not use it, she lost it'.[15]

That such disclosures might set Patrick Pearse spinning in his grave does not detract from the symbolic significance of the Irish language. *An Gaeilge* most likely will remain part of the patina of future Irish banal nationalism. As put by Iarfhlaith Watson: 'To most Irish people the mere existence of the Irish language is a sufficient marker of distinctiveness. For them, the maintenance of the language in the Gaeltacht and its symbolic use by the state is enough.'[16] The 1960 Broadcasting Authority Act committed the national broadcaster Raidió Éireann, which became Raidió Telefís Éireann (RTÉ) in 1961, to 'national aims of restoring the Irish language and preserving and developing the national culture' but was mostly vague on the extent to which it should commit to such goals. Only one section of the Act went into specifics: advertisers who used the Irish language in their advertisements could be charged lower rates.[17] In November 1960 the first Director General of RTÉ stated at a press conference that viewership figures would determine the kinds of programmes that would be broadcast. The promotion of national identity was a secondary consideration.[18] Only a small proportion of radio and television programmes broadcast by RTÉ were in Irish. The weekly amount between 1963 and 1993 averaged between two and five hours per week with a low of as little as 35 minutes per week during the summer months, when the sole programme in Irish was a five-minute news bulletin.[19] Still, even daily exposure to small doses of Irish-language news bulletins served to reinforce a distinct sense of Irish identity.

One analysis suggests that the Irish language could only be pushed up to a certain point by a national broadcaster seeking to create a unified national audience: 'In order to retain the idea of the unity of the nation, the audience had to be assumed to be undivided, with the Irish language being pushed into a largely symbolic role, detached from everyday use (the fact that Irish was compulsory in schools but yet very few children grew up to use it illustrates this point).'[20] All-Irish language programming was only ever going to appeal to a niche audience. It was not until 1966 that an Irish-language television station was set up, and not until 1972 that the Irish state established Raidió na Gaeltachta, as a response to a linguistic minority. A 1994 study identified 2 per cent of the population as native speakers and a further 9 per cent as either fluent or 'near fluent'.[21]

One reason perhaps why the Gaelic revival stalled after 1922 was that linguistic distinctiveness was no longer functionally necessary once independence had been achieved. A comparison here might be made with the Welsh language, which has continued to play a central role in Welsh identity and politics in the absence of independence from Britain. A second reason is that English has been arguably the predominant language of Irish nation-building for all that Gaelic has retained a symbolic importance. In an 1843 article Thomas Davis, the intellectual leader of the Young Irelander movement and writer of the popular ballad 'A Nation Once Again', listed what he saw as some of the most powerful weapons of cultural nationalism:

> *National* books, and lectures and music – *national* painting and busts and costume – *national* songs, and tracts, and maps – *historical* plays for the stage – *historical* novels for the closet – *historical* ballads for the drawing room – we want all these, and many other things illustrating the *history*, the resources and the genius of our country, and honouring her illustrious

children, living and dead. These are the seeds of permanent nationality and we must sow them deeply in the People's hearts.[22]

It was necessary that most such materials, including Davis's popular ballad, be produced in English. His list did not include the Gaelic language, although its restoration became a central plank of a later phase of cultural nationalism. English remained the language of Irish modernity as well as being one of the main vehicles of Irish cultural nationalism.

Whilst nineteenth-century nationalist politics were, as Anne Kane put it, 'bedevilled by factionalism and internecine warfare amongst contentious groups', it was also the case that different kinds of nationalism reinforced one another and produced what she calls nationalist master narratives within folk memory. Kane gives the example of the 1880s Land War, which meant different things to different class and interest groups amongst the Catholic majority. For the post-Famine peasantry insecurity of tenure remained an existential threat. Prior to the Land War the 'master narrative' of British domination, with all its subplots – the conquest by England, the confiscation of land by Protestant landlords, the Act of Union, Catholic repression, Catholic 'emancipation' – had long explained to the Irish their individual and collective subjugation. The tenant farmer understood his constant struggle for survival within the narrative of British conquest and confiscation; the Famine came to be culturally understood as a form of British control and oppression. The British government may not have been directly to blame for the Famine but claims that it was became integral to subsequent nationalist narratives. But Irish nationalism also acquired a strong conservative strand. A Catholic 'strong farmer' class had already emerged that would come to dominate conservative parliamentary nationalism into the twentieth century. Against this, an elite tradition of revolutionary nationalism had emerged out of the political vacuum left by the death of Daniel O'Connell and the failure of parliamentary nationalist politics to repeal the Act of Union with Britain. Between 1879 and 1891 activism against landlords and British rule brought together parliamentary and revolutionary nationalists, peasants, well-to-do farmers and many Catholic clerics into a temporary alliance – a 'brief but perfect storm' – that defined the cultural master narratives, discourses and symbolic contours of subsequent political and cultural nation-building.[23]

A coalescence of different strains of nationalism during the war of independence was followed by a civil war on the issue of partition. The post-1932 dominance of the Irish state by Fianna Fáil under de Valera coincided with a reassertion of unifying nationalism symbolism. With an Irish nation-state now established much of this exemplified what Michael

Billig calls banal nationalism. Banal nationalism, in essence, refers to a tapestry of unconsciously shared points of reference woven from a range of sources. In thinking about de Valera's post-independence vision for Ireland there is a tendency to reach for a few handy quotations, especially from the so-called dream speech broadcast in 1943 extolling the virtues of Irish rural life. But the symbols de Valera evoked were everywhere.[24] These were to be found in Paul Henry paintings of the rural landscape, on Irish bank notes, in the plays of John B. Keane and many others, in John Ford's movie *The Quiet Man*, in tourism advertising campaigns as well as in intellectual texts such as *The Hidden Ireland* by Daniel Corkery.[25]

The second main plank of the cultural nation-building project that did much to define post-independence representations of Irish identity was Catholicism. Amongst some intellectuals, cultural de-colonisation goals and Catholic antipathy to the Reformation and the Enlightenment sat well together. Insofar as Catholicism infused much of the symbolism and day-to-day life of post-independence Ireland and dominated the school system it was central to the apparatus of everyday taken-for-granted banal nationalism. In 1932, the same year that de Valera came to power, Dublin hosted the 31st Eucharistic Congress. On arrival, the Pope's legate Cardinal Lauri travelled with his cortege along nine miles of decorated streets flanked by 36,000 school children whilst a squadron of planes from the Air Corp flew overhead in a crucifix-shaped formation; 100,000 children attended a special children's Mass, 200,000 women attended a special women's Mass and 250,000 men attended a special men's Mass. A further Mass in the Phoenix Park drew a crowd of somewhere between half a million and one million men, women and children at a time when the population of the Irish Free State totalled just below three million. The Eucharist Congress showcased the triumphal fruits of the devotional revolution that had commenced eighty years earlier. The orderly, regimented crowds who took place in various processions were, according to one analysis, 'a source of pride for Irish journalists, clergy, politicians, and others who were happy to explode the myth of the inefficient and disorderly Irish'.[26] Its sermons and symbols commemorated the rise of Ireland as a Catholic nation. These proclaimed that Irish national distinctiveness was rooted in the Catholic faith of its people. But there was also a concern that a national identity so rooted in religious faith and ritual needed to be protected from the outside world. As captured in 1932 in a Dundalk newspaper:

> When you go down a narrow little street of tiny houses, beautifully whitened and spick-and-span for the occasion, hung with flowered garlands

and bunting that must have called for hours of work, with an inspiring altar at one end and miniature altars in many windows down the way you realise that here indeed lives the fervent Catholic faith of the Irish, whose survival is one of the world's miracles – that here the flood of Modernism has not touched the creed in which these children of the poor were raised.[27]

Irish identities rooted in Catholicism found expression in communities as well as through the kinds of national Catholic pageantry exemplified by the 1932 Eucharistic Congress. Schools, churches and Gaelic sports all organised at a parish buttressed one another in shaping the citizens of the Irish nation-state. Intellectual life after independence (see Chapter 6) was also rooted in Catholicism. That de Valera referenced Catholic ideas and values explicitly in his 1937 Constitution is hardly surprising. For a number of decades Catholicism proved to be a stronger national adhesive than the Irish language has been. However, just as Gaelic lost out to English during the nineteenth century so also the devout prac-tice of Catholicism became a minority pursuit. Although Irish society became more secular, the Church retained control over most of the school system. Religious vocations declined and most school children came to be taught by lay teachers. Catholicism in many of Irish schools became a thinner veneer but it has hardly faded away.

Cultural nationalisms variously seeking to protect Catholicism and restore the Irish language were trumped from the 1950s by economic nationalism in a context where the nation-state was up and running. Both Catholicism and the Irish language remained symbolically impor-tant. However, the survival of a distinct national identity no longer depended on either. A distinct economic nation-building project can be dated from the 1950s (see Chapter 1, Chapter 10 and Chapter 15) although its core element of economic liberalism could be traced back to at least a century before as a constituent element of Catholic nation-alism. Catholicism proved to be literally and metaphorically a broad church that included progressives as well as conservatives anxious to keep the modern world at bay.

The shift in overt emphasis from cultural to economic nation-building owed much to Fianna Fáil, which, as a catch-all nationalist party, proved adroit at reflecting dominant conceptions of Irish identity. The party founded by de Valera was in government for sixty-one years of the seventy-nine-year period between 1932 and 2011, when it suffered a massive electoral defeat. Under de Valera's leadership the party stood for economic protectionism, cultural nationalism, the ideal of a united Ireland and the practice of Catholic values and in doing so remained in government from 1932 to 1948. In the decades after 1958 it came to articulate a distinct twenty-six-county economic nationalism that was no less successful as a political ideology.[28] Ireland's economic nation-building project was hardly unusual. However, the extent to which it seems to have pushed aside other nation-building projects might be. That economic and social modernisation worked to undermine Catholicism is hardly surprising. Many studies link rising levels of education and urbanisation to a decline in religiosity. However, in the Irish case it might be argued that the Church lost much of its influence because of the degree of emphasis it placed on the control of sexuality.

Ireland became more prosperous and secular from the 1960s onwards. Family patterns and norms also shifted. Feminism and the women's movement, the sexual revolution, changes in gender roles due to more and more women engaged in employment outside the home, the existence of contraception, new models of parenting and new thinking about childhood and children's rights all worked to undermine the influence of traditional Catholic teaching.[29] What was referred in previous chapters as a Catholic moral monopoly (Chapter 3) or as Catholic public morality (Chapter 4), concerned with the regulation of sexuality and marriage, became diluted by the liberal modernisation of Irish society. The Church also lost much of its moral high ground following revelations of extensive clerical sexual abuse and disclosures about the mistreatment of unmarried mothers and vulnerable young people in institutions it ran partly because it had been unwilling to sanction interference by the state in their care.

A 1983 Referendum approved introducing a constitutional ban on abortion supported by 67 per cent of those who voted. A 1986 Referendum on removing the prohibition on divorce set out since 1937 in the Constitution was rejected by 63.5 per cent of voters. A second referendum in 1995 on the same issue was won by the narrowest of majorities: 50.28 per cent voted to change the Constitution. A 2002 Referendum on whether abortion should be permitted in cases of a risk of maternal suicide was defeated by a narrow majority of 50.4 per cent of those who voted. All this pointed to an ongoing influence of Catholic ideas and values.

More recent referenda results suggest that this influence may be further declining. The Protection of Life Act (2013) permitted abortion in limited circumstances when the life of a woman is deemed to be at risk. Unease about abortion under other circumstances has persisted. A 2012 referendum on children's rights, which challenged the emphasis on family rights in Articles 41 to 44 of the Constitution, was passed by 58 per cent of those who voted. It was not until 1993 that the Criminal Fraud (Sexual Offences) Act decriminalised homosexuality. A number of European Social Surveys conducted between 2002 and 2009 found that more than 55 per cent of Irish Catholics either agreed or strongly agreed that gays and lesbians should be free to live life as they wished.[30] In 2010 a Civil Partnership Act was passed. In 2011 the first openly gay TDs were elected to the Dáil. In January 2015 Leo Varadkar became Ireland's first openly gay cabinet minister. In May 2015 a referendum permitting same-sex marriage was passed by 61 per cent of those who voted. All political parties in the Republic of Ireland and even political leaders who strongly identified with Catholicism, most notably former-president Mary McAleese, declared their support for a right to marriage equality for same-sex couples.

In a July 2011 speech the Taoiseach Enda Kenny gave a speech that was excoriatingly critical of the failure of the Church to face up to its responsibilities for clerical child abuse in Ireland. His government then closed Ireland's embassy in the Vatican.[31] All this strikingly contrasted with the status quo around the time of the 'Mother and Child Scheme' crisis (see Chapter 12). Yet Kenny described himself as a 'faithful' and practising Catholic. According to the 2011 census 3.86 million people, or 84 per cent of the population of the Republic of Ireland, defined themselves as Catholic and just 270,000 defined themselves as being of no religion. European Social Survey data from 2009–10 found that 51.1 per cent of Irish Catholics attended Mass at least once a week and that only 3.2 per cent never attended Mass. These figures do not take account of attendance at religious services on special occasions: Christmas, first communion ceremonies, confirmation ceremonies and funerals.[32] Although Ireland has become more secular it is likely that for a majority of the population Catholicism will continue to be a significant identity marker and that even those who describe themselves as having no religion are likely to encounter Catholic symbolism routinely at communal events. Catholicism, for most of Ireland's population, is still part of the fabric of Irish identity and is likely to remain significantly so into the future.

Banal nationalism is a term used to refer to the ways in which membership of a nation is imagined, often subliminally, on an everyday basis. It is contrasted with 'hot' or atavistic kinds of national chauvinism that may exist on the margins as fringe ideologies but at certain times and places have taken centre stage.[33] For Daniel Binchy (see Chapter 7), who had observed the rise of Adolf Hitler first hand, nationalism was dangerous, volatile stuff. However, most Irish nationalists in the decades after independence viewed nationalism positively. It is not always easy to distinguish unequivocally between into good and bad or safe versus dangerous manifestations of nationalism. Violent nationalist revolutions may come to be routinely commemorated. Yet the politics of the Irish nation-state has been at times preoccupied with the potential volatility of nationalist symbolism. Ongoing calls for a united Ireland were the stuff of most political stump speeches during the decades after partition. These were predominately aimed at audiences in the Free State / Republic of Ireland.

Political sensitivity amongst parliamentary nationalists to the dangers of hot nationalist rhetoric came to be influenced by the 1956 IRA border campaign. This had followed a period of overt united Ireland propaganda by the Republic of Ireland that included calling on the United Nations to compel Britain to bring about a united Ireland (see Chapter 6). The fiftieth anniversary of the 1916 Rising in 1966 witnessed the publication of a number of essays (also see Chapter 6) that were critical of Pearse's evocation of nationalist blood sacrifice. The post-1969 Northern Ireland crisis also inhibited some mobilisation of symbolism that might be seen to legitimise conflict or cause offence to Unionists. For example, the Irish Rugby Football Union commissioned a song 'Ireland's Call', written by Phil Coulter, that is played instead of the Republic's national anthem, 'Amhrán na bhFiann' ('The Soldier's Song') at international matches played by the all-island Irish team. The lyrics of 'Ireland's Call' are apparently not much less martial than 'A Nation Once Again' ('We will fight until we can fight no more / For the four proud provinces of Ireland') but, unlike 'Amhrán na bhFiann' or 'A Nation Once Again', it does not have an association with strains of Irish nationalism that threatened Northern Irish unionists.

Indifference or lack of consideration of the aspirations of Protestant Unionists by many Irish nationalists who supported a united Ireland pre-dated the establishment of the Free State. Acceptance of the partition of the island by the Free State triggered a civil war. However, partition came to be normalised. What in Chapter 2 is referred to as methodological nationalism exemplifies how day-to-day life and identity politics are to some extent bounded by administrative borders. Many people living in the Free State arguably had little interest in or knowledge of the north until the post-1969 Northern Ireland conflict became daily headline news. Then, the grievances of Catholics, the Bloody Sunday killings, the hunger strikes, nationalist and Unionist terrorist atrocities, statements by Unionist politicians that they would neither retreat nor surrender, the slow minuet of the peace process and the torrents of international praise heaped on northern politicians who engaged with it – all of this became, through daily newspaper, radio and television coverage, common points of reference for citizens of the Republic of Ireland. During the decades of the conflict these citizens might have imbibed a few minutes of Irish-language programmes on television and radio every day. If they tuned into RTÉ radio at noon they would have heard the daily Catholic call to prayer that is the Angelus. However, day in day out, news pro-grammes led with coverage of the north.

The northern crisis may not have directly affected the lives of most citizens of the Republic. However, it exerted considerable influence over Irish politics not least as an object lesson on the dangers of whipping up nationalist fervour. In various ways Irish, Northern Irish and British governments have sought to dampen down 'hot nationalisms'. Insofar as the Irish State was founded on partition and was cemented by a civil war, it has opposed expressions of nationalism that challenge its legiti-macy. For example, under Section 31 of the Broadcasting Authority Act the government could instruct RTÉ not to broadcast any material that promoted an organisation advocating violence as a means to attaining its objectives. During the northern conflict RTÉ was prevented from interviewing IRA and Sinn Féin spokespeople.

Since the end of the northern conflict commemorations of the revo-lutionary origins of the Irish state now seem to be expressions of banal nationalism. However, top-down attempts by the Irish state to shape such commemoration can also be identified. The government minister appointed to oversee the centenary of the 1916 Rising may not have been able to speak Irish. She was, however, a Protestant from a border county and her appointment, like the official visit of Queen Elizabeth II to Ireland in 2011, is symbolically significant. In the north flags and parades could hardly be defined as banal expressions of identity.[34]

In a number of European countries manifestations of strong anti-immigrant nationalist chauvinism can be identified. Mainstream politi-cal parties in some countries, seeking to compete with far-right anti-immigrant parties for votes, have at times engaged in anti-immigrant populism. In the Irish case almost 80 per cent voted in a 2004 Referendum to remove a constitutional right of Irish-born children of immigrants to Irish citizenship. Polls have found about 20 per cent of the population to be strongly opposed to immigration (see Chapter 17). However, Irish political parties have assiduously avoided anti-immigrant populism. It may be the case that decades of sensitivity to the dangers of hot nationalism could partly explain this.

The previous chapter offered somewhat optimistic assessment of Irish responses to immigration during the economic crisis that followed the Celtic Tiger era. The 2004 Referendum result suggested the persistence of a strong sense of Irish national identity that excluded immigrants. A decade later it seemed that institutional barriers to immigrants becom-ing Irish citizens had been significantly reduced. Those who became new Irish citizens were welcomed into a nation held together mostly by the glue of banal nationalism. Newspaper accounts of citizenship ceremonies report the positive statements of political leaders but also how such events, typically attended by a few thousand new citizens, feature a performance by the Garda band: its repertoire on such occasions has included '(Is This the Way to) Amarillo' and songs popularised by Michael Bublé and Amy Winehouse.

Immigrants by their very presence, as a significant proportion now of the Irish population, will inevitably affect perceptions of what it is to be Irish. Through television programmes and in other ways Irish people are increasingly, if not yet constantly, being reminded that they live in a diverse society. This book has not focused on the role of literature in re-defining understandings of what it is to be Irish in a diverse society. But a recent collection of essays, *Literary Visions of Multicultural Ireland* (2014) edited by Pilar Villar-Argáiz, has done just that.[35] Irish literature and drama have begun to grapple with immigration just as they have previously tackled emigration and the return of emigrants and their descendants. Much of this literature, according to Bisi Adigun, the founder of the Dublin-based African theatre company Arambe, views the experiences of migrants through Irish eyes.[36] An example of this is Roddy Doyle's short story collection *The Deportees* (2007). Doyle and Adigun collaborated on an adaptation of *The Playboy of the Western World* (2007) that re-imagined the main protagonist Christy Mahon as a Nigerian asylum seeker. Compared to high-profile Irish writers like Doyle, immigrant writers are still marginal. Overall, such literature has barely scratched the surface of twenty-first-century multicultural Irish society, because it is just simply 'too new'.[37] The same also holds for sociological research. To date this too has grasped only fragments of the experiences of immigrants and those of the host society that is coming to terms with recent immigration.

Yet all such work attests to the diversity of Irish society. Immigrant characters are now commonplace if generally peripheral figures in Irish television drama and cinema. For example, the soap *Fair City* has featured many immigrant storylines.[38] It may be only a matter of time before immigrant celebrities and sports stars join 'mixed-race' icons of Irishness such as the rock star Phil Lynott, the soccer star Paul McGrath or the hurling star Setanta Ó hAilpín. For example, the Ethiopian-Irish actress Ruth Negga has starred in a number of films in which she has played an immigrant or a refugee. However, she was also cast in the 1970s-set *Breakfast on Pluto* (2005) and in the television series *Love/Hate* as an Irish woman who just happens to be mixed-race. One of the lead actors on the 2014 crime drama *An Bronntanas* (The Gift) on

TG4, the Irish-language television station, was Polish. He played an immigrant living in a Gaeltacht area who was learning Irish. Such real and fictional representations will most probably proliferate as artists, writers and journalists play catch-up with the ordinary everyday diversity of twenty-first-century Irish society and may well contribute to a re-imagining of what it means to be Irish that proves no less influential than the Irish literature that defined a cultural nation-building project more than a century ago.

Notes

1 Joseph Stalin, 'The Nation', in John Hutchinson and Anthony D. Smith (eds), *Nationalism* (Oxford: Oxford University Press, 1994), p. 20.
2 Stephen J. Brown SJ, 'What is a Nation?', *Studies*, 1.3 (1913), 496–510; Stephen J. Brown SJ, 'The Question of Irish Nationality', *Studies*, 1.4 (1913), 634–655.
3 Brown, 'What is a Nation?', p. 503.
4 Ernest Renan, *Qu'est-ce qu'une nation?* (Paris: Calman-Levy, 1882), p. 26.
5 Brown, 'What is a Nation?', p. 509.
6 Benedict Anderson, *Imagined Communities: Reflections on the Origins and Spread of Nationalism* (London: Verso, [1989] 2006).
7 Michael Billig, *Banal Nationalism* (London: Sage, 1995), p. 95.
8 Gustav Lehmacher, M. Sheehan, Osborn Bergin, F.W. O'Connell, Thomas F. O'Rahilly and T.O. Maille, 'Symposium', *Studies*, 12.45 (1923), 26–44.
9 Lehmacher et al., 'Symposium', p. 35.
10 Lehmacher et al., 'Symposium', p. 28.
11 Lehmacher et al., 'Symposium', p. 36.
12 Lehmacher et al., 'Symposium', p. 36
13 Donal Flynn, *The Revival of Irish: Failed Political Project of a Political Elite* (Dublin: Original Writing Ltd, 2012), p. 48.
14 Hugh O'Connell, 'The New Gaeltacht Minister Is not Fluent in Irish', *Journal. ie*, 15 July 2014.
15 'Gaeltacht Minister Defends Her Level of Irish', *RTE.ie*, 16 July 2014.
16 Iarfhlaith Watson, 'The Irish Language and Television: National Identity, Preservation, Restoration and Minority Rights', *The British Journal of Sociology*, 47.2 (1996), 255–274, p. 257.
17 Section 17 and Section 20 of the Broadcasting Authority Act 1960.
18 Watson, 'Irish Language and Television', p. 261.
19 Ellen Hazelkorn, 'Ireland: From Nation Building to Economic Priorities', in Miquel de Moragas Spá and Carmelo Garitaonandia (eds), *Decentralization in the Global Era: Television in the Regions, Nationalities and Small Countries of the European Union* (London: John Libbey, 1995), p. 103.
20 Mike Cormack, 'Minority Languages, Nationalism and Broadcasting: The British and Irish Examples', *Nations and Nationalism*, 6.3 (2000), 383–398.
21 Cited in Watson, 'Irish Language and Television', p. 256.

22 Thomas Davis, *The Nation*, 9 September 1843.

23 Anne Kane, *Constructing Irish National Identity: Discourse and Ritual during the Land War, 1879–1882* (New York: Palgrave Macmillan, 2011), p. 224.

24 Tricia Cusack, 'A "Countryside Bright with Cosy Homesteads": Irish Nationalism and the Cottage Landscape', *National Identities*, 3.3 (2001), 221–236, p. 233.

25 Daniel Corkery, *The Hidden Ireland: A Study of Gaelic Munster in the Eighteenth Century* (Dublin: Gill and Macmillan, 1970).

26 David G. Holmes, 'The Eucharistic Congress of 1932 and Irish Identity', *New Hibernia Review*, 4.1 (2000), 55–78, p. 68.

27 'Bravo Dundalk! Your Decoration's an Inspiration', *Democrat and People's Journal*, 25 June 1932, quoted in Holmes, 'Eucharistic Congress of 1932', p. 71.

28 Kieran Allen, 'The Irish Political Elite', in Tom Inglis (ed.), *Are the Irish Different?* (Manchester: Manchester University Press, 2014), pp. 59–61.

29 Tony Fahey, 'The Irish Family: Different or Not?', in Inglis (ed.), *Are the Irish Different?*, pp. 69–71.

30 Eoin O'Mahony, *Practice and Belief among Catholics in the Republic of Ireland* (Maynooth: Irish Catholic Bishops' Conference, 2011), p. 23.

31 'Enda Kenny Speech on Cloyne Report', *RTÉ.ie*, 20 July 2011.

32 O'Mahony, *Practice and Belief*, p. 5.

33 Billig, *Banal Nationalism*.

34 Anna-Kaisa Kuusisto, 'Territoriality, Symbolism and the Challenge', *Peace Review*, 13:1 (2001), 59–66.

35 Pilar Villar-Argáiz (ed.), *Literary Visions of Multicultural Ireland: The Immigrant in Contemporary Irish Literature* (Manchester: Manchester University Press, 2014).

36 See Amanda Tucker, 'The New Irish Multi-cultural Fiction', in Villar-Argáiz (ed.), *Literary Visions*, p. 52.

37 See Katherine O'Donnell, 'The Parts: Whiskey, Tea and Sympathy', in Villar-Argáiz (ed.), *Literary Visions*, p. 52.

38 See Zélia Asava, *The Black Irish Onscreen: Representing Black and Mixed-Race Identities on Irish Film and Television* (Bern: Peter Lang, 2013).

Select bibliography

Adshead M. and Millar M., *Public Administration and Public Policy in Ireland: Theory and Practice* (London: Routledge, 2003).

Allen, K., *The Celtic Tiger: The Myth of Social Partnership in Ireland* (Manchester: Manchester University Press, 2000).

Anderson, B., 'Exodus', *Critical Inquiry*, 20.2 (1994), 314–327.

Anderson, B., *The Spectre of Comparisons: Nationalism, Southeast Asia and the World* (London: Verso, 1998).

Anderson, B., 'Western Nationalism and Eastern Nationalism', *New Left Review*, 9.2 (1998).

Anderson, B., 'To What Can Late Eighteenth-Century French, British, and American Anxieties Be Compared?', *The American Historical Review*, 106.1 (2001), 1281–1289.

Anderson, B., *Imagined Communities: Reflections on the Origins and Spread of Nationalism* (London: Verso, [1983] 2006).

Arensberg, C. and Kimball, S.T., *Family and Community in Ireland* (Cambridge, MA: Harvard University Press, 1940).

Balakrishnan, G. (ed.), *Mapping the Nation* (London: Verso, 1996).

Bartlett, T., *Ireland: A History* (Cambridge: Cambridge University Press, 2010).

Beck, U., 'The Cosmopolitan Perspective: Sociology of the Second Age of Modernity', *British Journal of Sociology*, 51.1 (2000), 79–105.

Beck, U., 'How Not to Become a Museum Piece', *British Journal of Sociology*, 56.3 (2005), 335–343.

Bellamy, R., *Victorian Liberalism: Nineteenth Century Political Thought and Practice* (London: Routledge, 1990).

Bhreatnach, A., *Becoming Conspicuous: Irish Travellers, Society and the State 1922–70* (Dublin: University College Dublin Press, 2006).

Billig, M., *Banal Nationalism* (London: Sage, 1995).

Binchy, D., *Church and State in Fascist Italy* (Oxford: Oxford University Press, 1941).

Blanchard, P., *The Irish and Catholic Power: An American Interpretation* (Boston: Beacon Press, 1954).

Breuilly, J., *Labour and Liberalism in Nineteenth-Century Europe: Essays in Comparative History* (Manchester: Manchester University Press, 1994).

Breznitz, D., 'Innovation and the State: Development Strategies for High Technology Industries in a World of Fragmented Production: Israel, Ireland and Taiwan', *Enterprise and Society*, 7.4 (2006), 675–685.

Breznitz, D., *Innovation and the State: Political Choice and Strategies for Growth in Israel, Taiwan and Ireland* (New Haven: Yale University Press, 2007).

Burke, E., *Letters, Speeches and Tracts on Irish Affairs*, ed. Matthew Arnold (London: Macmillan, 1881).

Cahill, E., *The Framework of a Christian State: An Introduction to Social Science* (Dublin: Gill and Son, 1932).

Calhoun, C., *Nations Matter: Culture, History and the Cosmopolitan Dream* (London: Routledge, 2007).

Carlyle, T., *Past and Present* (London: Chapman and Hall 1843).

Chernilo, C., 'Social Theory's Methodological Nationalism: Myth and Reality', *European Journal of Social Theory*, 9.5 (2006), 5–22.

Cooney, J., *John Charles McQuaid: Ruler of Catholic Ireland* (Dublin: O'Brien, 1999).

Corkery, D., *The Hidden Ireland: A Study of Gaelic Munster in the Eighteenth Century* (Dublin: Gill and Macmillan, 1970).

Cormack, M., 'Minority Languages, Nationalism and Broadcasting: The British and Irish Examples', *Nations and Nationalism*, 6.3 (2000), 383–398.

Crafts, N. and Toniolo, G., *Economic Growth in Europe Since 1945* (Cambridge: Cambridge University Press, 1996).

Crotty, W. and Schmitt, D.E. (eds), *Ireland and the Politics of Change* (London: Longman, 1998).

Crowley, N., *Hidden Messages, Overt Agendas* (Dublin: Migrant Rights Centre Ireland, 2010).

Curtis, L.P., *Apes and Angels: The Irishman in Victorian Caricature* (New York: New York University Press, 1971).

Cusack, T., 'A "Countryside Bright with Cosy Homesteads": Irish Nationalism and the Cottage Landscape', *National Identities*, 3.3 (2001), 221–236.

Daly, M.E., 'Women in the Irish Free State 1922–39: The Interaction between Economics and Ideology', *Journal of Women's History*, 6.4 (1995), 99–116.

Dudley Edwards, R., *Patrick Pearse: The Triumph of Failure* (Dublin: Irish Academic Press, 2006).

Durkheim, É., *Suicide: A Study in Sociology* (New York: Free Press, 1951).

Durkheim, É., *The Division of Labour in Society* (London: Macmillan, 1984).

Ellman, R., *James Joyce* (Oxford: Oxford University Press, 1959).

Engels, F., *The Condition of the Working Class in England* (London: Allen and Unwin, [1892] 1943).

Fahey, T., 'The Catholic Church and Social Policy', in Seán Healy and Brigid Reynolds (eds), *Social Policy in Ireland* (Dublin: Oak Tree Press, 1998).

Fanning, B. (ed.), *Immigration and Social Change in the Republic of Ireland* (Manchester: Manchester University Press, 2007).

Fanning, B., *The Quest for Modern Ireland: The Battle of Ideas 1912–1986* (Dublin: Irish Academic Press, 2008).

Fanning, B., 'From Developmental Ireland to Migration Nation: Immigration and Shifting Rules of Belonging in the Republic of Ireland', *Economic and Social Review*, 41.3 (2010), 395–412.

Fanning, B., *Immigration and Social Cohesion in the Republic of Ireland* (Manchester: Manchester University Press, 2011).

Fanning, B. (ed.), *An Irish Century: Studies 1912–2012* (Dublin: University College Dublin Press, 2012).

Fanning, B., *Racism and Social Change in the Republic of Ireland*, 2nd edition (Manchester: Manchester University Press, 2012).

Fanning, B., *Histories of the Irish Future* (London: Bloomsbury, 2015).

Fanning, B. and Garvin, T., *The Books that Define Ireland* (Dublin: Merrion, 2014).

Fanning, B., Howard, K. and O'Boyle, N., 'Immigrant Candidates and Politics in the Republic of Ireland: Racialization, Ethnic Nepotism or Localism?', *Nationalism and Ethnic Politics*, 16.3 (2011), 420–442.

Fanning, B., Kiely, G., Quin, S. and Kennedy, P. (eds), *Theorising Irish Social Policy* (Dublin: University College Dublin Press, 2004).

Fanning, B., Kiloran, B. and Ní Bhroin, S., *Taking Racism Seriously: Migrants' Experience of Violence, Harassment and Anti-social Behaviour in the Dublin Area* (Dublin: Immigrant Council of Ireland, 2011).

Fanning, B. and McNamara, T. (eds), *Ireland Develops: Administration and Social Policy: 1953–2003* (Dublin: Institute of Public Administration, 2003).

Fanning, B. and Munck, R. (eds), *Globalisation, Migration and Social Transformation: Ireland in Europe and the World* (London: Ashgate, 2011).

Fanning, B. and Mutwarasibo, F., 'Nationals/Non-nationals: Immigration, Citizenship and Politics in the Republic of Ireland', *Ethnic and Racial Studies*, 30.4 (2007): 439–460.

Fine, R. and Boon, V., 'Cosmopolitanism: Between Past and Future', *European Journal of Social Theory*, 10.1 (2007), 5–16.

Fine, R. and Smith, W., 'Jurgen Habermas's Theory of Cosmopolitanism', *Constellations*, 10.4 (2003), 469–487.

Finn, T., *Tuairim: Intellectual Debate and Policy Formation: Rethinking Ireland, 1954–1975* (Manchester: Manchester University Press, 2012).

Flynn, R., *The Revival of Irish: Failed Political Project of a Political Elite* (Dublin: Original Writing Ltd, 2012).

Fukuyama, F., *The End of History and the Last Man* (London: Penguin, 2002).

Garner, S., 'Ireland and Immigration: Explaining the Absence of the Far Right', *Patterns of Prejudice*, 41.2 (2007), 109–130.

Garvin, T., *Preventing the Future: Why Was Ireland So Poor for So Long?* (Dublin: Gill and Macmillan, 2004).

Gellner, E., *Thought and Change* (London: Weidenfeld and Nicolson, 1964).

Gellner, E., *Nations and Nationalism* (Oxford: Blackwell, 1983).

Gellner, E., *Culture, Identity and Politics* (Cambridge: Cambridge University Press, 1987).

Gellner, E., *Encounters with Nationalism* (Oxford: Blackwell, 1994).

Hall, J.A. and Jarvie, I.C., *Transition to Modernity: Essays on Power, Wealth and Belief* (Cambridge: Cambridge University Press, 1992).

Hayek, F.A., *The Road to Serfdom* (London: George Routledge, 1944).

Helleiner, J., 'Gypsies, Celts and Tinkers: Colonial Antecedents of Anti-traveller Racism in Ireland', *Ethnic and Racial Studies*, 18.3 (1995), 532–535.

Holmes, D.G., 'The Eucharistic Congress of 1932 and Irish Identity', *New Hibernia Review*, 4.1 (2000), 55–78.

Hoyle, F., *Ossian's Ride* (New York: Harper, 1959).

Hutchinson, J. and Smith, A. (eds), *Nationalism* (Oxford: Oxford University Press, 1994).

Inglis, T., *Moral Monopoly: The Rise and Fall of the Catholic Church in Ireland* (Dublin: University College Dublin Press, 1998).

Inglis, T. (ed.), *Are the Irish Different?* (Manchester: Manchester University Press, 2014).

Joppke, C., 'How Immigration is Changing Citizenship: A Comparative View', *Ethnic and Racial Studies*, 22.4 (1999), 629–632.

Kane, A., *Constructing Irish National Identity: Discourse and Ritual during the Land War, 1879–1882* (New York: Palgrave Macmillan, 2011).

Kennedy, F., *Cottage to Creche: Family Change in Ireland* (Dublin: Institute of Public Administration, 2001).

Kennedy, S. (ed.), *One Million Poor? The Challenge of Irish Inequality* (Dublin: Turoe Press, 1981).

Keogh, D. and McDonnell, A. (eds), *Cardinal Paul Cullen and His World* (Dublin: Four Courts Press, 2011).

Kofman, E., 'Citizenship, Migration and the Reassertion of National Identity', *Citizenship Studies*, 9.1 (2005), 453–467.

Larkin, J., *In the Footsteps of Big Jim: A Family Biography* (Dublin: Blackwater Press, 1995).

Lee, J.J., *Ireland 1912–1985: Politics and Society* (Cambridge: Cambridge University Press, 1989).

L'Estrange, S., 'Commentary: Excavating Nationalism in Archaeology', *Archaeological Review from Cambridge*, 27.2 (2012), 189–205.

Lukes, S., *Emile Durkheim* (New York: Harper Row, 1972).

McCashin, A., *Social Security in Ireland* (Dublin: Institute of Public Administration, 2004).

McKenna, L., *The Social Teachings of James Connolly* (Dublin: Catholic Truth Society, 1920).

McRedmond, L., *To the Greater Glory: A History of the Irish Jesuits* (Dublin: Gill and Macmillan, 1991).

Mac Suibhne, P., *Paul Cullen and His Contemporaries*, vol. 4 (Kildare: Leinster Leader, 1974).

Malesevic, S., *Nation-States and Nationalisms* (London: Polity, 2013).

Malik, K. *Strange Fruit: Why Both Sides are Wrong on the Race Debate* (London: One World, 2008).

Mann, M., *The Dark Side of Democracy: Explaining Ethnic Cleansing* (Cambridge: Cambridge University Press, 2005).

Martineau, H., *Letters from Ireland* (Dublin: Irish Academic Press, 2001).

Matthews, K., *The Bell Magazine and the Representation of Irish Identity* (Dublin: Four Courts Press, 2012).

Mitchel, J., *The Last Conquest of Ireland (Perhaps)* (Dublin: University College Dublin Press, [1861] 2005).

Murray, P., *Oracles of God: The Roman Catholic Church and Irish Politics 1922–37* (Dublin: University College Dublin Press, 2000).

Newman, J., *Studies in Political Morality* (Dublin: Scepter, 1962).

Newman, J., *Conscience Versus Law: Reflections on the Evolution of Natural Law* (Dublin: Talbot, 1971).

O'Brien, C.C., 'A Sample of Loyalties', *Studies*, 46.184 (1957), 403–410.

O'Brien, C.C., *Memoir: My Life and Themes* (London: Profile, 1998).

O'Brien, M. and Larkin, F.M. (eds), *Periodicals and Journalism in Twentieth-Century Ireland* (Dublin: Four Courts Press, 2014).

O'Faoláin, S., *King of the Beggars: A Life of Daniel O'Connell, the Irish Liberator* (Dublin: Poolbeg, 1980).

O'Hearn, D., *Inside the Celtic Tiger: The Irish Economy and the Asian Model* (London: Pluto Press, 1998).

O'Mahony, E., *Practice and Belief among Catholics in the Republic of Ireland* (Maynooth: Irish Catholic Bishops' Conference, 2011).

O'Malley, E., 'Why Is There No Radical Right Party in Ireland?', *West European Politics*, 31.5 (2008), 960–977.

O'Riain, S., 'The Flexible Developmental State: Globalization, Information Technology, and the "Celtic Tiger"', *Policy and Politics*, 28.2 (2000), 157–193.

O'Riain, S., *The Politics of High-Tech Growth: Developmental Network States in the Global Economy* (Cambridge: Cambridge University Press, 2004).

O'Riain, S., 'Social Partnership as a Mode of Governance', *The Economic and Social Review*, 37.3 (2006), 311–318.

O'Riain, S., *The Rise and Fall of Ireland's Celtic Tiger: Liberalism, Boom and Bust* (Cambridge: Cambridge University Press, 2014).

O'Riordan, M., *Catholicity and Progress in Ireland* (London: Trench, Trubner and Co, 1905).

Ó Síocháin, S. (ed.), *Social Thought on Ireland in the Nineteenth Century* (Dublin: University College Dublin Press, 2009).

O'Sullivan, D., *Cultural Politics and Irish Education since the 1950s: Policy, Paradigms and Power* (Dublin: Institute of Public Administration, 2005).

O'Toole, F., *Ship of Fools: How Stupidity and Corruption Sunk the Celtic Tiger* (London: Faber and Faber, 2009).

Pearse, P., *Collected Works of Pádraic H. Pearse: Political Writings and Speeches* (Dublin and Belfast: Phoenix, 1917).

Plunkett, H., *Ireland in the New Century* (New York: Kennikat Press, [1904] 1970).

Renan, E., *Qu'est-ce qu'une nation?* (Paris: Calman-Levy, 1882).

Ryan, D., *Remembering Sion* (London: Arthur Barker, 1934).

Skidelsky, R., *John Maynard Keynes: The Economist as Saviour 1920–1937* (London: Macmillan, 1992).

Smith, A.D., *Nationalism in the Twentieth Century* (Oxford: Martin Robinson, 1979).

Smith, A.D., 'Nationalism and Social Theory', *British Journal of Sociology*, 34.1 (1983) 19–38.

Soysal, Y.N., *Limits of Citizenship: Migrants and Postnational Membership in Europe* (Chicago: Chicago University Press, 1994).

Suskucki, A.M. (ed.), *Welfare Citizenship and Welfare Nationalism* (Helsinki: Nordwel, 2011).

Tanner, M., *Ireland's Holy Wars: The Struggle for a Nation's Soul 1500–2000* (New Haven: Yale University Press, 2001).

Thompson, A., 'Nations, National Identities and Human Agency: Putting People Back into Nations', *The Sociological Review*, 49.1 (2001), 18–32.

Titley, G., 'Media Transnationalism in Ireland', *Translocations*, 3.1 (2008), 29–49.

Tyrell, P., *Founded on Fear* (Dublin: Irish Academic Press, 2006).

Villar-Argáiz, P. (ed.), *Literary Visions of Multicultural Ireland: The Immigrant in Contemporary Irish Literature* (Manchester: Manchester University Press, 2014).

Walker, G. and English, R. (eds), *Unionism in Modern Ireland* (Dublin: Gill and Macmillan, 1996).

Watson, I., 'The Irish Language and Television: National Identity, Preservation, Restoration and Minority Rights', *The British Journal of Sociology*, 47.2 (1996), 255–274.

Whitaker, T.K., *Economic Development* (Dublin: Stationery Office, 1958).

Whitaker, T.K., *Interests* (Dublin: Institute of Public Administration, 1983).

Whyte, J., *Church and State in Modern Ireland 1923–1979*, 2nd edition (Dublin: Gill and Macmillan, 1980).

Wimmer, A. and Glick Schiller, N., 'Methodological Nationalism and Beyond: Nation-State Building, Migration and the Social Sciences', *Global Networks*, 2.4 (2002), 301–334.

Wimmer, A. and Glick Schiller, N., 'Methodological Nationalism, the Social

Sciences and the Study of Migration: An Essay in Historical Epistemology',
  International Migration Review, 37.3 (2003), 576–610.
Woo-Cummings, W., *The Developmental State* (New York: Cornell University
  Press, 1999).

Index